Autumn Moons and

Whitetail Dreams

Autumn Moons and Whitetail Dreams

Portraits of the American Deer Hunter

by Michael L. Duarte

Safari Press Inc.

P.O. Box 3095, Long Beach, California 90803

Duarte, M. L.

First edition

Safari Press Inc.

1998, Long Beach, California

ISBN 1-57157-109-4

Library of Congress Catalog Card Number: 98-60683

10 9 8 7 6 5 4 3 2 1

Readers wishing to receive the Safari Press catalog, featuring many fine books on big-game hunting, wingshooting, and sporting firearms, should write to Safari Press Inc., P.O. Box 3095, Long Beach, CA 90803, USA. Tel: (714) 894-9080, or visit our Web site at www.safaripress.com.

Contents

Acknowledgments

Some parts or passages in this book were previously published in the short essay format of outdoor magazines. Grateful acknowledgment is made to the editors and publishers of the following magazines that made it possible for portions of those essays to be reprinted in book form: *American Bowhunter, Buckmasters, Deer & Deer Hunting, North American Whitetail,* and *Whitetail Strategies.* Thanks are also due to Ludo Wurfbain of Safari Press for taking a chance with this book and patiently guiding me through the publishing process.

Foreword

There are many folks across this land who can live without the autumn woods and white-tailed deer—and a good many who cannot. This chronicle is the ambrosial experiences and imaginings of one who simply cannot. Divided into three parts—September, October, and November—*Autumn Moons and Whitetail Dreams* aspires to capture the essence of old-time hunts and hunters, and the feel and taste of the autumnal woods.

Hopefully, the spirit of the little township is all-reaching, transcending the gap between hunter and non-hunter. It is not a place of chaos, the killing fields of animal-rights hysteria, but rather a quiescent landscape of much grace and compassion, embodying all things grand about the world of whitetail hunts.

Though I'm certain many readers will recognize or share a commonality with some whitetail experience in this portrait of autumn's days and nights, it is my fondest wish to reach those hunters who do not. Merely maintaining the right to harvest the bounty of North American wildlife demands our vigil; I seek to take the next step: keeping the spirit of the hunt—its quintessential hues and its ephemeral moments—alive in the rich character and grace so common to the old hunters of my childhood and this book. The reflections of an act often outshine its actuality.

To the new hunter, especially those without mentor or who lack experience reflecting the charm and earthy warmth of an earlier age, this chronicle offers a fleeting look into the soul of passionate deer hunting. And it is an important look, one to absorb, taste, and, it is hoped, to emulate in some small way. I can't help but believe that the future of legal hunting in this country rests in the hands and self-generated image of our up-and-coming generation of hunter. And that the fateful decisions of present and soon-to-be lawmakers will be wholly influenced by the character of the hunter—not the hunting itself.

To those readers growing a bit long in the tooth, blessed with much hunting experience and sweet memory, just enjoy this somewhat quirky reflection of whitetail encounters and long-passed hunters. They involve folks of small renown, but wildly passionate in heart and broad of spirit. And if you recognize Harland Corners, or catch some tiny reminiscence of a place you might have once lived—or wish to forever live—I have succeeded in my endeavor.

Michael Layne Duarte
The Canadian Border Country
April 10, 1997

Prologue

It was August 20 when Rolly first noticed the light. The old man hobbled over to the knotty-pine wall and placed a large X on the calendar date. A smile spread across his weathered face. He dug through the old steamer trunk in the spare bedroom and flipped through the stack of twenty-odd calendars. The earliest date was August 9; the latest, August 28. It had arrived.

The autumnal light rays that trigger the hormonal shift in the white-tailed deer also, silently and softly, affected the old man. The nearly imperceptible change in their angle of deflection, unnoticed by most, leaped across the heavens to the searching eyes of Rolly Harper.

Standing on the faded cedar deck overlooking the small pasture, he squinted, studying the slight orange glow in the late August sky. Though the daytime temperatures were still in the high 70s, Rolly walked to the woodpile and split a handful of pine kindling, grabbed a few small logs of birch, and carried them to the house. He would build a fire tonight, needed or not—just as he did every year to celebrate the arrival of the light. The incense of birch smoke would drift about the rooms of the old house and fill the nostrils of the old man, flooding the whole of his ancient body with visions of a coming autumn.

That night, with the crackling of pine and birch serving as his private symphony, the old man took down the .270 from its lofty perch on the wall. It wasn't that the rifle needed cleaning; Rolly Harper simply desired the scent of Hoppe's No. 9. Its sweet, pungent odor danced through the room and mixed delightfully, naturally, with the aroma of birch smoke. When he walked out on the deck later that night, he felt the slightest chill in the late summer air. He smiled again. It was nearly time.

It was a week later, the eve of archery's opener, when he noticed the greatest change in the light. The lack of intensity— a result of the changing angle of sun ray—was obvious now. There was a new softness, a glowing hue to the woods.

He would miss the bow season, and envied the archers who now slept restlessly awaiting the morn. Last season, at age seventy-nine, with crippling arthritis in his shoulder, Rolly gave up his great love affair with the bow. Now he had only sweet memories to savor. But he still had the rifle season. He still managed the rifle easily, and, by boning the meat in the field, he could pack the venison home without asking for help. But rifle season was forty-five days away, a tiny eternity. He would fill these days with hikes and scouts and preparations—his nights with dreams of frost and whitetails. The light grew softer.

Later that month, during the first cold rains of September, the trees began their ritual metastasis. Slowly, a small streak here, a little splotch there, the woods too began to glow with the light. Rolly pulled the buffalo plaid shirt and gray wool pants from the trunk. It was time to hang them in a sack with the fresh boughs of pine and cedar cut earlier in the day. He would freshen the sack twice a week, eventually adding his gloves and hat.

The second week of October found the old man gazing from the worn deck at the haze of woodsmoke filling the valleys and canyons, penetrating the reaches of his remote homestead. The light was in all its glory now. Softened even further by the drift of woodsmoke, it seemed alive with the gold and scarlet explosion of the woods. Rolly lifted his gnarled fingers to the air, as if he could almost touch the colored light. He smiled to himself and finished putting the new edge on his knife. Next Friday would open the season, and he held the honed edge up to the autumnal glow pulsing about the old cabin. Staring out at the woods, he pictured the big buck with the double drop tines he'd watched for two years. He had passed up a shot at the buck last year, settling instead for a nice eight-pointer that offered an entire year's supply of red meat. He knew the growing drop-tine buck would blossom in another year to near trophy class. After eighty years, Rolly Harper knew patience and self-discipline. Like Job before him, he knew them well.

Last winter, during a rough bout with pneumonia, he wondered if he'd waited one season too long. Not now. The light was back. The season of soft glow was a panacea for all his ailments. The pains of age seemed to disappear, drifting wasted through the autumnal hue. The youthful strength of wild optimism vibrated in his chest. It was time.

On opening morning, the old man quietly, carefully, moved through the darkened woods. With his .270 and backpack, he settled into his ground blind. He had built ten of them, each location meticulously chosen to take advantage of wind and weather changes—and of morning and evening light. It was a grand time to be alive. Of this he was certain.

Seeing only two does that morning, Rolly ate his lunch and drifted in and out of a restful nap until, near sunset, he heard the sudden popping of dry, frosted leaves. With a perfect wind in his favor, the old man saw the drop-tined buck as it stepped off the faint trail leading down the ridge. With a graceful, arching bound it leaped into the small clearing. A fluttering veil of golden leaves tumbled down from high above the buck's head. One leaf drifted slowly, settling on the swollen neck muscles of the deer. Rolly slowly, silently raised the rifle. Snugging it to his formerly aching shoulder, the old man hesitated. A sweet and clear vision came forth. Again, it was the light. The magnificent buck stood unaware, framed by the gold and scarlet, illuminated by the glowing light.

Rolly Harper knew in that moment that he would leave the buck for one more year. One more year for it to pass on its superior genes. One more year for an old man to dream, a dream worth living passionately for.

There was no hunting pressure on his remote place, and there were many younger bucks from which to choose. He knew he'd take a fine one, but not the double-drop. Not yet. As long as he had the buck to hunt and dream about, he would again weather the racking winter flu that ravaged his lungs, weather the crippling arthritic pains of another wet spring, weather the dust and heat and insects of summer until finally on a quiet August morning, while staring from the faded deck, Rolly would see again the slightest change in the declination of light, unnoticed by all others. The first soft glow of autumn—the light of life.

Dedication

This book is dedicated to the memory of Tom and Mary Jayne Duarte. Their lifelong encouragement and support of an always dream-chasing son made it possible. And to Rhona Sue, whose untiring work and belief in my abilities gave it life.

September

"Deer ain't rocket scientists, hoss. Just 'cause they outwit you so dang easy don't mean they got any intelligence."

Pokey Corbel, 1974

Chapter I

Come September, few people in Harland Corners have failed to notice that light. Perhaps even fewer have failed to catch the slight shift in aroma—the birch and pine woods leaking the first musk of a coming fall. And the apples. The sour-sweet smell of vinegar and cider rising from small presses working the apple harvest fills the air. And by September, all of Harland Corners, much like Rolly Harper, will have savored the scented drafts of woodsmoke. The slight evening haze floats about the valley now, and will remain until the returning warmth of late April, until the times of fresh budding tree and crocus and daffodil. But we rarely speak of those times—not here. Our time is now, for Harland Corners, population 1,200, is the unofficial whitetail hunting capital of North America.

Don't ask me how it happened. It was like this when I first arrived here as a young boy in 1957. It remains so today, and, I hope, forever. It is not so much this grand capital because virtually every resident of Harland is a deer hunter, or because the small weekly paper sponsors a yearly deer contest featuring the picture of every successful hunter with their fortune—be it doe, spike buck, or Boone and Crockett trophy. The weekly pictures give birth to the constant cafe patter of: "Hey, see that picture of the nice buck Harold Wadkins got last week?" or, "You see the picture of my granddaughter with her first doe?"

No, Harland is the deer-hunting capital not simply for those reasons but because the folks of the Corners truly live for the season, for the first splash of gold mottled through the green of deer woods. They live for the first signs of autumn. The hint of a coming frost. The first wisp of chimney smoke. By September, a good month and a half before firearm season, Meyer's Hardware and Sporting Goods, the one down on the right past the blinking four-way stoplight, is already alive with embellished tales and grand plans for the approaching season. If you're a longtime whitetail hunter, you may know the type of stories, told by your own people. People like Gus Porter, right now probably leaning over the gun counter at the store, drinking free coffee from a Styrofoam cup and, of course, not intending to buy a damn thing from Tip Meyer.

"Seen the tracks of that old buck again," Gus might casually mention. "Yep, it's the old crooked-foot buck. He's still alive, and I aim to take him this year. If I'm lying, I'm dying."

Now Old Man Meyer, being the consummate storekeeper—ambassador-like and unwilling to upset a friend and sometime customer like Gus—might be certain that Old Crooked Foot is long dead, since Gus first mentioned those tracks twenty years ago. But he'll still nod his head and mutter, "I'll be damned, Gus. Maybe this'll be the year."

And then Tip Meyer might scratch his head and add his own embellishment: "You know, Gus, Phil Speaker stopped in yesterday and claimed he spotted a big ten-pointer across from the Miller farm. Claims that buck was all swollen in the neck, rut-like, already. Think it's possible, Gus? Awful damn early. It's only September."

And on it goes. Sure, there's the gratuitous mention of the weather. Maybe a rhetorical question about how good (or bad) the Harland High football team will be this year. The standard niceties. But quickly the conversation will revert to the coming deer season. And not just at Tip Meyer's Hardware. Visit A-1 Groceries. The Four Corners Cafe. Harvey's Bar & Grill. Walt's Texaco. It matters not the place, the buzz is ubiquitous, floating like the evening woodsmoke. A haze of deer talk. There are two things of certain consequence in the Corners—apple cider and white-tailed deer. The former brings in the necessary cash for life. The latter offers the reason to live that life.

But I waste time describing the nuances of Harland Corners. Its physical description is of little import, its location even less. It is its soul, perhaps the last warm vestige of true hunting spirit still pulsing in this land, that merits some attention. The eternal light of autumn. A grand and sweet thing—like wandering safe in the comforting veil of a Norman Rockwell painting.

That compelling spirit is best visited through the lives of these folks, most of them a long time gone. Some I knew well; others I know only by tales and anecdotes, by feats famous and infamous, or by the ancient and tattered mounts hanging in every business establishment in the Corners. Gracing even the walls of Viola's Kut & Kurl, the beauty salon catering to a mix of giggling prom girls and silver-haired ladies of wise mind, are three nice shoulder mounts circa the 1940s. One, a nice but smallish buck was taken five months before Gene Hansen's death in the Italian theater of World War II. Of course, I never knew Gene Hansen, with my birth coming a few years after the war. But I know his buck.

Above the cash register, next to the lavender-trimmed, beveled mirror, hangs Viola's own buck. Not her best but, more important to Viola, her first. Viola just might be one of those in the handful mentioned previously—those few who, by September, might not have noticed the changing autumnal light, the sign of a coming season. She would certainly know the frost—by now her tomatoes would be lost and the reality of fall would pulse a bit in her veins. But the light? Probably not. Whitetails are her hobby, not her passion.

A Proper Deer Gun

Now, you'd see passion in Ed Timmons. Like Rolly, Ed also would have noticed the softer light in late August. He was Viola's uncle, and his buck hangs over the doorway of the Kut & Kurl. It's not a particularly large or grand thing, but it has an incredible symmetry, a perfect balance, much like Old Man Timmons himself. The finest feature of the buck is the odd brow tines. At least seven inches long, they both curve inward in a rainbow-like arc, nearly touching tip to tip and forming a perfect half-circle.

If you drive north from Viola's, past the blinking red light, past Meyer's Hardware and Sporting Goods, and head up the highway about five miles, you'll see County Road 8. Take that graveled road another two miles and you'll come across the old Timmons place. Or what's left of it.

Nearly forty years have drifted by since I last saw Old Man Timmons. Yet in a moment of reflection it all seems so incredibly nigh. Nostalgia has a way of bending time, of disrupting the linear measure of it, compressing the great span of human longevity into tiny units—like dog years or even less.

He lived down the road from us, ran a small dairy passed down from two previous generations of Timmonses. Although he had no children of his own, his driveway marked the official end of the county road and, in consequence, was the school bus turnaround. The school district determined it imprudent to venture another quarter-mile on our neglected, rut-ridden section of the road. Timmons was not merely our closest neighbor, he was our only neighbor.

For the first fourteen years of my life, he was simply the gray-haired old man I waved to from the bus stop most every morning during the school year. But that soon changed. After my father's untimely and premature passing, Old Man Timmons took it upon himself to become my surrogate—my outdoor guardian.

That first fall after my father's death, Timmons began to meet me at the bus stop in the afternoons, always toting a bottle of pop or a glass of lemonade for my pleasure. Our roadside conversations spanned the gamut of outdoor adventure. He spun incredible tales, none of which I ever doubted, about battling cow-killing wolves in turn-of-century deep snows, outwitting chicken-killing foxes, and once, in the cool air of a spring evening, fighting off a four-hundred-pound black bear in the calving pens with only a pitchfork and a chunk of 4x4 post. Three jagged, foot-long scars ran from his knobby shoulder across his chest in a certain and chilling testimonial.

Three weeks into our new friendship, near the end of September, he invited me up to his house to look over his collection of ancient wolf traps. As we walked up the steps to the mud room, he licked his finger and held it up like some fleshy thermometer.

"There's gonna be a frost tonight," he ventured. "Soon be time for a boy to go deer hunting."

I hated to point out his small error, but felt compelled to impress him with my small knowledge. I sheepishly told him deer season had been open for the last week.

"You don't say," he muttered. "Well, I never respected no man that hunted deer while the leaves were still green. Nope. I figure the Lord scattered them deer around to be chased in the true colors of fall. I'm figuring He wanted man to walk alone in the October woods. There's something about the shimmer of gold and scarlet, the silence of frosted mornings, that plum draws out the best in a man. It plain humbles a regular human being. No, son, I never cared to hunt whitetails in the green leaf."

While we both walked the long driveway back to the county road, Old Man Timmons asked if I'd like to hunt his wooded quarter-section behind the pastures.

"Loaded with deer back there," he offered. "Birch trees oughta be turning color by next week, if we get a hard frost."

I answered in the affirmative, and told him I'd immediately start practicing on tin cans with my .22, sighting it in.

"A .22? Hell, boy, that ain't no proper deer gun!" The old man shook his head in disgust. "And dangerous with my house and livestock so close by. If a boy's gonna hunt on a farm, he oughta have a shotgun. What happened to your Pop's old 12-gauge?"

I explained that it had originally been my grandfather's gun, kind of an heirloom, and had gone to my uncle by an old agreement.

"Well, lad, I'll have to withdraw my offer of hunting the quarter-section. A .22 ain't a proper deer gun."

With a small amount of embarrassment, I walked home, still planning on at least practicing on tin cans and dreaming of deer hunting. I could always hunt the large tract of public land at the end of the road.

As two weeks wandered by, each morning deposited sparkling prisms of ice on the browning fields. The once-dark woods began to wiggle in shades of crimson and gold—colors filtered and softened by the haze of woodsmoke from evening fires. On those afternoons when Timmons would meet me at the bus, he seldom failed to mention the autumnal ritual, seeming more animated each day, waving a hand toward the riotous spray of birch and maple across the valley and popping rhetorical questions.

"I'd say it's almost time, eh?" or, "I feel them bucks calling me. Ain't you getting the itch?" or, "Them woods are surely becoming inviting, wouldn't you say? A man might wander in there and never want to come out, eh? Believe that's just what happened to old Ed Parker back in '29. He used to grouse hunt up on Popknee Ridge—him and that old dog of his. Every day, I'm telling you. Then one time, he just never came out. They found his Model A up there along a logging road, but never a sign of Ed and that old dog. Damn search party spent the whole month of October looking for him. Him and that dog were both long in the tooth, and I figure they just up and decided not to come out. What do you think, son?" I shrugged and offered that it seemed a bit farfetched to me.

"Hell's bells! That's what the October woods can do to a man. It's pulling on me right now as we talk. Don't you feel it, lad?"

Of course I agreed with him, though I didn't truly feel a thing. Not then. Not like I do now—now that I, too, have grown somewhat long in the tooth. Now that I notice the first and slightest gold creeping through the woods in early September. And it pulls on me.

To an old deer hunter, one who knows too well that a limited number of Octobers remain for his pleasure, the first frost, the first evening breeze carrying the sweet aroma of maple smoke from a chimney, are events not to be taken for granted.

And I've decided that the little 12-gauge single-shot collecting dust in my closet for these many years should not be taken for granted, either. I've cleaned and oiled it, and even bought a new box of slugs. Come October, I promise to set aside my precision-crafted .308 and hunt the proper little gun again. I found it on my porch nearly forty years ago, wrapped in tissue paper, two dried dew claws tied on its trigger guard with a length of buckskin thread. A small note, scrawled on a piece of cardboard, was fastened to the sagging tissue paper:

"This is a proper deer gun for a boy. May it serve you well.

Your friend,
Mr. Timmons"

Chapter 2

September always seems to bring another man back to life—if not in all the Corners, then at least in my mind. Another man long passed but hardly forgotten.

There has always been much argument in this town concerning just who was/is the best whitetail hunter. After each citizen's lobbying effort for his/her own prowess, after the always-respectfully mentioned handful of ancient and departed souls, the argument tends to narrow down to Harry Ault and Pokey Corbel. My money goes on Harry.

Perhaps because I was just a twelve-year-old boy when I met him (he passed on a few days before my fifteenth birthday), I'm partial to Harry Ault. A young boy or girl is often overwhelmed by the demonstrated knowledge of an ancient one—and in my case, especially if it was woods or whitetail knowledge. The average twelve-year-old might think his father is, without question, the smartest man in the world, only to discover some years later that Dear Old Dad, while still a good man, just might not be the sharpest knife in the drawer. Because a twelve-year-old's own knowledge and experience are so limited, a half-wit of any small experience can seem positively brilliant. I don't think this theory applies in my assessment of Harry Ault. Yes, I was young and much impressionable, but so many in Harland tend to agree with my assessment, it essentially validates my claim. Harry's buck hangs in Walt's Texaco station—last stop on your way out of town. It is one of the truly huge mounts in the Corners and the only mounted Boone & Crockett specimen. Unfortunately, Harry never bothered to have it measured in his lifetime and didn't really care about the record book. In fact, besides myself, only a handful of town folk had ever seen the buck until after Harry's passing.

September was Harry's month, as he was one of Harland's small group of archers. Disdaining the camaraderie of the hunting fraternity or the company of friends (the latter was of little consequence since, other than me, Harry had no friends), Harry took to the woods on September 1 with a homemade recurve and the cheapest shafts Tip Meyer's store offered. The early archery season, opening forty-five days before firearm season, combined with our dearth of bowmen, allowed Harry the full privacy of the woods. Until recently, with the surging popularity of archery in the "under forty" set, most folks in Harland would scratch their scalp, make the practiced queer face, and slowly shake their heads at the thought of bowhunting. Especially in September. If a man was intent on handicapping his chances with a bow, he ought to at least wait and hunt the November rut, they would pontificate. No reason to go wigging out in September after whitetails. Even the most anxious of whitetail hunters know that September is apple-harvest and grouse season. A time to talk deer, to think deer, but not to hunt them. Or, as Old Man Timmons might dishearteningly question: "Hunt deer in the green leaf?" The whole practiced concept of Harland fit Harry's lifestyle like a finely tailored suit. He had the deer woods to himself.

Harry the Horn Man

Harry Ault was a special man, unique among the hunting fraternity for his unequaled knowledge of whitetail habitat. To the gawking delight of Harland's "town boys," his woodsmanship went totally unappreciated. We were simply amused to see his battered old truck, hood and tailgate decorated with deer antlers, chug down Main Street in a cloud of blue smoke. We named him Harry the Horn Man. That deer grew antler, not horn, was of little import to twelve-year-old boys. We considered it a fitting name, evidence of our sharp wit, and truly thought the old man a full-blown lunatic.

This perception changed when, on a dare, I rode my bicycle out to his remote cabin, intending to snoop around and spy on the madman. Oddly, to the dismay of my buddies, Harry and I hit it off grandly. A meeting of little minds, I suppose, and I soon became his friend and apprentice.

Long before I knew what an aphrodisiac was, before I could spell the word, I fully understood its financial value.

"Two dollars a pound, boy," Harry wheezed. "That means two dollars for a big • 'un, four bits for a little forkie."

To a twelve-year-old boy, in 1959 money, it was a tasty sum. In the long-forgotten land of ten-cent soda pop and nickel candy bars, a "two dollar horn" was a rare and celebrated find. To add an element of intrigue to my new after-school occupation, the Horn Man made me swear an oath of secrecy concerning the value of antler.

Harry lived in perpetual fear that others might discover his tiny gold mine and horn in on the fixed supply of antler sheds. He had little to fear—the town folk had long ago written him off as an eccentric hermit. They knew he collected antlers, but suspected he only built odd sculptures with his woodsy finds. Strange artwork was Harry's cover operation. Sure, he had a mailbox post of intertwined antler and covered the front of his cabin with wild patterns of various-size sheds, but it was simply a diversion. No one but I knew that yearly Harry secretly hauled a small load of antlers in his faltering Chevy truck all the way to Chicago and a Korean exporter. In that rusted '46 Chevy, held together with baling wire and electrical tape, it was a harrowing two-day round trip. Other than a very small, monthly disability check from the Veterans Administration, antler was his only income.

At first, I was aghast at the small fortune he allowed to waste away in his "cover art." I questioned him on the waste.

"Them's porky-chews, child. They's hardly worth spit. My buyer discounts hard for mice and porky-chews. All the way down to two bits a pound," he squawked. "A shed hunter has gotta get to the bone before the porcupines and varmints. You gotta have fresh bone, slick horn, boy."

In short order, I learned from Harry the single most important secret germane to white-tailed-buck hunting: Simply know where the bucks live. Each evening in that spring of 1960, we drove the backroads and highway, glassing for early feeding deer. It mattered not that the bucks were without antler at that time of the year. To my stunned appreciation, Harry could determine a rack-less buck from a large doe simply by

14

movement—how the animal carried itself or moved its hindquarters. It mattered even less that the worn county map decorating his kitchen wall was dotted with a hundred favorite and prime locations he called his "hotspots"; Harry continually scouted for new zones.

"It all changes, child. No feed zone stays the same year in and year out. Fires, logging, farming, and floods can change primary feed zones. It ain't people 'at move whitetails out of a range, it's food. I've seen fall rains mold and destroy entire mast crops, seen overbrowsing wipe out one-hundred-acre plots of young popple. Deer move on or die."

We worked every feed zone discovered. Without fail, each plot was the centerpiece of a large trail network. And Harry worked the trails. He explained how bucks rarely used the heavily trodden doe trails, preferring to flank these runways by a good distance. We simply walked these well-traveled doe trails, constantly swiveling our heads to study the ground running out fifty yards to the left or right. Few sheds were found on the main doe trails, but the flanking brush was a mother lode.

Harry the Horn Man knew his whitetails well. Over a period of years, he collected nearly identical sheds from the same bucks, often following their antler growth from yearling to trophy-class proportion. Contrary to much published opinion, I learned that white-tailed bucks are nearly immovable from their chosen home range. Harry and I tramped through the same bedding areas on a weekly basis, spooking the same deer from the same beds. The bucks never bothered to move from the area.

One particularly thick 320-acre plot of hardwoods was a veritable network of trails and beds. Harry had collected some thirty sheds from that plot over a period of five years, indicating it was home base to at least four bucks. It was a certain moneymaker. The following year, the half-section was clear-cut by its lumber-company owner, and I was sure the area would be a loss. Not Harry. Upon investigation, he pointed out where the bucks had merely moved their bedding areas a scant one hundred yards into the untouched timber and brush, casually resting there while chain saws and skidders worked a short distance away. That spring, we collected seven sheds from those very same deer in that same half-section. In fact, Harry's prized rack, the only one he bothered to have mounted, came from a buck that lived the majority of its life in a twenty-acre wooded ravine separating two farms. Harry collected the yearly sheds for several seasons, spotting the buck time and again, before finally asking permission to hunt the deer. That fall, he took the massive animal from where it daily bedded, less than fifty yards from a noisy machinery barn.

Although white-tailed bucks might travel a bit farther for special mast crops and farm plots, or stretch boundaries during the rut, these excursions are generally one-night trips. Like most creatures of habit, trophy bucks are far more comfortable with the familiar sights, sounds, and scents of their home base.

I learned a great many things from the Horn Man, Harland's own and only "madman." Yet it's his quaint expression that memory most often feeds back: "If they ain't living there, ain't much use a hunting there."

Chapter 3

One of the most misunderstood and blasphemed characters in the North American woods is the whitetail trophy hunter. Even in Harland, an occasional unflattering word is hissed behind someone's back—the "hissor" usually being a disgruntled or casual hunter, one who regularly settles for a yearling doe or a forkie and always adds with a smirk, "You can't eat them horns." If Harry the Horn Man was still among us, he might pause the moment and offer a small argument. Or it might come from old friend Carl, who recently turned down a thousand dollars from a collector for a beautiful, unmounted, nontypical rack he managed to take last fall. Last I looked, a thousand dollars still bought a carload of edible grocery—even at the always overpriced A-1 store. Actually, the aphorism is false. In a roundabout way, in a metaphorical sense, you can eat "them horns."

But I've never met a whitetail trophy hunter who gave more than a moment's consideration to pecuniary reward. It is simply the great challenge, the grand accomplishment. Although often surrounded by respectable bucks in his own territory, the average hunter can easily go a lifetime without seeing a trophy-class deer in season or in good shooting light—or ever. Most trophy whitetails are taken by pure and certain luck. By accident. Not that the successful hunter isn't a crafty sort who put in hard work and long hours, but it's highly likely that he or she didn't even know that particular buck existed.

There are still a few in Harland, purists, who dedicate themselves to locating a large buck long before the season and often, as in my own case, pursuing the same buck over a period of years. Why? Why Moby Dick? Why chase sixty-one homers? What is this seeming inherent yet often maddening drive to attain the impossible? It is no small thing, this thirst for perfection, a thirst responsible for great architecture and medicine: the technologies of the human being. And though seeking perfection in the deer woods hardly equates to the analytical pursuit of a quantum physicist, it is essentially the same concept—attaining the implausible.

The trophy hunter is so often miscast as a dispassionate sort, out of touch with the true and ancient reasons of the hunt. Reasons of meat and filling the larder; providing for family. This perception is a gross generalization bordering on myth. Though a fisherman might be wholly concerned with catching his supper, it is always the talk of his fourteen-pound bass that fills the smoky air of the corner tavern or cafe. There is no mention of the full bucket of nice eating-size perch his family shared for supper last night. The silence about the smaller fish reflects neither embarrassment nor lack of heartfelt appreciation. It is simply the predictability, the ease of accomplishment in the full bucket of small perch. Not so the giant bass. It is always the bass. The double-drop-tine buck. Moby Dick.

Trophy hunting is merely the natural evolution of the pursuit. A different plane. Not better, just different. A challenge accepted.

Peter Wilson discovered it many years ago. He came to Harland Corners in 1951, carrying a young bride and long-held dreams of an apple empire. Finding that stumping 160 acres of cut-over pine and hardwood in orchard preparation was a bit more costly and labor-intensive than he'd dreamed, Peter went to work for the county, retiring just last year.

His buck, a beautiful 190-class nontypical just inches shy of Boone & Crockett entry, hangs at Will Armor's barbershop, right next to the Four Corners Cafe.

Molded Leaves and Wild Beasts

Peter Wilson became a trophy hunter in the autumn of 1973. His previous twenty years of chasing game had always ended in success—his limit of ducks, a goose or two, and always a fine young deer for winter meat. He often wiggled a crooked smile when reading stories about distant fellows spending small fortunes chasing a trophy. And he was perfectly dismayed that some men, while seeking a trophy buck, actually passed up shots at lesser deer, failing to fill their tags. Born into a poor family of eight children, Wilson was raised a meat hunter. There was little choice. Trophy hunters were frowned-upon city folk, wealthy eccentrics. Peter was a woodsman, a farmer of 160 acres, and above all a very successful deer hunter.

Until 1973

The woods were damp and quiet that November day. Having already bagged a yearling doe on opening day, Peter moved slowly through the birch and alder thicket, the double-barreled 12-gauge at the ready. A Sunday supper of grouse was the anticipated reward of the afternoon hunt. Having failed to flush a single bird in an hour, Peter opted for a comfortable seat under a large fir and reflected on an earlier suggestion to his wife.

"Don't take nothing out of the freezer, honey. Think I'll go grouse hunting."

How many times had he put himself in this embarrassing position? Before the small thought finished its run, the sound of snapping branches popped the drizzly silence. Peering through the leafless alder, he watched the doe move slowly by him. She walked haltingly, spastic tremors twitching her flanks, stopping with every stride to paw the ground with a forefoot. To her right, the glint of antler caught Peter's eye. Like a mis-proportioned bloodhound, its nose clearing the ground by only inches, a small buck followed close behind.

Although priding himself a woodsman, Wilson had never been privy to the autumnal courtship of whitetails. With his heart pounding, seeming to climb high in his throat, he tried to stifle the rapid breathing, fearful that these deer, some twenty yards distant, would spook. It was in that held-breath moment that Peter Wilson first saw the beast. Through the wet and leafless alder emerged an ancient and massive buck.

Peter had seen a large buck or two before. To make ends meet on the stump ranch, he'd taken work with the county. Driving a snowplow at a lonely and dark 5 A.M., he'd witnessed a trophy or two freeze in the flashing brightness of his headlights, but never in daylight, never this close, and never this huge. Peter stared at the uplifted sweep of main beams. Small beads of moisture glistened off the foot-long tines of each beam. It is hard to accurately judge size at a distance, but he was certain the main beams were as thick as his stout wrists. The buck leaped across the small trail, thrusting its swollen neck and massive head toward the younger buck. The little buck squatted, tucked its tail tightly between its legs, and quickly bounded out of view. Having dispensed with the competition, the beast turned its attention to the rutting lust.

In an instant, the beast was alongside the doe, rubbing its swollen neck over her back, nipping at her twitching shoulders. Obviously in the deep of heat, the doe allowed the beast to mount her. Peter felt his back pressing into the bark of the fir tree. To be a spectator at a nearly sacred act of the woods would be his defining moment. He stared mindlessly, breath held long and hard.

Quietly, some twenty yards off in the brush, the small buck sneaked back toward the scene of passion. Stomping and pawing at the forest floor, he promptly, loudly, demonstrated a show of faux-courage. The huge buck completed his act in a few quick thrusts and without a moment's hesitation hurled his heavy frame off the doe and bounded toward the intruder. Realizing his error, the little buck again backed slowly off into the thicket.

As Wilson quietly watched, a small shift in wind threw two of the performers into a quickening panic. Suddenly the doe froze at attention; a small tremor visibly ran across her rib cage as she thrust her nose upward, screwing her nostrils for the scent of man. The little buck quickly circled behind a large cedar. Not so the beast. The huge buck simply dropped low, thumping its belly against the once gold but now mottled and molded leaves. With another quick scenting of human odor, the little buck broke in panic to Wilson's left, the doe darting off to the small buck's flank. In a heartbeat, the explosion of their exit became a deafening silence.

Wilson's eyes pierced the leafless thicket the beast had dropped into a moment ago. Minutes wiggled by as he squinted into the skeletal maze of naked branch. And there, in those moments, in his twentieth year of deer hunting, Peter Wilson became a trophy hunter. He watched in awe as the huge buck remained silent, its jaw nearly buried in the damp, rotting leaves of late autumn, its huge rack tilting into the tangle of leafless maple brush in total camouflage. The buck was lying flat and motionless, outwitting and outwaiting the scent of danger that bolted the other two deer in panic.

In those quiet moments, as Wilson watched the mesmerizing drama of life and death—of greatness—a small thought raced forward. Tiny shivers raced along his neck and back as the great deer crawled silently on its belly into the deep brush and out of sight. Many thoughts and images crashed about Peter's head. Of any thousand hunters happening on this scene, not one would have even glimpsed this magnificent animal. The doe was tardy in flight, probably offering most hunters a full sighting, possibly a shot. The smaller buck offered only a glimpse of antler and white tail as it bounded through the thick woods. But not a soul, not a single hunter, would have been aware of the incredible beast lying motionless in the alder and maple brush. "Beast." The word rolled slowly off his tongue as images of darkness and ancient tribes, primordial and strange, flooded his senses.

On a cold, drizzly day in November, it came to Peter Wilson that such wild beasts exist. In these friendly and familiar woods so near his farm and home, there existed more than just the generic deer. There also existed beasts quite unknown to most men. Bucks that spend a lifetime out of human sight. Mysterious bucks that move only by night, with a cold cunning germane only to predators, spending their lives in the dank and dark of deep-wooded sanctuary. Rippled bodies of strength and twisted beams of antler—a prowess that stamps them as dominant.

Peter unconsciously pressed his back harder into the fir's cold bark and peered into the growing darkness and drizzle, taking a long, deep breath. And in that breath he knew many things. He knew he'd found a new dream. A new pursuit. He knew he'd never again hunt up at Dempsey's abandoned homestead, its small clearing and overgrown orchard a mecca for young deer. Nor would he hunt the clear-cut on Popknee Ridge that flat guaranteed at least one good shot a day.

No, those were the generic-deer hunting grounds, the bright and friendly openings in the huge network of dark sanctuary. He knew the beasts would never be seen there. Only in the dark of night would they chance a risky step into those friendly clearings. And above all, in that same wiggling moment, he knew the days of autumn would now push him from the warm sun and pleasantries of the common hunting grounds, push him far into the swamps and molded-leaf draws of choking brush and alders, push him into the darkness and silence of deep woods.

It was no small challenge.

Chapter 4

The Scenting Game

I'm sure this argument of a deer's scenting and reasoning ability goes on outside the Corners, but I'm not certain any gathering of whitetail enthusiasts carries it out with such heated opinion, panache, and pigheadedness. We are a simple folk, but passionate in belief. Of course I'm talking about human scent and the deer's ability to make use of scent's warning siren.

It is somewhat ironic that my hunting fraternity screams foul at the antihunting crowd's penchant for anthropomorphizing all animals, gifting them with sentience and the full range of human emotion or intellectual predisposition. We find their proposition wholly laughable, rife with ignorance, a concept that simply doesn't survive the cold, razor-edged reality of life and death in the food chain. We feel quite superior in our realist approach. Yet we hunters, especially the whitetail folk, are perpetrators of very similar myths. Or worse.

No one gifts the white-tailed deer with more savvy, cunning, and analytical reasoning ability than the failed hunter. If the deer possessed half the reasoning ability we imagine, in worst-case scenario, it would easily be the second most dangerous predator on earth—in best case, they would drive cars, write books, and warm their tawny hides next to a roaring, natural-gas fireplace.

After spending a large chunk of my life daily observing deer behavior in a natural environment, I can only quietly snicker, much like old friend Pokey Corbel, at the wild exaggerations of whitetail intelligence. And scenting ability? Even more embellished than intelligence is the deer's olfactory associations. There are many hunters who wouldn't dream of invading the deer woods after the middle of September, so fearful are they of depositing the trace of human scent. "Don't trample up the hunting area with the stink of man," they proclaim with much certainty. "Not with the season so close."

Again, much like Pokey Corbel, I quit arguing with them years ago. I watch a few folks of Harland, along with the majority of North American hunters, spend millions on expensive, five-dollar-an-ounce cover scents while depriving themselves of all-important pre-opening-day scouts and wondrous walks in the autumn woods.

Two critters taught me very important lessons on the scent and reasoning ability of whitetails. One was the cautious red fox; the other, the first, was Pokey Corbel. Though Pokey now lives outside Tucson, Arizona, and hasn't lifted a snow shovel in fifteen years, he did agree to leave a beautiful twelve-point hanging on the far wall of his brother's Farm Insurance office. It is a strange-looking thing with an exaggerated narrow spread, long in tine and very tall, giving the appearance of leafless trees reaching skyward. Since Mr. Corbel first enlightened me about the ill-service of worrying too long on an uncontrollable thing like scent, the lesson of the fox can wait for the moment.

He was a difficult man to speak with, preferring the private company of his wife and his thoughts, rarely venturing out to mingle in Harland's community life. And though he always spoke softly with much warmth of character shining through, it was his biting wit, a harmless yet taxing sarcasm, that left many folks preferring the safety of distance. As happens so often, the

24

fear of challenge, the fear of a candid conversation, kept many from knowing a good man.

The Small Winds of Success

Pokey Corbel was the most successful buck hunter in all the Corners. Few argued the veracity of this pretentious title; his grand collection of trophy-class antlers and mounts provided certain testimonial. How he managed the feat, however, was a bone of constant contention. For Pokey, despite his remarkable yearly scores, defied every logical premise of hunting success.

To the discriminating archer or rifleman, Pokey was the consummate hunting nerd. He never owned a stitch of camo or bothered with any modern accouterments. His bow was an incredibly unbalanced and noisy homemade recurve requiring the strength of a small Samson to bring it to full draw. His rifle, a nearly smoothbore .303 of war vintage, sat idled, collecting dust and soot above the mantel for eleven months of the year. His hunt planning appeared so haphazard as to border on quirky spontaneity. He would close his small auto repair shop next to Viola's Kut & Kurl whenever the mood struck—be it noon or 3 P.M.—hop in his truck while still dressed in gasoline-soaked coveralls, and drive the fifteen-odd miles to one of his spots. To thumb a fair measure of insult at us scent-free, properly prepared Nimrods, Pokey smoked while hunting. Chain-smoked.

Try as we might to pry snippets of information from him, he always managed to outwit us, giving up nothing. He was KGB material. We would crowd around him on a rare appearance at the cafe or Harvey's, slap him on the back, shake our heads in admiration, and lavish jealous praise on his skill. It never worked, and as soon as the old man left our sight, with all the grace of feeding hyenas, we would tear him to shreds in wanton character assassination. Being short on facts but long on jealousy, our accusations were cruelly certain, fired by great imaginations and, of course, a few beers.

"He's probably a poacher. Notice how he's always out until way after dark?" the verbiage might begin.

"He most likely hunts over bait—illegal, you know," it would easily continue.

"I once heard of a fellow down South that leg-snares bucks at night along rub lines—that's probably what he does."

And on it went. The more dastardly the accusation, the more certain we became of our own hunting prowess and the consequence of our just-poor-luck. This went on for years until finally one evening Pokey informed us that he was retiring and moving to the desert Southwest. It took nearly a month to scratch up the courage to ask or, if necessary, beg for his whitetail secrets. Late one afternoon, a six-pack of his favorite brew in hand, I mustered the temerity to pull into the soon-to-be-closing auto shop.

"I don't have any secrets, son. I just use common sense, that's all," began the conversation. "But since I've always noticed you're a little short in that department, sure, I'll share my thoughts a moment."

Pokey quickly popped open his can of elixir and smiled.

"So, you ask why I hunt in these greasy overalls? Why not? Deer aren't afraid of grease. I've never read where grease has preyed on whitetails for ten thousand years, like man has. Have you? It's the scent of man that scares 'em. Hell, don't they come out every evening and browse right next to Charlie Perk's tractors in the field? Those rigs reek of diesel and gas. When I was logging years ago on Parker Ridge, them deer would come down on winter nights and lick the grease off the fittings on my skidder. These deer are plenty used to the odor of machinery."

"Aha!" I smugly interrupted. "My point exactly! And when you're hunting, the deer associate this smell of gas with man and flee the covert!" I had him on this one.

"What do you think they are, rocket scientists? They associate the smell of man to man, that's all. You think if a deer finds a pencil in the woods, it'll automatically figure you been writing a letter home to mother? Damn if you don't gift the critters with a mighty big brain. Plus, I always use a little skunk essence for extra cover."

"Skunk essence?" I questioned. "That's no good. What's the first thing a deer thinks when it smells skunk spray, Pokey? They know skunks spray at danger. Skunk odor has got to mean trouble and danger."

"There you go again, hoss. Deer don't think, least not like a man; they react. They don't have an analytical process like us. They don't sit down to reason and draw logical conclusions. If it's not programmed in their DNA, it goes right over their head. Once, I was watching a buck feeding down by the river when a rabbit-chasing coyote ran right by that deer. When the coyote caught the rabbit, the squealing was a loud and terrifying thing. You think it bothered the buck? Hell, he went right on eatin' like it was none of his business—and it wasn't.

"If deer could reason, why, hell, they'd probably be sacking groceries at the A-1, like you. Deer ain't smart, hoss. Just because they manage to fool you often enough don't mean ya gotta gift them a great intelligence. They survive by scent and sight, that's all. Take those away from them, and they ain't no brighter than that cardboard box in the corner. It's their incredible sense of smell, their awareness of place and motion that beats us. It's not intelligence, son, it's hypersensitivity to predators. I always use the wind, worry only about human scent, and sit perfectly still. And then, of course, I only hunt where the bucks live."

"Oh, swell tip," I mugged. "That's easier said than done."

"Not at all, hoss. You boys run out in the woods a few weeks before deer season and hunt down a rub line, or put up stands along beaten-down trails used only by does and yearlings. You have a better chance of seeing a trophy buck along the freeway down south. Every spring, when you boys are out playing softball or telling lies down at Harvey's, I'm out hunting sheds. There ain't a canyon or swale, not a field or woodlot between here and the county line that I don't walk once. From sheds, I know 'most every decent buck in the area. I even give 'em names in my notebook. I build three blinds at every shed area—not just one. I always own the wind. That's my secret, hoss, know your buck and own the wind."

Later that week, during a gathering at Harvey's Bar and Grill, the boys were hot to press me for the secrets of Pokey Corbel. "There is no secret," I lied between sips of a cold one. "The man has no secrets. He's just lucky, I guess. Sorry, I tried, fellows."

They shook their heads sadly, reconciled somewhat by the confirmation of luck playing the large role in Pokey's success. Such is the way of foolish jealousy, easily cooled with the salve of false credulity. With a sly smile I quietly added: "Oh, by the way, boys, I won't be able to play on the softball team this spring. My trick knee has been acting up lately. Think I'll take the spring off and let it rest."

Lessons of the Fox

Twenty years ago, I somewhat foolishly attempted to fulfill a childhood fantasy, thinking I could shape and build a lasting reality. As a young boy during the 1950s, my favorite magazine was *Fur, Fish & Game*. Thanks to that fine periodical eagerly awaited each month, I dreamed every outdoor boy's dream. I wanted dearly to be a wilderness trapper. I would read each story over and over again, study each advertisement closely, even the tiny classified section in back. Each winter's night, with that month's magazine resting safe on the floor alongside my bed, I would drift into sleep, imagining my someday grand exploits along the Yukon River or the Rocky Mountain wilderness. In time, by pestering my father to buy a couple of No. 1 longspring traps, I brought the first step of the dream to fruition. It was a good investment, I argued wisely with Pop. With the money I earned from trapping muskrats at the nearby slough, I could buy my own school clothes, saving him a bundle, the argument continued. And though he finally did buy a couple of traps, his smirking face was welded in the doubting "Yeah, sure look." As usual, he was right.

The slough running behind Carlin's pig farm lacked the misty wilderness spirit a budding trapper requires. Wading knee-deep in ice-cold backwater rich with pig urine had none of that imagined Yukon River charm. Though I did manage to secure a few pelts and receive the princely sum of six-bits a hide for them, I soon discovered a dream is a far better thing than a reality. To my calculating, sly credit and Pop's chagrin, I wasted not a penny on school clothes, spending my hard-earned income wildly with a handful of friends on milk shakes and nickel candy bars and more magazines of dream.

Years later, knowing too well that in some tiny crevice of boyish nostalgia I still harbored this trapping dream-fantasy, I tried again, this time seriously—dedicated and determined. The target was now the overwhelming abundance of fox in our county. Given a decade of poor fur prices, and trappers becoming a nearly extinct group, the fox population had boomed. In Harland, the scuttlebutt garnered from the few trapper-type geezers still haunting the late nights at Harvey's set me hot on the trail of certain success.

"A man could easily take seven hundred fox in a season if he'd be willing to work. Never seen so much sign. They're everywhere!" would begin the standard hype. "Wish I was young again. Yes, sir. I could take a thousand fox this year with no help. Mark my words," the talk would continue.

It was much too much for my barely continent and yet always scheming brain. Even at rock-bottom prices, seven hundred fox would more than equal my current year's total wages—and all for an engaging two month's work. It was time to give notice at the mill. I was destined to be more than someone's forty-hour monkey. I was a man of vision.

After explaining my new plans to a very apprehensive and doubting young wife, I began to study in earnest, buying every "bible" on fox trapping written by the old and great masters. In an act of pure kindness, I'll leave these authors of paranoia unnamed. They might have grandchildren out there somewhere, and no one likes the stray branch of the family tree rattled and remembered.

What does all this have to do with white-tailed deer? Scent is the common denominator. In every one of those fox bibles, written by the legends of the fall, nothing is more demonized than scent. The preparations advised to avoid "scenting up" an area were incredible; the warnings of danger in lingering human scent nearly hysterical. And I bought it all, believed every word.

For the edification of readers lacking any trapping acumen, to run a longline in hopes of taking seven hundred fox in a two-month season is a herculean task. Since a good catch ratio is one for every ten sets, the trapper needs at least one hundred sets and must be able to check all one hundred daily, while moving and resetting about thirty per day in keeping with the rule of seeking new or hot territory. This challenge, of course, is in addition to the all-night skinning, stretching, and drying sessions to process the daily catch.

I followed these masters' instructions to the letter—and failed miserably. It was not their offered set designs or general information on fox behavior that caused my downfall. It was their scent paranoia. The masters demanded that all aspiring trappers cloak themselves in rubber, preferably hip waders and rain gear, to prevent any human scent from "leaking out." One had to carry two sets of elbow-length rubber gloves and, please, never touch the outside of any glove with a fleshy finger.

One set of gloves was for digging, the other for handling bait or lure. Try putting on or removing elbow-length gloves without any flesh touching the precious outside. In addition, each book carried the admonition that all digging tools—screens, traps, hell, everything used—must not be touched, breathed on, or carried in the scented cab of the pickup. The new trapper was forbidden to chew gum (strange aromas might mist and settle to the ground), smoke (same theory), or sneeze, cough, or fart (again, same theory). The pinnacle of scent paranoia arrived with this warning: "Never breathe on the set area. Always hold your breath as long as possible. When needing to breathe, quickly get up from the set and expel breath downwind of set area before continuing work."

Thanks to following these paranoid ramblings, I was scarcely able to get in ten new sets per day; each new set consuming nearly an hour of precious time. I waddled slowly across fields and forests, sweating hard in my rubberized outfit and staggering under the load of many sealed containers of tools, traps, and bait. I felt like the boy-in-the-bubble. The season was half over, and, due to my inability to quickly place new sets, I was exhausted and had caught only a few fox.

But how could I doubt the word of legends? Though these books were written in the 1920s and '30s, they were the gospel. They clearly warned about the fox's keen scenting ability—about how it could pick up human odor three days after the fact and how the fox would "naturally" associate the odor of chewing gums or cigarette smoke with man.

At that very time, by way of some minor miracle, I was reading an article buried in the back of our state-sponsored tourist magazine. It concerned a crowd of bloodhound breeders sorely disappointed by the cancellation of this state's regional field trials. It seemed that intermittent rain, combined with unseasonably cold temperatures hovering at 32 degrees, doomed the field trials. Due to weather and temperatures, no bloodhound was able to pick up the trial's required eight-hour-old scent trail!

I've never been mistaken for a member of the intelligentsia, but it requires no large reasoning ability to look at my thermometer, registering 28 degrees, and put two and two together. If the famous bloodhound failed to pick up an eight-hour-old scent at 32 degrees, why was I worrying about the fox? Out the window went the books of legend, the sealed containers and rubberized sweatsuit. I carried all my gear in one bucket and quickly, unsanitarily, pulled on and off my one set of gloves. I smoked, I chewed, I spit and coughed. I breathed wherever and whenever I wanted, and I reset forty locations a day. And I caught fox—lots of fox.

To this day, many of Harland's better hunters still gift the whitetail with wildly potent scent-reasoning powers. Although I hardly advocate smoking under any circumstance, it is foolish to think deer will associate the smell of smoke with humans. They just don't have that reasoning ability. The lack of a fully functioning prefrontal lobe, that cursor of analytical reasoning, makes it nearly impossible. By repetition of occurrence, perhaps in Pavlovian dog fashion, after being exposed to it a thousand times, they might begin to relate smoke to man—but I doubt it. As with the fox and the bloodhound, if your woods are wet and cold, or filled with the musk of autumn, your buck is not going to be easily aware of your presence a day after the trespass. Exceptions to this rule exist in hot, scent-holding climates, or if you choose to urinate about the area. The hormonal scent traces found in body wastes are, because of their oil-based composition, long-lived.

Several years back, I decided to test Pokey Corbel's theory on diesel and gas odors. In an unused pasture about two hundred yards from our remote home stand two ancient apple trees. From late August through October, the falling fruits attract many does and yearlings, young and foolish, brazen enough to sneak from the sanctuary of woods and feed daily in daylight. Like clockwork, they faithfully appear every afternoon around four o'clock to check for new-fallen apples. My own fresh footprints—scent "leaking" through leather boots—around the trees failed to bother them. Neither did the spittle of chewing tobacco on the ground. On several afternoons we tied a diesel-soaked rag on one of the trees. It caught their attention, and the deer momentarily screwed their noses to the air, drafting the strange scent, but it failed to deter them. They still came in to feed. We tried it all—burning sandalwood incense sticks, hanging strips of bacon and open cans of sardines. The deer noted each new aroma, hesitated, then calmly walked in to feed.

But to Pokey's credit and great knowledge, all hell broke loose when I draped a sweat-soaked undershirt on the branches, one used while splitting a cord of firewood earlier in the day. First, the small group of does refused to leave the safety of woods, and we watched them mill about nervously until dusk. Finally, a young doe gathered the necessary courage to venture closer to the trees. When it approached within twenty yards, the full realization of its foolishness hit home. With a strong scenting of the shirt, the little doe leaped into the air and, with a whistling snort, bounded back into the tree line, prompting the others to scatter behind her.

For a week we alternated a freshly sweated undershirt with an identical one laundered with the sweetness of fabric softener. The result was predictable. With some caution, they slowly approached and ate with the sweet-scented shirt hanging above them. But each day we hung the shirt wasted in the fresh sweat and glandular secretions of man, the deer refused to leave the safety of the tree line.

Pokey Corbel was right—too often the hunter becomes preoccupied with remaining completely scent free, an impossibility. The small glands of the face, neck, and behind the ears emit powerful human odor, as does every breath expelled. It hardly matters that your jacket or pants may smell like that morning's fried bacon; it is your ever-present emission of glandular human essence that will always fail you.

It is a far better thing to forget cover scents and concentrate on the wind. With a breeze as light as three miles an hour in his favor, a hunter can chance to enjoy a tuna sandwich and a slice of strong cheese and top it off with a Cuban cigar. With no breeze, or the wrong direction of flow, the hunter can scarcely afford to even breathe.

Chapter 5

If one were to stop in our little town—that is to say, if one did not blink while traveling north on Highway 12 and miss it completely—this stop would more than likely be at the Four Corners Cafe. It is here that the traveler would first discover he had entered a small zone of whitetail Americana. There are at least two hundred faded photographs on the yellowing walls, photographs of hunters and their bucks dating from the 1920s to the present. No matter the season or weather, at least one group of men or women sitting in the booths or at the counter would be talking deer.

But it is up a side street, Alder Lane to be precise, that the traveler would encounter the true hub of gossip and tall tale. There, tucked in the shade of elm and pine, surrounded by a graveled parking lot, sits Harvey's Bar & Grill. Built in the late 1930s out of the county's last huge logs, the old watering hole immediately leaps out at the stranger's eye, as if one had stepped back in time a half-century.

It is not just the outside appearance—the moss-covered shake roof and small stream tumbling softly by the back door, or the faded deck of hand-hewn log benches flanking the creek—

that captures the eye and heart. It is the magnificent interior as well. The long bar and all the tables are crafted from rough logs, hand-sawed and sanded, stained and varnished at least twenty times over the years. They seem alive, and the first move of any stranger is to softly rub his fingers over the worn surface, as if to secretly reassure himself that it is all a real thing. Against the far wall stands a massive fireplace of native stone. Even in the heat of summer, long months since the old fireplace last crackled a warming symphony, the room smells of woodsmoke, a sweet, pungent aroma covering well the standard odors of kitchen and bar.

Harvey's has always been the receptacle of Harland's hunting crowd. Even the most pious, teetotaling opponents of alcohol consumption, the temperance zealots of town, find in themselves a necessary pardon of Harvey's Bar & Grill, and can be witnessed sitting a November night by the fireplace enjoying a charbroiled steak sandwich and cup of coffee amid the clatter of pool tables and the aroma of brandy. It would be a difficult thing to live in the Corners and be a deer hunter while finding too much fault or sin at Harvey's place. It has always been this way.

First opened in 1937 by Orville Pert, it took only a few months before it became a Nimrod's heaven. That first autumn, next to the front door, Orville built a huge scale of 8x8 wood beams. Although the scale is now frozen useless with rust, the old frame still serves as trellis for a patch of climbing vine and a sacred reminder of days past.

In those lost days of the food-scarce '30s, during the long climb out of the Depression, most folks of Harland prided themselves on the weight of the buck, not its horn size. A three-hundred-pound whitetail was a large blessing to a hungry family, and a wildly better thing than a tiny yearling.

Orville Pert started Harland's first official deer contest. With that just-built scale, he offered the owner of the heaviest buck a First Prize of a reconditioned .303, a box of shells, and a steak dinner for two. Price of entry was fifty cents, and there were second- and third-place prizes of wool shirts and dinners, and even fourth-place prizes of pocketknives and pitchers of beer. This continued until the more prosperous times of postwar 1947, when Orville became fascinated with the Boone & Crockett style of deer records and changed the contest.

Unfortunately, in 1988, years after Harvey Mott inherited the place from Orville, the state ruled the contest illegal. By then, its reputation was large, and the prizes had evolved with inflation into all-expense-paid, guided elk hunts in Colorado, new rifles, trail bikes, and cash. Somehow, probably with much

jealousy because it failed to get a "piece of the action," the state attorney general's office ruled the contest an illegal form of gambling, and the days of the great deer contest, a fifty-year tradition, came to an end. Governments and gods always seem to demonstrate a cold sense of benevolence when watching over their children.

Orville Pert called the place "The Hideaway," and at that time it was truly hidden. Far off the main street, Highway 12, in 1938, it was the only business on Alder Lane and was safely, warmly hidden away along the creek and among the trees. After Orville's death in 1974, his "grandson," Harvey Mott, came to the Corners with the intention of investigating his recent inheritance.

Having lived the first thirty years of his life in the Nevada desert, Harvey fully intended to sell The Hideaway and happily return home to the desert state with a pocketful of cash. He had barely known his step-grandfather, Orville Pert, was surprised by the inheritance, and referred to Orville by the odd name of Grandpa No. 10. Harvey's small mistake, the little slip in judgment that married him helplessly to Harland Corners, was the time of his arrival.

It was October, and, in defense of Harvey's weakness, one does not spend an October week in the Corners without falling victim to its mesmerizing spell. The magic of autumn—the nearly surreal beauty of October woods and field, the pulsing throb of the ubiquitous whitetail hunting spirit—is often too large a thing for the average soul to ignore. And if one is a deer hunter, even a Western mule-deer sort like Harvey, it is impossible to remain disinterested. Harvey quickly postponed the sale and moved into the large living quarters above The Hideaway, opting to run the place himself for a year—just long enough, he claimed, to become eligible to legally hunt the Corners and live a year in the land of eternal autumn spirit. That was in the fall of 1974, and Harvey Mott, now 55 years old, still lives happily above the bar and grill that carries his name.

Of course, many folks first refused to call it by its new name, Harvey's Bar & Grill. We are like that in the Corners, so perfectly contented with past and present that we resist all change, even subtle ones like business names.

Though Walt Thompson died in 1968, his service station still displays the large sign, "Walt's Texaco," its legal affairs are still conducted with that moniker, and it is referenced only by that name. Jimmy Wheeler, a lifelong resident of Harland, took it over, bought it outright at Walt's passing, and never considered changing the name. It had been Walt's Texaco all Jimmy's life; he'd filled his first bike tire from Walt's air hose, bought his first Nehi grape soda from Walt's vending machine, and was perfectly satisfied and proud to now own and operate Walt's. Silly? Maybe. But it is the way of life here, and we are fine with this silliness. I doubt the next generation will be much different.

I guess what made the nearly impossible transition from Hideaway to Harvey's a bit easier on us was Harvey Mott himself. If he had been a different type of man, a regular sort, it would still be secretly called The Hideaway. But Harvey Mott possessed such a quirky personality, the product of a strange and passionate childhood, that he was impossible to dismiss. Harvey leaks this quirkiness on all he touches, rendering his acceptance an act easy and natural, something that seemed to fit in so properly. It didn't hurt that he became the most impassioned whitetail man in town and quickly began to live each moment in that fine dreamscape.

It isn't easy for us to accept an outsider like Harvey in the Corners. It's not snobbery, for we are mostly a warm and friendly people, but rather that we have little experience at the job. New folks are a rarity here. In consequence, we all seem to have a mutually shared background, a commonality of life experience that, without malice, leaves new folks out of the loop. Most conversations are prefaced by the simple rejoinder, "Remember when?" Or, "This reminds me of the winter of '67 when . . ." The very nature, the spirit of this valley discourages growth, and we have little reason to maintain a chamber of commerce.

The general area is mostly state land; the few large private tracts are family orchards and dairies handed down from generation to generation. Without a growing industrial base and the new jobs it would provide, there is hardly reason to subdivide and build housing tracts, soliciting new settlers. There are simply just enough jobs to keep us alive at the present population, and these only pop up at someone's retirement or death.

One unfortunate by-product of this sameness involves our youth. So many graduates of our small high school (38 in this year's class) move off to larger areas of growth and opportunity, returning home only for holidays and hunting season. But on the upside, those youngsters who choose to remain and stick it out are the truly passionate ones, the heart and soul of Harland's perpetuity, not willing to give up what they recognize as a grand lifestyle. Solely because of this passion, they keep the Corners as it always has been. They are the new gatekeepers of this spirit, willing to live austerely, working fill-in or part-time, waiting patiently for a permanent job. Or willing to daily commute the fifty or more miles to a job in a larger city, willing to trade three hours a day in lost drive time to live in the veil of Harland's comforting mystique. It is for this reason that we are woefully inept at accepting new folks: we have little experience at it.

Although we thoroughly resented the name change to Harvey's Bar & Grill and secretly continued to call it The Hideaway for a few years, we took to Harvey Mott like a duck to water. It mattered not that he came from a faraway place called Nevada; he possessed our identical values and wit, our penchant for things rare and sweet and real. Perhaps it requires a certain background to nurture these values, a childhood link to the joys of simplicity that seem so alive and pervasive here. And Harvey possessed this requisite background in abundance.

This history is best illustrated in a small story we've all heard many times about Harvey's childhood, of how he met Orville Pert and came to call him Grandpa No. 10. And though it fails to involve whitetails—a rarity when talking about Harland Corners—it is an important story of coyotes and life in the mostly magical world of rural childhood, and it helps to define the shared spirit that binds us together in this small place of Harland.

As Harvey Mott stands example, it is who we are, not the time or place of our birth.

To try to explain all the factors and little nuances that drew us immediately close to Harvey, helped us take him in as if he were always ours, would fail to touch upon the true reason: his shine of character, sculpted from childhood. And to know of Harvey's childhood, to know the how and why of his long-ago, kismetic meeting with Orville Pert, Grandpa No. 10, we need to visit Nevada and Grandpa No. 9.

Grandpa No. 9

There was a great page missing from the tome of Harvey Mott's life. Or, if not a full page of posterity, then a paragraph of reflection, a sentence of wonder. Or a word: grandparents. Harvey was simply the child of his mother and father. For eleven years, his sense of family history seemed to involve only his parents, as if posterity began in that moment of conception. His maternal grandparents, the Corbitts, were long dead by the snowy dawn of his birth, and there existed no reference to them in his family. Somehow, their entire significance seemed relegated to the fertilization of a semiprecious egg that was his mother. As he gazed at the old tintype photos on the shelf, his questions about them would provoke only reserved and safe responses from his mother.

"Oh, your grandfather passed away when I was a baby, Harvey. I don't recall him at all," she would whisper. "Your grandmother? She was a fine and simple woman." That was the whole of it.

He never once suspected there was a history hidden away in them, some half-gnawed bone of contention collecting dust in a corner of posterity. Nor did he feel slighted by this glaring lack of genealogy. In fact, it opened an entire range of speculative possibilities for an imaginative lad of eleven years.

Knowing one or two minor details, such as that Grandfather Corbitt hailed from Texas and Grandmother Corbitt from Chicago, he was well equipped to fabricate any history that might serve in a game of playground one-upmanship. While huddled around an important game of marbles, he could easily top Billy Cartwright's boorish brag about his grandfather's feats with: "My grandpa was a Texas Ranger. Probably fought Billy The Kid. Go ask my ma if you don't believe me." Or, if the occasion required the pinnacle of embellishment: "Oh, yeah? My grandpa fought at the Alamo. Go ask my ma."

Harvey knew so little of chronological history that he placed his unknown grandfather at all the more important events of the great West. That his grandpa would have required a birth in 1750 and a full life of two hundred years was completely lost on Harvey's tiny brain. Fortunately, his pals were hardly any brighter, and his tales were rarely challenged. Of paramount importance to this lack of real challenge was the rejoinder, "Go ask my ma if you don't believe me." It was the infallibly perfect dare, for the simple reason that not a single neighboring chum would ever visit him.

Though he had many school friends of both genders, none ever accepted the invitation to sleep over. Surely, the whispering of their sagacious parents conveyed the warning to stay away from the Mott clan. It might have been due to his father's odd moneymaking schemes of cooking illegal booze, gambling, and capturing wild mustangs in the desert for the Reno livestock yards. Or it could have been a matter of the nine Mott children running barefoot through the dust and chicken crap around their tarpaper house.

But more than likely, it was the fear of his fourteen-year-old sister's problem. Young Ruthie, with a deteriorating mental illness, was often inclined to strip bare-naked and, in her budding womanhood, chase and bark at any passing vehicle venturing down the county road in front of the property. This was in an era before snooping social workers and government largess became routine. If not, poor Ruthie would have been expeditiously removed to the loneliness of the nearest state asylum. Her odd behavior didn't go unnoticed or unappreciated, as the local sheriff visited often, claiming some official business but mostly snooping about in hopes of a chance to gawk at the girl.

42

God, in His sardonic sense of justice, took Ruthie a few short years later, and to this day Harvey is certain she is now a soul of refined bearing in some celestial parlor, or, worse, chasing those same Packards and Fords across a heavenly landscape without the complicity of a lecherous sheriff. If Harvey felt a certain shame in her obtuse behavior, he was at least reconciled by the use of his often repeated dare: "Go ask my ma if you don't believe me." It offered tremendous advantage in the schoolyard wars of braggadocio.

In their poverty and obscurity, the Mott clan was not without morality and discipline. Harvey had been properly switched on the rear and had his mouth pasted with Fels-Naptha on the few occasions of that common childhood malady of "re-creating" the truth. But about his unknown grandparents, he was not lying. Wasn't there a chance that Grandfather Corbitt was really a Texas Ranger? Hell, he was from Texas, after all. And Grandmother Corbitt? Wasn't there a slim chance that she, as Harvey often claimed, was milking Mrs. O'Leary's famous bovine when it kicked over the lantern to burn old Chicago? After all, she was born in Chicago.

Presented to an imaginative child, one struggling with low self-esteem, was a veritable gold mine of possibilities in one-upmanship, the battle ax of young boys. Harvey was guilty only of mutating supposition into fact, probability into certainty. Are not some priests and admired scientists guilty of this same childish quirk?

But enough of the unknown Corbitts; it is Harvey's once-unknown paternal grandparents, blinking into his life for two memorable days, that eventually pointed his road in Harland's direction.

Granny Layne, Harvey's other grandmother, was a southern belle miserably displaced in the graceless West. Sagebrush could never replace the flowering dogwood; beer-drinking cowboys and dusty tramp miners could scarcely fill the tailored silks of her former Kentucky beaus. Yet it was this same crude landscape she chose to wander during the early years of this century. Perhaps the verb "chose" is used somewhat gratuitously—she had little choice. It wasn't simply her decision to carry off Harvey's month-old father from the grandstand of the Louisville racetrack in 1909, nor the fact she'd just swiped a $500 wager that Harvey's wealthy and blooded grandfather had won that day, spiriting both money and child to the railroad station in a selfish attempt to escape the bond of matrimony. No, her self-imposed banishment to the troglodytic West was equally necessitated by her acquisition of at least ten husbands over the next forty years. In an era when divorce was scandalous and a woman's grace demanded fidelity to one husband in flesh, memory, and grave, Granny Layne played the field.

She married this one for money and that one for love, and another for escape from love and still another for power, and one because he was a soldier (she was very patriotic), but she married Grandpa No. 9 because, at age sixty-three, she was plum wore out from the chase.

Harvey never had the pleasure of meeting Grandfathers 1 through 8, nor had he ever truly met Granny Layne; her last visit came when he was a tiny lump of newborn baby. Still, he sensed the coming visit would be an event to remember. On hard questioning, his father would only reply: "Your Granny Layne is an angel, Son. She's real partial to boys. You'll like her fine." Then at night, through the tarpaper walls, he would hear his mother's voice: "That woman ain't nothing but a gray-haired old tart. You know it's a fact, Papa. I don't want her and this new Grandpa No. 9 hanging 'round here. I got the children to think of, and I won't tolerate her kind of un-Christian behavior. It would be a scandal."

Let's not forget that this woman bemoaning the embarrassment of scandalous behavior found little wrong with a fourteen-year-old girl, naked in growing womanhood, chasing and barking at passing autos. Suffice it to say, there was an energy crackling through the dry Nevada air as the family awaited the arrival of Granny Layne and Grandpa Number 9.

The old Chevy pickup kicked up the August dust as it traveled down their long driveway. On its back sat a wooden house with shake roof and a small chimney smokestack. This was 1952, when Winnebago was either a town or a tribe and not some generic term for motorhome. The family had seen a house trailer or two out on U.S. Highway 40, but a camper, as we call them today, was a rare sight. The family stood near the chicken house and feed shed, mouths agape and eyes wide, waving a welcome to the approaching truck.

"I'm warning you, Papa. This oughtn't be more than a overnight visit. I won't tolerate more," Mrs. Mott whispered at Harvey's father.

"We'll let the cards fall, that's all." Harvey's dad shrugged, kicking the toes of his boots in the dust. "Now wave a little. Smile, for God's sake."

Harvey was immediately disappointed. His childish imagery had conjured a grand dashing dame with feathers and ruffles, a sweeping stride, and a flippant toss of a hankied hand. Out of the '49 Chevy scampered a gray-haired, ancient imp. No more than his own height of 4 feet, 10 inches, she was clad in pink pedal-pushers abruptly collared by silver-sparkled cowboy boots. At the top of this mess was a lime-green blouse, unbuttoned just enough to arouse and frighten an eleven-year-old boy with its exposure of sagging, blue-veined breasts—huge breasts waiting to wrap their jiggly business around a boy's throat when his turn for introduction and hugging came around.

"Now, you must be little Harvey!" she cried as his turn at the swinging gauntlet arrived. Her alcohol-rich breath blew a stink up his nostrils. Her Philip Morris cigarette singed the hair above his ears.

"Fletcher, come now," she hollered. "Get outta the truck and meet your new family!"

If Harvey had been mildly disappointed by the southern belle's appearance, then Fletcher, Grandpa No. 9, stole the show. The children had been told by Papa that Fletcher was a retired cowboy and had chased many a rustler in his day and probably hanged a few, working for all the big outfits in Montana. From an earlier letter of Granny's, they knew that Fletcher always wore shiny rattlesnake-skin boots. The children weren't so naive as to expect John Wayne or Gene Autry—something in the line of

Randolph Scott was all they required. It was not to be. From the running board of the truck jumped Jimmy Durante's twin brother, a twin brother who must have misplaced his razor. With a gray-whiskered stubble, a toothless smile, and a half-full bottle of Pabst Blue Ribbon beer, Grandpa No. 9 sheepishly hobbled toward the Mott clan.

Moments before, Harvey had been worried that Ruthie, in her uncontrollable excitement, might rip off her dress and start barking, spoiling this great event. Now, he half-wished that Mama would let go of Ruthie's hand so she could properly run off these impostors. Where was the great white Stetson hat he had expected? In its place atop the balding head was a soiled brown baseball cap. The frumpy little man was covered in grease-stained overalls. Even little brother Charlie, at age six, knew cowboys didn't wear overalls. And the great rattlesnake-skin boots? The old man wore black tennis shoes like any little kid might wear, except Fletcher's were pockmarked with little holes. From each jagged corner poked shrunken, sockless toes.

The southern belle turned to Harvey's father and smiled. "Son, I want you to meet your new pa, Fletcher Wibley."

Harvey's dad shoved his big hand out toward the little man and nodded. "Glad to meet you, sir. Mind if I call you Fletcher?"

Before the overalls could answer, the southern belle leaped forward in astonishment. "Now, John P. Mott, I'm ashamed, truly I am. This here is your new-pa. You call him by a family name; come on, Son."

Harvey's dad frowned a glance at Granny, and just as his eyes began to narrow in that look of anger nine Mott children knew to fear, his face broke into a grin. His withdrawn hand again reached to No. 9.

"Glad to meet you, New-pa," he smiled.

The little gnome leaped forward like a trained monkey, clasping Papa's hand while at the same moment splashing beer over Harvey's shoulder and head. No. 9's tiny hand—not a hand that once hanged rustlers, Harvey quickly decided—was swallowed up in Papa's big fist.

"The pleasure would be all mine, New-son. And you too, New-daughter and Grandchilds." The "cowboy" smiled a toothless grin at Ruthie, and she squeezed next to Mama's dress when the little man moved toward them.

"Now, Ruthie," Harvey whispered. "Let him have it with both barrels. Bark, Sis, please, now," but not a single growl escaped her lips. Harvey frowned when his mother poked her thin hand out to the reaching fingers of No. 9. He had little choice but to focus a stare on his dusty toes when his turn at the handshaking arrived. He wasn't about to gaze face to face with this cowboy impostor. He was suddenly, immensely grateful for his unknown Grandpa Corbitt, the long dead and famous ex-Texas Ranger. The gnarled little hand of No. 9 was now on Harvey's beer-soaked shoulder.

"So, you'd be Harvey, eh?"

As the boy felt the pressure of knobby fingers squeeze his shoulder, No. 9 busted out with a fart the whole family could hear. Charlie and Ruthie burst into giggles. Harvey was too ashamed to laugh.

"It's your Granny Layne's fault, Son. She won't let your new grandpa drink nothing but this-here farting beer," he laughed, turning to meet the scowl on the freckled face of Harvey.

"You ain't my grandpa, sir," Harvey snapped. For an instant, he let his eyes meet the shiny blue spots squinting out from No. 9's stubbled face.

"Harvey! Shame on you!" his mother hissed.

Harvey knew that later, out of sight and sound of the visitors, he had a good whipping coming. The fierce eyeball of Papa, staring over at him, foretold the future. He was doomed. At least he'd stood up to the fraud, and he silently vowed to not even cry when the later whipping commenced.

"Hell's bells, Sonny. You come with me to my little truck house over there and I might change your mind about this grandpa business." The "cowboy" pointed to the truck. "Of course, I won't be insisting you call me Grandpa. You can call me Mr. Wibley if it suits you, boy."

Harvey wasn't about to follow the little gnome anywhere until a hard shove from Papa propelled him against Fletcher's hip. With a frightened face, he turned to watch the rest of the family stroll off toward the tarpaper-wrapped house. A shiver of fear tickled down his back when realizing he was being abandoned to this farting, fake-cowboy grandpa. He quickly turned to motion little Charlie to stick with him, but Charlie had already spun about to hang on Papa's belt loops.

No. 9 flopped down a set of hinged steps and opened the camper door. "What do you think I got in here, boy? Come on up and take a peek."

Harvey was squinting, trying to focus on the pointing finger, when his eyes spotted a calendar hanging on the wall of the camper. It was the dirtiest picture he'd ever seen. Of course, by today's standards it was quite tame. But the huge naked breasts on the young cowgirl smiling over AUGUST 1952 * COMPLIMENTS OF EDNA'S CORNER BAR * HAVRE, MONTANA to this day remain Harvey's second-strongest memory of No. 9. The first and most important recollection was obscured by the overwhelming odors of cheap perfume, stale cigarette smoke, and strong urine from a porcelain pisspot stashed in the corner by a kerosene stove.

"Over here, boy. Look what Fletcher and Granny brung ya."

In the dim light he saw her sitting calmly on the mattress, adding to the complexity of odors in the small enclosure. It was a genuine Australian cow-working shepherd dog.

"She's all yours, Harvey, me boy."

"She?" Harvey's heart immediately sank. "Papa won't allow us to keep no she-dog, on account of the trouble they cause when they go into heat. And all the pups we gotta shoot, too."

No. 9 stared down at the boy's obvious disappointment. "Well, I figure your pap will make an exception with this here dog, this one being prideful to own and whelp outta. She belonged to an old pal of mine who just passed away, and she comes from a long line of cow-working dogs. Why, a boy could expect to get ten dollars for one of her pups, if

48

ya got another Aussie to breed to. 'Course, maybe you don't
need no ten dollars. Maybe you Motts is rich folk."

"Well, we ain't got another Aussie, sir. Just two old curs
that don't do much but bark and tear stuff up."

"Then how's about coyotes? Bet you got plenty of them
running these hills. Up in Montana, we breed a good Aussie to
coyotes. Call em Kai-dogs; sharpest and cunningest-looking
pups you ever saw. Worth a bit a money, too."

A light came on in Harvey's tiny brain. Kai-dogs? Maybe
he could salvage something out of this fake-cowboy-grandpa
fiasco. Maybe he was a bit hasty in his judgment of Old No. 9.
Harvey could easily picture his newfound wealth and status.
Harvey Mott, the Kai-dog man. "You think ten dollars might
be too much to ask for a Kai-dog pup, GRANDPA?" Harvey
hoped the old man noticed the nice grandpa thing.

"I figure ten bucks would be a good price, son. Got any
potential customers?"

"Plenty. You sure she'd take to breeding with a
coyote? What if they ain't interested in an Aussie? What's
her name, Grandpa?"

"Hold on, boy, one question at a time. Her name's
Mattie, and of course she'll take to coyotes, and them to her.
It's nature, boy. You just put her out in the hills when she
comes in heat—stake her out real good with a bucket of
drinking water, and presto, overnight she'll get knocked up
by a peckering coyote, maybe even a wolf. Got any wolves
around here?"

"Naw. They was poisoned out long ago. Pa thinks he saw
one on McClelan Peak a year ago. Would a wolf-Aussie dog be
worth more than a Kai-dog?"

"Hell, boy, a sight more. 'Course, not as much as a bobcat-
Aussie cross." No. 9 smiled long, and slowly scratched his
stubble. "I knew an old boy outta Billings that bred a bobcat
with an Aussie. Was offered two hundred bucks for that pup,
and that being 1915 money."

"What happened, Grandpa?" Harvey was beginning to
see many redeeming features in No. 9.

"What happened was trouble, boy. That little pup spent all day chasing and barking at himself, running crazy in circles. Wasn't interested in cows or sheep, neither. Right when that pup run enough circles to figger he'd caught himself, hell if he wouldn't roll over hissing and spitting and clawing at his own eyes, like he was all cat. The pup was a perpetual cat-and-dog fight, peculiar behavior, for sure, and that old boy that bred it finally up and shot the thing to put it outta its misery. 'Course, you won't have that problem with Kai-dogs—same natural family and all."

No. 9 gave a quick wink and tossed the boy's red hair with a knobby hand. Harvey knew a wink from his father meant he was joshing, but he didn't know about No. 9's wink. The story sounded real enough, and he knew that cats and dogs hardly got along. This was turning into a good day after all.

Then Grandpa No. 9 looked at the boy and smiled. "I'll fix this up with your pa. He'll know a good dog when he sees one. Meanwhile, you might figger on keeping her locked in that feed shed you got over there. The way she's squirming around, and the way them two curs of yours keep sniffing and growling outside, I think she's in heat right now."

The old man handed him Mattie, and Harvey carefully backed down the hinged steps accompanied by the growls of the two male dogs. Glancing up to beam a smile, he saw the new grandpa take a long pull off a whiskey bottle, then quickly hide it in a worn-out cowboy boot. A cowboy boot! Hey, maybe this guy used to be a cowboy after all, Harvey mused, or at least knew one well enough to get close and steal his boots.

Somehow, much to Harvey's surprise and joy, No. 9 convinced his father of Mattie's value. And he was correct about her coming into heat. Harvey spent the rest of that summer afternoon bouncing rocks off the two curs' heads whenever they sneaked the feed shed, trying to muscle in on the coming puppy empire.

There was one large setback in the new operation; there was to be no coyote breeding or staking out of Mattie. To Harvey's dismay, Papa Mott, the know-it-all, forbade it. He told the boy—right in front of the new grandpa—that coyotes wouldn't be interested in breeding with her. Hadn't he heard of Kai-dogs? Harvey was racked with disappointment in his father's ignorance and turned to No. 9 for support. But the old man seemed to be busy at that moment, studying the antics of a housefly strutting on his arm. For that moment, No. 9 seemed suddenly struck by a speechless daze.

"All a coyote would be interested in is a meal," the know-it-all had continued. "Coyotes will eat anything, dead or alive. And who the hell would want a goddamn coyote-dog cross, anyhow?"

Ha, he didn't even know enough to call them Kai-dogs! Harvey was stunned by his father's obvious stupidity. Still, no coyote nonsense was the order. Papa said he'd find a proper mate for Mattie next year.

"Fat chance," Harvey sadly whispered, knowing well his father's proclivity to forget and postpone.

There often comes a time when a boy measures the risk against the reward and flat-out defies his father. Harvey's moment of childish rebellion had arrived. It was his dog, and he'd find a way to do just as No. 9 had suggested. There was no reason to wait a year for the coming ten-dollar bills. He figured to move fast, as there seemed to be a strange lull in discipline, spankings, and even chores as the southern belle's visit continued. Although this was a first experience, he was beginning to understand the unspoken value of grandparents. He could easily use a visit from them on a weekly basis.

On the second night of the visit, through the tarpaper walls separating the bedrooms, Harvey heard his mother's ultimatum to his father. It would force him to make a quick play.

"I warned you, Papa. It's been two days, and I've already had all the fussing and putting on airs that I'm able to stomach outta that woman. And that new Grandpa, No. 9, the way he leers at the girls, I'm afraid if Ruthie had one of her spells, he'd leap right outta them filthy overalls and be chasing 'round after her. It turns my stomach."

"She's my mother, for heaven's sake. You want me to boot 'em out?"

"Mother? That sniping little gargoyle stolt you away from a wealthy and decent father. Cut you off from a rightful inheritance."

"Well, she had to birth and raise me—through tough times, too," his father whispered. "I owe her the decency of a visit, at least."

Through the din of bedside radio and the rustle of fresh sheets, Harvey bore witness to the only cussing he could ever recall from his mother: "Raised you? The hell you say! Of all the damn tripe. She pitched you into one Catholic boarding school after another. You was raised by nuns, you old fool. She was too damn busy promenading and castrating every man west of the Alleghenies."

"Well, Mama Mott, aren't you a sharp-tongued lass tonight," his father hissed. "I've gotta run up to Winnemucca in the morning and haul some horse for Ed Bryan. If I see them in the driveway, if they're awake in the camper, I'll say something. If not, I'll deal with it when I get back in the evening."

When the house fell silent with sleep, Harvey made his move. It was a long hike in the dark, a quarter-mile through sage and greasewood to a low ridge where coyotes ran nearly every night. Mattie came along grudgingly, whining and snarling as he pulled her through the sagebrush using his Gene Autry belt, a Christmas gift, for a leash.

"Come on, Mattie," he whispered. "You're gonna meet your new husband tonight. You'll be a happy new-ma real soon."

She failed to respond in the eager manner he imagined the new queen of the Kai-dog empire should, and in his nervous flight, he'd forgotten her water dish. It was a minor setback; he figured her to be bred by morning light and safely returned to the feed shed with no one the wiser. The chore was accomplished in Jeffersonian fashion, and he returned safely before midnight, shoving Charlie over in the bed and crawling under the covers.

The night was spent in sleepless toss, listening to the never-heard dark sounds of night—every snore and nightmare, every fart and cough, every sneaking mouse and creaking board, even the cries, snorts, and giggles from Ruthie's room as she played and fought with the ropes his mother tied her down with at night. Chasing cars in the buff was merely her daylight pleasure; what she accomplished in midnight creeps, if not restricted with tie-downs, was never spoken aloud in the Mott family.

Finally, near dawn, came the heralding cries of coming wealth. Louder and bolder than a winter's hunting pack, the howls and yips of coyote crashed through the tarpaper walls. Wide awake, eyes shining in the darkness, Harvey envisioned the nuptial orgy. An eleven-year-old farm boy might know little of human sexuality, but animal husbandry is thrust in his face the moment he takes a first wobbly step toward the barn. Harvey wondered if God might be just a little pinched at him over the images conjured in his calculating brain.

With the chorus of howls and screams floating down from the ridge came visions of several large coyotes nipping and snarling at Mattie's flanks. He pictured them mounting her, and wondered if they got stuck together like the town dogs he and Billy Cartwright had tried to pull apart. "Probably not," he mused. Coyotes were smarter than town dogs and had to get off the female in a hurry if a jack rabbit ran by. Harvey had it all figured out, and drifted off into sleep with visions of dollar bills and Kai-dogs.

With the grog of two hours of sleep clouding his head, Harvey remembered little of awakening, but he did recall his mama's yelling and Charlie's harping that breakfast was cold. Mattie! The midnight escapade crashed back through the grog. Harvey dressed quickly to dash into the kitchen.

"Where's Papa?" he mumbled, snatching three cold flapjacks off the platter on the drainboard.

"He's talking with your Granny Layne out in the driveway. Then he'll be heading out for Winnemucca. What's with you this morning? It's almost eight o'clock."

The first of a coming crowd of necessary deceits slipped his lips. "I saw a little mustang colt up on the ridge this morning right where the coyotes always run. Thought I might slip up there real quick, Mama. I'll be back for chores in no time," Harvey mumbled, suddenly proud of his newfound mendacity.

She started to object, but he dashed toward the screen door before a lecture on "chores first" rang out. Shoving a cold flapjack in his mouth, he jumped the two worn porch steps, nearly landing on her little patch of marigolds.

"Speaking of the ridge," he heard her voice trail off in the kitchen, "coyotes were as loud this morning as I ever can recall. You hear them, Harvey? Harvey?"

Just like one of the amorous curs, Harvey sneaked behind the feed shed to avoid the eyes of his father, presently engaged in animated conversation with Granny and No. 9 in the long driveway. Sneaking through the tall sage, he overheard the southern belle bawling and caterwauling some plea about family honor. Climbing the small ridge, he saw his father hop in the stock truck and point its nose toward the highway. He was safe.

Growing up in the rural West can bring moments of shattering ruin, not quiet disappointments but rather explosive shots, like some aunt's precious crystal goblets you accidentally bump and send crashing from a manteled perch. Moments of pure terror, real or imagined. After climbing the last twenty yards of the ridge, heart pounding from exertion and excitement, Harvey's life exploded into tiny shards. There was no tail-wagging Mattie softly whining her pleasure at his rescue. What leaped up to his suddenly moist eyeballs was the savagely ripped carcass of a small dog. The stench from freshly shredded intestines raced up his nostrils, and he turned to vomit the three cold flapjacks. Little black and orange beetles were already wiggling in her stomach fluids spilled on the desert sand.

"The bastards!" he screamed. "They ate her alive!" His eyes ran with tears; bile and mucus flooded his mouth and dripped from the tip of his nose.

Like all coyote feedings, they had started at the anus, eating their way through intestines and liver, leaving the carcass to taint a bit before cleaning it up at the next night's feeding frenzy. Splatters of blood and yellow gall juices soaked his Gene Autry belt. He didn't bother to retrieve the belt or bury the dog; that could come later, if Papa allowed his life to continue. But at that moment it wasn't Papa, or Mattie and her bulging eyes clouded with death, that raced about his mind. It was Grandpa No. 9. That phony monkey of a fake cowboy had practically murdered the new dog with his stupid stories. Practically forced him to defy Papa—and lied like a common sonofabuck. And Harvey's role? He was innocent, of course, tricked. Of this he was certain.

Feeling the hot blood pulse his temple, Harvey squinted at the tiny speck of the camper parked in the long driveway a quarter-mile distant. The conversation through the tarpaper walls last night crashed back through his brain, and it quickly came to him that the caterwauling he overheard was the result of Papa's eviction. He scrunched his wet eyeballs to focus on the truck. Was that a wisp of blue smoke rising from the tailpipe? They were leaving!

Of course, he'd never struck an adult in his short life, and, in fact, had hit only one boy his own age—purely self-defense—over a disputed marble shot. But he was going to pummel the new grandpa. Through the tears, he almost smiled when imagining his little fist smacking the old lying goat in that messy stubble of whisker. Harvey quickly pictured the shock, the southern belle's cry of pity, and the trouble it would bring him. What did it matter? He was already a dead boy, breathing borrowed air, thinking on borrowed time. Papa would never tolerate or forgive his open defiance of fatherly orders. He suddenly glanced down at Mattie, picturing his own small head on the torn carcass.

Turning to leap over the first sagebrush in his way, the boy dashed down the steep slope. Blinded by tears and snot, he misjudged the steepness, crashing headfirst against a granite outcrop. With torn jeans, a bloody gash on his forehead, and a strawberry scrape running down his arm from elbow to wrist, he scrambled back afoot and sailed down the hill. The camper-truck began to slowly move down the long drive, and the boy angled his pursuit to cut it off before it reached the county road. With lungs seared from exertion, tiny flecks of blood rising from pumping arms and splattering his tee-shirt, Harvey raced after them like a crazed warrior from the desert past. His life was over; nothing but childish rage was of any import. And then it all became a lost cause. He wasn't going to catch them, lacking at least fifty yards as they pulled onto the graveled county road.

Collapsing in the driveway dust, Harvey quickly grabbed handfuls of rock and, nearly separating his shoulder, flung missiles at the little camper moving off toward the north. As he slumped to the ground exhausted and emotionally drained, bemoaning the great loss of Mattie and fearing the certainty of a large whipping, he vowed to wreak havoc upon No. 9 on the next visit.

But it was not to be. That was the last time Harvey ever saw Fletcher Wibley. Two years later, a day after his thirteenth birthday, the southern belle again arrived at the long, dusty driveway, this time with Orville Pert, Grandpa No. 10.

* * * * *

Such is the way of sculpting hands, the childhood experiences that one day help to fill the measure of who we are. It is not one single event but their aggregate that completes the process. Providence defies all reason, moving deftly, touching its little finger of anomaly on every child's head, then moving on to shape another's soul with some odd circumstance. And with good friend Harvey Mott, Providence visited often.

Chapter 6

September is a welcome yet strange month to us. Serving mostly the anticipatory role of harbinger, it becomes a nearly quirky mix of momentary joy and disquieting impatience. Like most of North America, Harland has an early archery season, opening September 1, forty-five days before firearms season. But we are mostly riflemen in the Corners, and sadly fail to share the archer's thrill. I suppose it's our notorious inability to change, to seek a new way, that guarantees a clean miss of bow season's joy.

For the majority, September is a time of harvest and grouse hunts, days to walk the woods in peaceful scout. The first rub lines appear, dancing chills up the back and neck, heightening the rebirth of the season. Hardly a September day passes without finding several folks wandering the woods, carrying the just-in-case grouse gun, but mostly seeking the pleasurable stir of fresh rub line. Time and again the September woods issue the large invitation: Come forward and join. It is the silent promise of bright and friendly openings no longer mosquito rife and summer-damp, an autumn place, kind and waiting.

Though we find our ways to enjoy September, I'm sure our pleasure is small indeed compared to the bowman's. We old-timers are a helplessly stubborn lot and satisfied with our firearms season, but soon this will all change. A new September spirit is quietly evolving in our area, adding new flames of passion. More and more of our youngsters take up archery each year, and I am pleased with this happening. To bow hunt the September woods, seeking a mature white-tailed buck without benefit of rut or late fall's restricted food plots, is an incredible challenge.

We have always enjoyed our few older archers, men like Harry Ault, Pokey Corbel, and Rolly Harper, but it is a changing world, even in Harland Corners. I believe this first came about four years ago, when the Miller boy took a spectacular eight-point in mid-September. He used an ancient long bow, and after that day there was hardly a youngster between twelve and eighteen years of age who didn't pester his folks for a bow.

It was a heavy deer, already showing the early neck swell of November's rut. Long in tine, the buck scored high enough for Pope & Young and, of course, made the front page of the *Harland Herald*, the Miller boy smiling wildly in the grainy photo.

I must stop a moment to explain why the lad is referred to as the Miller boy. With only small apology, I must admit I don't remember the boy's first name. I do recall hearing it once or twice but never had occasion to use it, so the name escapes me now. Although now nineteen, he was always referred to as the Miller boy by us simpleminded folk of cafe and bar gossip. But after twelve years of trying to have a boy, after their four lovely daughters joined our earthy crowd, Hank and Betty Miller finally had their son. In his great pleasure at the final happening, even Hank always referred to his son as "the boy."

"Did you see where the boy hit a grand slam in Saturday's Little League?" Hank Miller might ask when passing time at the Four Corners Cafe. Or if you came across Betty at A-1 Groceries, she might question: "You see in the paper where the boy made eighth-grade Honor Roll?"

It is not purely my fault that I always fail to recall his first name, although I have a strong hunch it might be Jim. It's not as if we know every child in town personally; we are a large county and there was little reason to remember it. The "Miller boy" served substantially well in place of any regular first name. Again, without apology, we are a town of old habits, long-toothed in our inability to court change.

It was a simple matter of fate, Providence's other name, that the Miller boy and eventually many of the rest of Harland's young folks got pointed toward archery. The boy's simple act of accompanying his parents on a Saturday ride up north to a neighboring town's plethora of yard sales brought the bowman's spirit back to live again in the Corners. I am happy for this event—it was a long time in the coming.

The Long Bow

The boy picked up the bow from the small table at the yard sale. Turning it over in his trembling hands, he studied the fine grain, trying to guess the species of wood. Dark and smooth, the homemade long bow had a worn leather grip and stood nearly as tall as the fifteen-year-old lad. Trying to mask his excitement (a yard-sale buying tip his father had once mentioned), he turned to the old woman seated behind the tables.

"How much for the bow, ma'am?"

The woman smiled warmly at the boy and spoke softly. "Ten dollars ought to do it. It's worth a sight more, but seeing you're just a boy, I suppose ten dollars is a mighty sum. Am I right?"

The boy let out a long sigh of relief, answered with a happy "Yes," and dug through his pockets for the exact ten dollars he'd earned yesterday moving irrigation pipe in the hot sun for Tom Gentry.

The old woman again smiled, then suddenly drew a stern expression on her tired face. "I can only sell this bow on one important condition, son. You must promise me to make good use of it. This is a hunting bow, not meant to hang on your wall like a decoration. It's got my late husband's hunting spirit—his father's, too. It should live on."

Later that night the bow stood in a dark corner of the boy's bedroom, invisible except for a single shaft of moonlight reflecting off its slight curve. Sleeping soundly, the boy was unaware of the ancient bow's history, unaware that on another warm night some sixty years before, the bow had gathered a similar shaft of moonlight. At that time, freshly finished and hand-rubbed for days with linseed oil, it had awaited the short season of 1934. Its talented maker had spent more than a week crafting it, dreaming of a young buck dancing about the morning dew of Mulhaney's apple orchard. A buck to feed a Depression-poor Midwestern family.

The man had not keenly and patiently crafted the bow simply for the thrill of an archery hunt. He would have preferred the certainty of the .30-40 Krag or the old Remington shotgun. In the hard-starving times of 1934, a certainty of any kind was a small blessing. But he'd sold both guns in the winter of '33 to pay the mortgage interest on the small farm. Paying the interest kept a roof over his head—paying on the principal was out of the question. Through the long, dusty summer, the man had practiced with his bow, using hand-carved arrows to plunk the straw bales. With little money, he couldn't risk damaging the two expensive, store-bought shafts equipped with broadheads.

By early fall, he could place all his thirty-yard shots into a worn-out baseball cap and was only worried about the rumors of a canceled deer season. The whitetail numbers, hard-hit by failing homesteaders forty years earlier, were now being cut further by the Depression's starving unemployed. There was talk in the capital of canceling the already shortened three-day season. Still, he launched at least fifty wooden missiles each evening from every position imaginable. Having seen only two does in the rolling hill country throughout the entire summer, he knew it might come down to only one chance. One shot leaves no room for error.

The boy stirred from his sleep, sat up quickly, and squinted in the darkened room, trying to focus on the bow. Although the season was still months away, the excitement of the find at that day's yard sale stirred dreams of the coming hunt. He'd dreamed of being on Carver Ridge amid the small grove of rare oaks, dreamed of drawing on an eight-point pawing at the mast. Staring at the fine bow in the moonlight, the boy decided it was at least equal in personal value to his treasured Hank Aaron baseball card. Ironically, it was back in 1954, Hank Aaron's rookie year with the Braves, that the bow last changed hands.

Twenty years after its maiden hunt in 1934, the bow left the dark confines of the attic and fell into the hands of its maker's son. After his father's passing, the middle-aged son remembered the bow and, in honor of his late father's memory, decided to try archery. All summer, he, too, practiced with the bow. Unbeknownst to the sleeping Miller boy, the new owner spent summer evenings listening to Hank Aaron play ball, his radio diligently tuned to the Braves' games as he targeted the backyard straw bales. And the bow served the son well, helping him take eighteen deer over the next thirty years. The cherry wood, penetrated to its core with linseed oil, remained resilient and elastic, alive with action, a harmonic balance that seemed to direct each feathered shaft in quick and accurate flight. Then, once again, after the recent death of the maker's son, the bow had escaped another dusty corner of posterity to reflect moonlight and hunt again.

Accustomed only to shooting a friend's small compound, the Miller boy was stunned by the strength required to hold a full draw. At first he was certain he could never hunt with it. Without a let-off relief, like the compound provided, he could never hold it perfectly still for that small eternity while a white-tailed buck moved into range. Still, he practiced holding the long bow at full draw every evening in the privacy of his room, feeling the sting of pain in his shoulder and the numbing cramp of hand.

"That thing's pretty enough, son, but it belongs on the wall," his father, Hank Miller, had commented. "Put away a little of your summer-work money, boy, and I'll match it. We can go to Meyer's and find a nice compound. That piece of junk ain't made for taking deer—it's mostly just a decoration piece, that's all."

But the boy persevered. Through the hot summer and the first cool nights of fall, his strength and confidence grew. There was a feel, an unexplainable vibration to the ancient bow, and the boy was certain that, in the hands of a skillful hunter, the oiled cherry wood would respond with unfailing accuracy. It seemed predestined for success.

There could be no turning back now; he would hunt with the long bow. Not just for himself—there was no point to prove—or to keep a promise to an old woman. But more importantly, somehow he knew the real reason was for the sake of the bow.

* * * * *

Come September, an odd change seems to come over the whitetails. For all of spring and summer, they seem to pop up throughout my place, waltzing carelessly about in the lush foliage of woods and green of pasture, courageous things risking full exposure in the bright of day. They wander the fields, drink from the spring, and are actually fearless enough to browse the flower beds near our house. Not so come fall. Seemingly overnight, the entire herd disappears—save for a few young does refusing to give up the falling apples in the pasture.

When we first bought these twenty acres of remote land and began the arduous task of building an old-fashioned log home, I was ecstatic. It was spring, and I'd never witnessed so many carefree deer. Throughout each day, while I chainsawed and axed—both loud and intrusive noises—the deer paid us small attention, casually wandering across the pasture and moving in and out of the tree line. I couldn't believe my luck. Not only had we finally found an affordable piece of land complete with privacy and small stream, but also the place was apparently thick with whitetails. We saw large groups of does each day and often good-size bucks in growing velvet. Visions of the coming season daily filled my foolish head. I imagined how grand it would be to hunt a mere one hundred yards from home. I imagined the large number of bucks that would rush

62

past my stand in their rutting search, intent upon tending my heated does. I imagined the thrill of seeing ten or more deer each day while hunting. And I imagined it all wrong.

By September the rapid hormonal changes in both buck and doe, sparked by the decline and angle of autumnal light, radically alters their spring and summer behavior patterns. They seem to lose the tame and careless manner, acting first cautious and then flighty and tense, until finally they just disappear. It caught me by surprise those first years, but in time I came to realize the ritual disappearance was predictable fall behavior and, I believe, a prime example of the powerful influence of hormones.

The whitetail enthusiast will have to bite the metaphoric bullet and take my speculation for what it is—simply speculation. Although I've researched many published deer studies, I've found no mention to support or deny my theory. Still, I remain confident that this presumption of hormonal-influenced disappearance is the only correct answer.

Many years back, I tried to scratch out a living by means of another childhood dream, training thoroughbred racehorses on the "bush" track circuit of middle America, racing at a dozen minor-league tracks during the spring and summer. If there is one legal substance that is abused in the small-time racing game, it is the hormone injection. I reference "legal" because a veterinarian can legally inject a racehorse with testosterone or estrogen without violating racing law. Since both substances are naturally occurring metabolites in the horse, they are not considered "drugs" and do not constitute illegal doping. Occasionally hormones can radically improve a racehorse's performance and health, with testosterone transforming a lazy or disinterested gelding into an aggressive racing machine, or estrogen changing a thin, poor-eating filly into a robust animal with large appetite and desire to run. Unfortunately, artificially increasing hormonal levels often carries a large downside.

Whether the hormones make a better racehorse is questionable. What is a certainty is their ability to make a horse wildly paranoid, as if evolution has been reversed. Gone are the ten thousand years of domestication, the careless nature that allows domestic animals the luxury of relaxation, their ability to eat and sleep without constant vigil and fear of predation. Horses loaded up on hormones rapidly revert to a seemingly wilder persona. Mares that recently stood droopy-eyed, heads poking out of stall doors and casually munching hay, are now flighty and tense. Nothing seemed to bother them last week, but now a windblown scrap of paper sailing by sends them crashing about the stall. A car's backfire or other sharp sound sends them through the roof. They tend to stay back in the darker shadows of the box stall during daylight hours, eating and becoming more active at night. Sound familiar?

After the six to ten weeks required for the long-lasting hormonal surge to flush out of its system, the horse reverts to a calmer, domesticated nature.

I am nearly certain this is the root cause of the late-September disappearance of once-carefree, open-feeding deer. They are still about, of course, but now, with the heightened alertness and stress-producing surge in hormonal production, they are far more cautious in habit.

It is my only reasonable explanation. At my place there is no change in available food sources, no increase in human presence, and it happens every year. Of course, I observe this behavior in a northern climate with its November rut. I am curious whether this disappearing act also occurs farther south, some sixty days before the peak of their later rut.

The end of September is a busy time, a transitory period that finds the heartbeat quickening and people readying wood for winter fires and wandering longer in the deer woods each spare afternoon. We work about homesites and farms, tying loose ends of responsibility together. In the Corners, we seldom wait too long on autumn's demand for preparation. It is best to rid oneself of nagging chores. Soon will come a time of celebration: the fleeting moment of life's gift to the woodsman and hunter. It is not a time to be mired in work or troubles.

Tomorrow comes October.

October

"... a lucky man is offered two miracles of witness in his short time here. To share the love of a good woman and, of course, to walk alone the October woods.

wooden sign above the bar at Harvey's

Chapter 7

There is probably a kind word to speak about every month in the Julian calendar. And for each of us, there is a particular month to cherish. To a bright-eyed child, the joyful anticipation of December's Christmas never sleeps quietly. To a bass fisherman, thoughts of sultry dog days on August lakes evoke a lingering smile of reminiscence. A lonely widow might dream sweetly of November's Thanksgiving, a time of family and loved ones rejoined, if only for a day. But to a hunter, to a whitetail purist, there is only one month, one brief span of time, one incredibly fleeting moment gifted by the muses. October.

It is not the first snows of late autumn or the November rut that stirs the soul. It is the simple beauty of October. The October woods secretly draw out the humility of the hunter. There is little room for arrogance in the golden hue of birch or scarlet glow of maple.

If Mother Nature, or Caesar of Julian calendar fame, had ever nocked an arrow or silently chambered a round while a white-tailed buck was stepping into view, the magnificent splendor of October would surely consume a larger span of calendar time. Instead, October quickly slips away, creeping and crawling somewhere about the universe until finally, after a torturously sluggish eleven months, it suddenly reappears in all its remembered beauty.

There is no way to truly capture it. Film does it a sad disservice. Words fall empty—hollow failures echoing from the keys of a typewriter. How does one describe a color that has no name? Or sweet and musty smell to the woods and fields that may exist only in the self-serving mind of the hunter? How does one photograph the warm pleasure of anticipation and camaraderie when traveling the highway with trusted friend, driving to an old deer camp or a new hunting ground? Many fine thoughts, like bounding whitetails, have been left without trace in the October woods.

How is it that a man hiking a logging road in the green leaf of May, surprised by the flight of grouse or the waving flag of white-tailed doe, is simply, merely, startled? How is it that in the crisp and colored 'scapes of October—even without weapon in hand or any ulterior design—on that very same road the grouse now leaps out in a spectacular staccato burst, twitching every sensory chord of the man? And that very same flashing tail of doe now sends shivers racing the nape of his neck? Why does a man who spends eleven months in teetotaling abstinence suddenly crave the ambrosial aroma of hot coffee laced with brandy when sitting around a battered woodstove on a frosty October night?

Even the Plains Indians rejoiced at the coming of October. The Falling Leaf Moon of the Sioux marked the time of keeping fresh meat. No longer would summer days quickly spoil a harvested animal. Gone were the hot days of dried jerky and half-rancid pemmican. Now the crisp night campfires of the Falling Leaf Moon could once again pop with the drippings of fresh roasting ribs and dreams of tomorrow's hunt.

And the mosquitoes? No, the damnable mosquitoes, biting flies, and no-see-ums are not allowed in October country. The pests that torment the boys of summer have thankfully fallen victim to the touch of October's frost. The hunter rejoices. The stinging, bloodsucking vermin of the dark, humid woods are gone, along with that very same darkness and humidity. The woods are now open and bright, pulsating in scarlet and gold. Free and inviting. What was once a tangled mess of mold, green leaf, and buzzing hell is now a breathtaking sculpture of naked alder, their skeletal limbs silhouetted by the frosted red of blackberry bushes.

The air is now light and easy to breathe. The weight and burden of age seem mysteriously lifted from the elderly hunter. The problematic, daily turmoil of the younger Nimrod is equally erased.

I once knew an elderly man who spent the spring and summer scurrying about his country home, cutting firewood and taking early care of all other autumn chores. He planned his time and saved his money with one simple yearly goal— October freedom. Not a single day of his sacred month would be wasted in common toil. The mundane was never allowed to encroach, spoiling his thirty-one days of celestial romp. It was a month only to eat and sleep and hunt. With so few years left in his life, he refused to allow the creeping perception of mortality to waste a single precious day of October—be it bright blue with sun or cool with misty drizzle. Of one thing he was certain. There is no greater panacea for physical or spiritual ills than to walk alone in the October woods. The great painters and musicians call the moment Rapture. The eastern priests call it Nirvana. To the whitetail hunter, that fleeting moment is simply, sweetly, October.

Life is simple there—forever cherished.

* * * * *

Come October, Harland is fairly alive with the color and scent of the coming season. It is impossible to not see and feel it, pulsating about the valley and surrounding hills, animating all who live within its soft glow. It is only fifteen days until the opener, and though we all prefer the certainty of good chance accompanying November's rut, few will pass up a gifted day of October hunting.

I plan to hunt it daily, as usual, and have cleared my work schedule and obligations to afford the coming weeks of pleasured life. What is most unusual about this year's plan is the nature of the hunt itself. For the first time in many years, I won't be October-hunting the wooded land of my own property and the adjacent tract of state land. For the first time ever, I will hunt the grounds of a remote deer camp, resting safe in the sanctuary of its weathered cabin. And for a special experience, I will hunt it alone.

One smallish drawback to living in the Corners, in the middle of a large valley surrounded by rolling hills of magnificent deer cover, is the proximity of good hunting. Town folk must suffer all of a ten-minute, early morning drive to the best of private or public parcels, while farmers and orchard folk hunt from their back doors. This is a drawback, you might question? How could such a blessing be perceived as a drawback? The question is easily answered in three words: the deer camp, or, more specifically, the lack of deer camps.

There are many residents here, myself included, who have spent their childhood lost in the pages of outdoor magazines, moving through stories of African safari and Alaskan caribou, searching tales of whitetails. In those magazines of long ago, a common denominator, a golden thread woven throughout all good deer stories, a thread tugging hard at the hearts of the hopelessly romantic, was the deer camp. It didn't matter whether the story was set in the deep forests of upper Maine, the rolling hardwood hills of Alabama, or the still waters of Minnesota's North Country; the deer camp described was always grand and special, a lodge where the same men gathered year after year to live a week at heaven's gate.

Not so in the Corners. One would be more than demonstrably crazy to venture on the long and costly journey to some faraway deer camp when a better buck sneaked about the apple trees of his own backyard—a backyard offering the quiet beauty of October hunts with the added bonus of mid-November's rutting frenzy. As both lads and adults, many of us stared at those black-and-white photographs: sagging meat poles heavy with huge bucks, the shadow of quaint, shingle-covered cabins filling the background. We all stared with great want and dream, but did little to bring it all close or real. All of us, that is, except Archie Weil.

Another of Harland's silly romantics, Archie was determined to spend his seasons in a camp, and to that end he searched the county far and wide in 1948, looking for a large piece of nearly inaccessible land, a place surrounded by state land or timber-company holdings. With the blessing of an inheritance from his uncle, Archie Weil was able to build that dream. In some moment of sane mind, he put half the money in a college fund for his then two-year-old son. With the remainder, he bought a few new tools for the machine shop he operated down the gravel driveway next to Meyer's Hardware & Sporting Goods. With much luck and the rest of the money, he found a remote 160-acre piece of hardwood and fir thirty miles north of the Corners—still in the county, but more than a two-hour drive over the rough, winding road that served as the only access and enjoyed no maintenance.

At $4,000, the quarter-section surrounded by lumber- and paper-company lands nearly cleaned Archie out, leaving $500 for cabin wood and pipe to develop the spring. To his benefit, this was 1948, and $500 stretched far in the hands of an industrious man, willing to and capable of doing all the work.

For forty-five years, Harland's only official deer camp served Archie, his only son, and a handful of old friends, now long passed, in all its intended and imagined glory. Unfortunately, in 1970 Archie's son did not return from his patriotic stint in Vietnam, and it is for this reason I am now temporary custodian and trustee of the place.

I never knew Archie Weil that well—a short but warm conversation when our paths crossed was the extent of our friendship. I had never visited the camp, or ever been invited. To solicit an invitation would simply reek of the kind of graceless audacity that we Corners folk care little for. But last winter, as a terminal illness ate at his tired body, Archie invited my wife and me to a first-ever supper with him. Afterward, around the warm fireplace of his little house in town, he explained his troubling dilemma. Though we were hardly good friends, he'd chosen me as his agent, simply because he'd heard I was an outdoor writer and an ardent protector of Harland's mystique—a keeper of the whitetail spirit. He was compelled by love and honor to leave the camp to his twenty-six-year-old grandson, living hundreds of miles to the south. But he worried hard that the grandson, not a whitetail purist, would immediately sell the place, severing the long life and dream of the camp.

Archie was hopeful to his last breath that the grandson, given a few more years of living the tense chop of city life, would finally see the great riches of the camp and keep it going. To ensure its short-term survival, I was legally appointed the five-year trustee, during which period the grandson could not sell the place. At the end of that five years of thought and decision, it was up to the grandson to sell or keep—whatever he wished. Although experiencing much trepidation in my answer, I was compelled to honor the wish. It is a way of life in which I believe and aspire to maintain—I had little choice in mumbling "Yes."

That was last winter, nine months ago, and I've been to the camp many times this summer and fall, learning the land and scouting hard. After hearing the story of Archie's last hunt and visit to the camp, I found it a difficult chore to tidy up the cabin; other than trapping a few mice and storing a little firewood on the small porch, I left it as found. There seemed to be a certain grace about the place, a welcoming softness that begged to be left alone. Its magic grew from a simple story Archie told on my second visit to sign the legal papers he'd arranged. It was the last I'd see of him; he passed on a week later.

It was a sweet story of reflection, told quietly as we sat near the living room fire. There wasn't a trace of sadness in his voice, not a hinted quiver; in fact, he seemed to pulse with joy in the telling, his sparkling eyes shining the fine light of contentment. If I could tell it like him, with that twinkle of purity and the choice of simple word, it would be a better story in the telling. But I am handicapped in remembering the details and forced to work it through as a third-person narrative. Still, it must be told, the honorable good dream of Archie Weil begs the chance of immortality.

The Ambrosia

He showed the wear of seventy-odd years in the slow, half-hitch of walk. Though slightly stooped, the old man was quick to smile, never betraying the pain wandering unchecked in

arthritic joints. And a smile now wiggled across the white-stubbled face as he walked from the truck toward the old cabin.

It was Friday, October 14, the eve of opening day, and the old man had the deer camp to himself, the way he liked it. The grandson, with his own friends from down south, would be driving up the following weekend. Until then, Archie would savor the seven perfect days of October's splendid hunt—and seven stone-quiet nights to dream of hunts past. He didn't mind the young men coming next week, and mostly enjoyed their company. But they sorely lacked appreciation of the hunting camp's spirited swell of old days.

The young men with whom he now shared camp were too easily satisfied just getting out to the woods three or four days a year—too quickly pleased with shooting the first deer encountered. They were too impatient to craft a careful still-hunt, and much intolerant of the frost and silence of sitting the necessary long hours on stand. But even more bothersome to the old man, they were far too anxious to call it quits and head back to the city for another year, with little remorse at the leaving. Not a woodsman among them—not even his grandson.

Forever gone were Archie's old friends and Jack, his only son, men who lived to hunt this mountain, old friends whose eyes misted in tear when the cabin door closed tightly for the long wait till next year. Men who would have made several trips to the camp over the last two months, searching out new rub lines and scouting new feeding and bedding areas—just as the old man had done over the last two months.

In the quickening dusk, the old man glanced at the ancient outhouse and leaning meat pole and the iron hand pump standing over the spring. Through his squinting eyes, the deer camp seemed like a soft painting, warm and beckoning. It was always this way.

"Grouchy" is what his grandson's friends good-naturedly called him. A strange thing to them, this old man who hunted hard the day and enlivened the evening tales with stout coffee and the float of strong spirits. In his grouchy way he'd barred the camp door to portable generators, battery televisions, and loud music, proud of his small sign hanging above the chipped porcelain sink:

GOD DIDN'T CREATE DEER CAMPS FOR ELECTRICITY,
FLUSHING TOILETS, AND ROCK AND ROLL

The light rain was letting up a bit as the old man carried the last of the week's grub inside the small cabin. Smiling, he glanced at the little forked horns on the wall above the cabin door. The whims of fate had taken his son Jack some twenty years ago, but one glance at the antlers brought to life a snowy day in 1960 and a proud father helping his son carry back a first buck. A trophy? There is no Boone & Crockett rack that could cast a more pleasing shadow than those tiny forks.

The cabin had been ransacked by vandals and thieves a few times over the last forty years, but even the most indiscriminate thief failed to bother with the puny rack that served as the cabin's headdress. No one but the old man could feel such unflinching pride and sweet remembrance in so pitiful an example of whitetail glory. With the light rain rhythmically pattering the metal roof, mixing perfectly with the crackling of a new fire, Archie paused a moment to stare at the little rack and take in the light odor of sweet pine smoke drifting through the cabin. That's a buck of a lifetime, he mused in a long smile, a trophy of the heart.

Much later, after a supper of woodstove-baked potato and small steak, the old man settled in on the lower bunk, the one closest to the fading warmth of the woodstove. He knew the top bunk offered the warmer sleep, but the frequent nocturnal calls of growing age demanded the colder but convenient lower berth. He needed no alarm clock to ring in tomorrow's opener. The farm habits of childhood clung to him like an old robe. He always rose long before first light.

In those last moments of evening, as he leaned from the bunk to blow out the kerosene lamp, he visualized that great day of thirty years past. His nostrils once more drew the scented draft of deer woods, of cedar and pine. Once again he was watching the ridge as young Jack, unaware his father's eyes followed every move, patiently stalked the little buck feeding quietly on the opposite slope. This was 1960: the seasons still short, the deer numbers slowly building in the state, bucks only.

He'd shared the boy's hard disappointment in not even seeing a buck in his two years as a hunter; a heartbreak for a young boy of sixteen who breathed and dreamed deer. But on that grand day, Archie watched from a hidden point as the youngster attempted to field-dress his first deer. Fluffing the pillow for comfort, the old man grinned while remembering Jack's head bobbing up every few seconds with a sour face, gasping for a breath of fresh air. He watched as the boy carefully wrapped the liver in the sheets of wax paper he'd carried folded and tucked deep in his coat pocket for just such a prayed-for and monumental occasion. Archie allowed the boy to struggle and curse, dragging that ceremonial first buck a good hundred yards before he whistled loudly, betraying his presence and offering help.

In the crackling of the coals from the stove, the old man could hear the wild bursts of young Jack's voice, the adrenaline-rich account of his first stalk. Unaware that his father had watched it all, the boy hashed and rehashed every minute detail that night until he finally fell happily asleep. The old pleas of the boy to hang the tiny rack above the door now echoed softly through the old man's tiring head. Sleep slowly began to mix with the faint scent of pine smoke. A sleep not accompanied by sorrow but rather washed in the pure joy of fond memory.

Later in the long October night, through the cracks around the warping door of the woodstove, the last embers of coal cast orange beams of glow on the tiny antlers—a flickering light to remind all passersby that a trophy is rarely measured in length or breadth alone but in soul and heart, in the ambrosia of its sweet recollection.

Chapter 8

Two weeks have slipped quickly by, as time always seems wont to do in this swift season, and the time of camp has arrived. This fine place needs little more description, except to say that for a whitetail man the lay of the land is close to perfect. The one-room cabin covered in faded planking and blackberry vine sits in a grove of birch overlooking a quarter-section of small benches and draws. These little worlds, nearly separate in their environments, patiently climb the face of the steep mountain identified on a topo map as Stone Ridge. I have scouted this Stone Ridge twice, finding it an impenetrable network of thick cover and deer beds. It is impossible to scramble twenty feet without stepping in well-worn areas so often used as bed that large depressions remain in the earth. It cannot be hunted without perfect patience or great luck, two attributes with which I'm rarely acquainted, but it does serve well the 160 acres spreading out below it.

There are many small openings on this land, hand-cleared by Archie and friends over the years and now growing back in young birch and aspen saplings. Grown up in the red-stem box elder and patches of clover, the half-acre clearings dotting the quarter-section offer abundant and private feeding grounds.

Archie Weil had described it well: "It's not a matter of taking a nice buck up at camp," he'd whispered to me that last night. "That's a certainty for a man who knows the place. The challenge is waiting for the right buck, and having the patience of Job. I enjoyed the place so, but always failed the proper wait."

I've chosen several sites for ground blinds, elevated areas that let me peek into small canyons and saddles, and a few other sites that flank lightly used and probable buck trails leading toward the clearings. There are so many rub lines— fresh and old—on both large and small cedars, that one is nearly forced to ignore them, checking only to confirm the travel direction they indicate.

If I were to hunt this place during November's rut, I would set up differently, concentrating on the heavier-used doe trails and taking full advantage of the views of food-rich openings. I would pay much attention to the travels of careless does, hoping to catch a rut-crazed buck in foolish pursuit. But the grandson and friends will be up here then, and, not knowing them at all, having spoken only with the grandson on the phone, I wouldn't dream of intruding on their time or pleasures of camp. There is one large buck near my own place, a wily old bugger I've seen twice before, that will wander the legal-hunting daylight only when made careless by rutting fever. I will hunt him, come November, and leave camp to the boys.

We are blessed with a season in this area that allows a hunter two bucks or does—one by modern rifle, the other by bow, shotgun, or black powder's primitive weaponry—and it opens the door to myriad delicious possibilities. Most younger folk or those with families and large appetites to consume much venison take the first nice deer they encounter, then spend the rest of autumn seeking some famous will-o'-the-wisp, some ancient buck they swear in all manner of high embellishment they've been chasing for years. The older folk, those with no children or family in need, are far more patient in the hunt, knowing well they will take only one deer. To take two would hint of waste. It is job enough to consume one three-hundred-pound whitetail in a year with a stomach of ever shrinking appetite and need.

For these folk, for the Archie Weils of Harland Corners, it was always a game of patience, of waiting for the good buck, holding breath and heartbeat, letting the lesser deer pass. A lost opportunity hardly mattered—with any small luck, they could always take a smaller buck or perhaps a doe before the final day's shadow grew long. To them, just as it now grows slowly in me, what matters most is only this great moment to be alive, this time of October's feel and taste and color.

I have yet to gain this sacred patience they talk of so highly. I am willing to await the good buck, but I hardly possess the old ones' stoic nature, the ability to sit long hours in perfect silence. There are many in the Corners who have but one or two locations, and in these semiprecious spots they spend the whole of autumn, enjoying food and coffee in the comforting grace of all-day stands, filled with the certain hunch of good bucks eventually coming their way. They have all of September and early October to walk the gold leaf in grouse hunt, scout, or pleasure-stroll, to seek new areas or visit the familiar haunts of boyhood hikes. Now it is a time of silence, a time to take a stand and wiggle only with large caution, aware of all life around them—the slow-crawling spider that failed to heed last week's warning of hard frost, the squeak of a tiny cedar waxwing flying from tree to tree, or simply the sibilant rush of a cool October breeze.

I am not there yet, always tempted to rise up and sneak the thickets in a careful still-hunt. I often do this for most of the early season, spending only late afternoon, the evening hunt, purely on stand. Later, as the rut moves closer with its chance of seeing mature bucks that have the temerity to wander in daylight, I will endure long hours on stand. Just like most simple happenstances of life, the stand harbors a secret value, a special moment often overlooked or under-appreciated.

The Silence

I'm certain that some of the more profound thoughts of mankind were conceived in the silence of the deer stand. At few other stops in life is success predicated on remaining absolutely motionless, frozen in body, while the mind is allowed to dance wildly in free association. On the stand, the hunter is at first completely absorbed by the stillness of the deer grounds. For the first twenty minutes he sits in awe of the soft vibrations of nature. The slightest breeze, the bark of a far-off squirrel, or the sound of a mottled leaf fluttering to the frosted ground is a large interruption. He peers into the shapeless shadows, begging his eyes to find the desired shape of deer, ears strained, searching, seeking the sound of a coming buck.

And then it happens—slowly at first, coming on and then fading, then coming on again—the arrival of the deep silence. In that eerie, chill-provoking silence, he first hears the sound of time passing, the silence of time wandering through trees and fields.

Many would suggest the ticking of a clock is the only sound of time passing. Let them believe it. The hunter knows different. When the hunter's ears are tuned sharp but absorb only deep silence, in that noiseless yet deafening zone he first hears the sound of time. He can compress it, expand it, drift with it. Only when the hunter is perfectly still and focused does the eternal hum of both ancient ones and the yet-to-be-born fill the senses. A thin and sharp silence, pulsating and rhythmic. The mind begins to drift in that vacuum until—wait—the smallest of sounds, the scurry of a vole, the snapping of a twig; like an explosion, the mind leaps from the intoxication of silence and crashes back on the landscape of the deer covert.

Has it happened to you? Of course. Though the uniqueness of our thoughts may be sacred, the sound of time passing is a common experience shared by all in the silence of the stand. It's an experience without boundary, running into tomorrows and yesterdays, moving up, moving down. Over the years many sagacious ones have suggested there is more to gain from the deer hunt than just the harvested buck. I am always captivated by the moments of complete and absolute silence on the deer stand. It seems to have a hypnotic effect, and I have drifted across the entire planet, lost in the silence of time, until I suddenly caught myself completely oblivious to my surroundings and intent.

Once, while free-floating in that silence, I came to realize I was staring at a small buck staring back at me. I hadn't the slightest idea of how it had arrived in my shooting lane. I had seen no movement in the stillness; heard no sound in the deafening silence. Had it been there long? Forever? I was so enraptured by the depth of thought and silence that I merely subconsciously acknowledged the presence of the buck and continued my mental drift. Somehow my subconscious reasoning must have decided the season was too young and the buck too small, as I felt no inclination to acknowledge the animal. This free-fall in thought continued for several minutes, the buck and I exchanging unblinking stares. Finally, a small leaf fluttered down, and its tiny sound was enough to break the spell of silence. This time, in my unblinking stare, I readily acknowledged the buck and also decided it was indeed worth taking. As soon as that thought registered in my brain, the buck bolted back into the dark of woods. There had been no shift in wind, and I had made not even the slightest movement. I am hesitant to make supermarket tabloid claims about any deer's sensing ability, but to this day I'm convinced this one knew precisely when my thoughts changed from benign to malevolent.

The silence, the ethereal sound of time, is not without its pitfalls. I have known more than a few hunters who could not stomach it. An old friend once confided he could take long hours on stand only if the woods were alive with distractions. If they were completely silent, he complained that verses from old songs or advertisement jingles would get "stuck" in his head until sanity was threatened. If the woods were not animated with chirping birds, barking squirrels, and sneaking deer, he would give it up and still-hunt. Still another hunter, a relative from the city, opined that the deep silence actually frightened him. He felt uncomfortable and alone, unfamiliar with the strange feelings and thoughts that accompany the sound of time passing.

I'll be the first to admit it's often a mind game to spend long hours on stand, especially if physical comfort levels begin to deteriorate. But if your intention is to take a truly decent buck, there is little choice.

In a world where action and speed have become minor gods, perhaps the stillness, the deep silence of thought in a deer stand, is a perfect tonic. Contemplating one's place in the universe is, of course, not an absolute requirement for mental health. Nevertheless, the avenues for pure thought and reflection are free and clear, inviting, in the silence of the stand.

* * * * *

It dawned very cold that first morning of camp, far sharper than any opening day of recent memory—a warning peek at coming winter, as if last week's unusual dusting of snow was not harbinger enough. I was immediately grateful for last night's decision to still-hunt the early hours, hardly ready for a stand with morning temperatures in the low teens this early in the season. Often, the first week of deer season arrives with a warmth that threatens spoilage of fresh hanging venison. But these are the temperatures of November's Thanksgiving, the cold that begins to stay longer each week, barely abating during the afternoon sun and guaranteeing a soon-to-be winter. The frozen leaf will make for a noisy walk, requiring more time in choosing steps than in moving feet, but walking will still keep down the chill.

I am always the coldest at this time of year, being unused to the bite, as if this cold had never once occurred in the past. By the nights of twenty-below January, I will have grown so jaded in acclimation to the damnable ice that I would lounge outside in shorts to celebrate these same "balmy" temperatures of October that I now find so cold. It will take a few days of chill before I finally accept the growing cold for what it is and mostly forget it for the rest of autumn. By late November's cold, one dresses warmer and, completely unaware, practices some obscure Zen principle of ignoring cold through thought and faith like the reverse of walking a bed of coals by disbelieving their heat.

By first light I managed to sneak a few hundred yards from the cabin and stood silently on the edge of a small bench; the funnel of a narrow draw separating this bench from another runs westward to join in a saddle at the base of Stone Ridge. A heavy and fresh rub line ran up this draw toward the bedding grounds of the ridge, but I was sure its maker was already secure in the impenetrable maze up the mountain. Still, it was a good place to begin at first light, and I sat quietly against the base of a large cedar, squinting to gain focus in the growing light.

The rise of morning thermals carrying the warmer air of the valley below was strong enough to feel as it carried my scent up the hill. There was little chance of seeing a thing up there, with my scent now drifting across the face of the small mountain, and I turned all attention to the gradual slope of the draw below me. Within minutes, the crackling betrayal of frozen leaf accompanied the small breeze climbing past my spot. A young doe and its more-than-likely first fawn slowly fed their way up the draw, passing my overlook at forty yards. Although most hunters would pass up such a twosome, there is nothing like the tingling rush of first seeing deer on opening morning. Without intent or design on them, my heartbeat still took off on a small, uncontrollable run, and I was fortunate this was not November's rut, when a decent buck might be slipping through the cover behind them.

Like the first cold of autumn that seems to overpower me, the first close encounter of the season sets off tiny waves of buck fever. I am not unlike a fourteen-year-old on his first hunt, and barely controlled the trembling as the doe browsed closer, a scant twenty yards below my feet. At long last she scented or sensed my presence and stamped a warning forefoot on the ground. With a false casualness, she and the fawn quit the feeding and moved quietly up the gradual slope of the bedding grounds. Soon my scent would cover them, and whatever suspicion she'd just demonstrated would be quickly confirmed. Though they were just a small doe and fawn, I was suddenly, wildly happy and forgot entirely the unusual chill of this morning.

Partly because I had a full fifty-two-day season in front of me, I decided a small celebration was in order and tore into the daypack for the thermos of coffee and rolling tobacco. Yes, as absurd an act as it remains, I am still a hopeless slave to nicotine. While most of those around me grew wise, demonstrating the admirable self-discipline to quit the nasty habit, I remained the fool, the dinosaur wandering a health-enlightened new age. Even in the heart of a changeless place like Harland, there are only a few spots where smoking is still allowed: Tip Meyer's Hardware, because Tip is never without a half-chewed and often-lit cigar in his mouth; the Four Corners Cafe, where a ban would dissolve the age-old forum of old-timers who gather each morning in the corner booths, drinking pots of coffee and telling the same stories of earlier times and the better days of youth; and, of course, at Harvey's, where the ever-present rich aroma of woodsmoke masks even strong perfume. To my very small credit, I at least quit buying packs of the nasty things years ago, forcing myself to stop and roll my own when the demons call. In this manner, I easily limit my intake to perhaps ten smokes a day, a far better thing than my earlier years of unconsciously reaching for the pack twice an hour.

For years I worried that this large vice might be the sole reason for my failing to connect with a monster buck, the certain giveaway, warning the always-alert trophy deer that I was about. And though smoking certainly doesn't help my chances, I've grown to believe, like Pokey Corbel before me, that it is only the wind that matters. The odors of smoke and bacon and coffee warrant little concern to a hunter who owns the wind. Perhaps if I'd ever joined the growing legion of archers, those determined folk who must coax a mature buck within spitting range, I would have shed this cavalier attitude about scent. Knowing too well that a whitetail can scent a small distance even against the wind, I'm sure I would worry hard about the tiniest odor. But a rifle is a forgiving thing. With a killing range leaping out to hundreds of yards, I am concerned only with the direction of wind and enjoying my time in the deer woods without excessive worries about the joys of sandwich, coffee, and smoke.

This day reflects my favorite version of still-hunting. Rather than continually sneaking the woods in the three-step-then-stop cadence, I move slowly, silently, stopping to search long only when the tiny hunch compels me to stop. I like to move about

84

in this manner until I come across a place that just feels right at that moment. The feeling is a nearly indescribable mixture of good sighting lanes that run to distant thickets, a perfect wind, and the loud but often erroneous sixth sense of impending encounter. When it all suddenly comes together, I like to sit amid a clump of brush or with my back against a tree and let the quiet settle for twenty minutes, then softly blow a fawn bleat or rattle the small set of horns I always carry. After a half-hour of no activity, I move on again.

Because this method has brought me only a handful of decent bucks over the years, I hardly recommend it. Nothing rivals the success of motionless silence and long hours in a permanent stand. But this moving about, this still-hunting method of taking many and varied short-term stands throughout a day, serves my purpose well. I am here in these woods only to savor the hunt. Soon enough will come the rutting moon of November, a time when I must scratch deep inside to find the requisite patience for an all-day stand. Not now. This is sweet October.

I came across a small clearing the first day and was quickly surprised by it. Having scouted this land all summer and fall, I was certain I could recognize all of Archie's man-made openings in the densely forested landscape. This one was different, clearly demonstrating the traits of a natural clearing. Few saplings or clumps of brush and berry had ever invaded to take advantage of bright sunlight—an anomaly of sorts in this wooded land. Precisely in the center of the clearing was an old sawn stump, a remnant of the 1940s logging boom. It gave the place a strange appearance, as if it had been placed intentionally, cosmetically, by some mad woodland landscape artist—a backyard garden setting lacking only a birdbath and a few marigolds.

There was another odd thing about the clearing, a humming presence of past lives, both human and beast, and I wondered if Archie or perhaps his son had often hunted this place. Nevertheless, it was a good feeling, soft; the whole area was flush with the warm sun of midday, and it was a perfect place for a short nap. I drifted in and out of light sleep and daydream for most of an hour, wondering about the history of the clearing, imagining ancient times of deer and wolves, of long-past Native Americans sneaking this same place, a hungry family camped below in wait. But what has stayed with me longest is the odd dream of flies I enjoyed in that sun-drenched nap—a sleeping vision of some similar clearing and stump. I am certain it was a different place, perhaps another woods or even a different state, but it, too, possessed the same vibrating presence, a montage of past lives.

The Deer Stump Dream

The hunter had worked the logged-over ridge all morning—three hours of frozen tree-stand silence, the rest in a hapless still-hunt. It was close to noon when he finally stopped to rest and eat a sandwich at a sawed cedar stump rooted in a sun-warmed clearing. He paid little heed to the two flies that had somehow escaped the killing frosts. Behind him, across the graying growth rings of the sawed stump, danced the amorous flies.

The large, greenish-iridescent one sat on a growth ring some eight inches in toward the heart of the tree, rubbing its appendages to release the pheromones of sexual attraction. Like the man beside it, the lusting fly was oblivious to the posterity of its chosen spot. That thin ring where the fly now tempted a mate was once, as were all the inner rings, the very outside of the cedar. This ring was outside when the cedar was only a six-inch-diameter young tree. At that time, forty years past, the tree had been visited nightly by a stout whitetail buck. Each October night in 1954, the huge deer had rubbed and pushed at the small tree, working its swollen neck muscles in anticipation of rutting combat. The sharp points of its brow tines had torn through the bark, gouging the soft cambium layer in mock combat. The nearly perfect circle of the growth ring was indented, wavelike. Where the buck had once sparred, the fly now sat.

That fall of the gouging scar marked the last year of the big deer, the dominant breeding buck of the small valley. His DNA had flooded the gene pool for five years until, later that fall, one month after scarring the small tree, the old-timer's muscled brisket had been punctured by a young buck that had made a lucky thrust. Within weeks, weakened by its rut-driven breeding frenzy and lack of attention to rest and diet, the buck slowly succumbed to the infection spreading through its shoulder and foreleg. Weakened and hobbled, the big deer was surprised on the edge of the clearing by a brazen bobcat that sensed its helplessness and chanced a risky attack on the much larger animal.

On the day after Thanksgiving, as the first snows of November slowly piled on the little clearing, the cat lay contented, suckling the warm blood and other life-giving fluids of the deer.

The smaller fly danced and dove at the fat greenish one, skipping over a few inches to land on the growth ring of 1965. On that spot was a jagged pocket filled with crystallized sap where a broadhead had sliced through the bark. The boy who had launched the missile had sat in his ground blind for five frosted mornings. It had been the finest buck he'd ever drawn down on—most likely a third-generation descendant of the old-timer of 1954. If an unseen branch had not deflected the arrow, the boy would have taken the state-record whitetail. Now, thirty years later, the fly sat on the long-healed broadhead slice and attempted to coax a mating mood out of its neighbor; one last attempt to propagate its species before a killing frost.

The arrow, much decomposed, still lay buried in the tall grass and vine near the stump. The boy hadn't bothered to retrieve it, spending the rest of the day in a fruitless attempt to track the buck. He had never seen a bigger buck, and the rush of adrenaline was not about to make him resign the monster to memory, leaving the deer to quietly bound off into posterity.

The smaller fly again leaped at its mate, stirring the air with the scent of breeding desire, this time landing near the heart of the tree. Again it frantically rubbed its appendages together in a gesture of invitation. The fly sat on the small ring of the tree's eighth year of life, 1939, when it was a six-foot tall sapling. The ring clearly showed its slow growth rate and the heavy scarring caused by desperate browsers.

A record winter snow fell that year and, combined with a constant south-sweeping arctic air mass, had been responsible for a tremendous winter kill. Not only rodents and ungulates but predators as well, succumbed to the torture of 1939's starvation. On a frozen January night, the small tree had been nearly stripped bare by two yearling does. One deer, pawing through the snow around the tiny trunk, had nearly girdled the sapling. And around that small sapling, so many other small trees had been destroyed by yarding whitetails that a small clearing had eventually formed. This one tree had survived to bear witness.

The large greenish fly raced across the rings toward its suitor. Each hurried step leaped years in the life of the tree and the clearing—years of buck rubs and tree stands, winters of whitetail starvation, and summers of fatted plenty. The tree had grown as does dropped fawns in spring and as predators hunted on cold nights—the tree had witnessed it all—from the crack of November's rutting battles to the sharp report of a .30-06 and the whistling hiss of an arrow's feathered flight. And then the tree itself had been harvested, along with others on that tract of land. The clearing had been a fine place to hunt. In time, it would again be that fine place.

The flies coupled momentarily, than flew the ten feet to settle on the top branch of a close-by new sapling. The man finally noticed the flies, wondered aloud how they had survived the frosted mornings, and slowly stood up to continue his hunt. As his pant leg brushed against the sapling, startling the flies into a frantic flight to another stump rich in deer history, he failed to glance down to his left in the tall grass and vine where the decomposing and faded yellow arrow still rested secretly.

Chapter 9

I had to laugh at myself on that second night in the cabin—it all seemed so like another man's déjà vu. There I sat in perfect contentment, mimicking the story Archie once told, the tiny antlers of Jack's long-ago buck casting shadow from the light of the kerosene lamp. Without intent or design, by some quirk of mutual tastes, I ate the very same meal as he had: a small steak, some warm brown bread and a foil-wrapped potato baked in the coals of the woodstove. The largest difference between our nights was most likely the piercing yip of a coyote pack running somewhere close. It is a haunting thrill of cries, prompting the chills of imagery to run the nape of neck, and I no longer wonder about the Westerner's attachment to it.

We had no coyotes in this country of my youth; our only coyote experience was the fake howls set in some low-budget western movie. Lord knows the how or why of it—even the Fish & Game offers little clue—but the critters have slowly moved into this country over the last twenty years, delighting many but disturbing a few worriers. As usual, in my practiced sense of pragmatism, I am caught on the in-between of the matter.

There are three sounds of the wild I deem sacred for their certain ability to immediately stop all thought or conversation and send me into the distant mist of primordial dream, a pleasant place thick with the warm rush of excitement: the summer call of a single loon, the flutelike bugle of a bull elk, and the hunting cry of a coyote pack.

Still, much like the other worriers, mostly our old ones who fear change, I wonder if the coyotes will play hell on our rabbits and hares, the good numbers of grouse, and, most important, our spring crop of precious fawns. It would be beyond shame, beyond all things ironic, and then beyond that again if these wild howls that stir much good in my soul threatened the very life and essence of who we are in the Corners. I suppose it will be up to nature, for I've often read that neither trapping nor hunting seems to dent the coyote's proclivity for reproduction, so I listen close to the piercing yips, swallowing the heated thrill with a small dose of apprehension.

Is it an odd or wrong thing, a cruel paradox, as the antihunting folks insist, that we worry so to protect and preserve the very deer we will soon kill? I have often wondered if we Corners folk aren't a bit jaded in our self-absorption with deer and place. But in truth it is us, the hunters, the keepers of this spirited way, who serve nature best. For all our charitable bent, we are still a selfish species that goes out of its way to protect something loved.

If we in Harland lacked this passion for autumn's hunt, I'm sure most landowners would subdivide their acres into homesites, a newly formed chamber of commerce would beg new industry, and the whitetail would quickly lose its much needed expanse of orchards, alfalfa fields, and quiet woods. Those that survived would be chased by the new and growing population, the casual and hurried hunters of modern life who would drive every road and search the skeletal remains of a once-grand place.

No, I see nothing paradoxical, no dichotomy in our desire to preserve our deer. We know this animal to be short-lived, to rarely survive five years without predator, accident, or winter's bite of starvation bringing an uncaring end. Our spirited harvest, the grand pleasure it embodies, and the welcomed food of winter's table are the defining reasons of preservation. Without this eternal vigilance, without this fine love, who would truly protect the whitetail as an entity, the zookeeper?

It is neither paradox nor dichotomy, because we never harm the whole of what we love. We harvest the single, the short-lived product of the eternal whole, and in doing so with such rare passion, we guarantee the survival of the whole. It is not someone boxed in a concrete and asphalt place a thousand miles from here, staring at a picture of a single deer and simply wishing to preserve that singularity; it is not this person who will guarantee a quiet land of whitetails. It is us, the impassioned ones, who safeguard the whole. Such is love and its ubiquitous companion of large spirit.

When tragedies of passenger pigeons and buffaloes occurred, it was hardly the fault of this spirit and love, but more the cold morality of the marketplace, of money and greed. If we visit history, we will always find the demands of commerce or impending human starvation as the culprit of animal depredation. Market hunters nursing wallet rather than soul and starving pioneers forced to shoot every living thing cared little for the consequence of their acts. Not so with Harland Corners folk or the several millions across North America who carry this passion of autumn's hunt. We are the gatekeepers of a hunting spirit that transcends the fashions of history and, hopefully, the onward march of time.

Simply stated, the antihunting crowd ventures far from truth and norm when putting picture to their argument of an evil bloodsport. I once saw an animal-rights television show that dramatized by "re-creating" the typical deer hunt. Three wild-eyed young men, fully bearded and dressed in military camo, were squeezed into a 4x4 truck driving some dusty mountain road. An incredibly loud Hank Williams Jr. song blasted from the stereo as the men drove slowly along, all three with an open beer in hand.

When a small doe was spotted, the truck came to a sliding stop and the three wackos leaped out to simultaneously open up with fifteen-round "assault" rifles. The TV simulation showed the doe being assailed by a barrage of rapid fire—and how they accomplished this scene without killing the doe is beyond me—until finally the small doe lay thrashing, blood spraying about, while the three goons hooted and hollered, high-fiving each other in some Salvador Dali surrealistic fashion. Where the hell does this ugly kind of behavior go on? If this is truth, then even I, as a gatekeeper of the spirit, must oppose its fiendish nature.

Just because I live behind the soft veil of Harland Corners, I am not so naive as to believe the deer hunting crowd is without some goons. How can it be any other way? In a contemporary society that worships the gaudy and trumpets the ostentatious, we are guaranteed our fair share of the goon element. The unforgiving nature of statistical probabilities renders the occurrence a certainty. But I'm sure the television hunt's behavior is at least rare and purely anomalous in the quaint small towns that dot much of whitetail country. It cannot happen in Harland Corners; it never has, and, pray help, it never will. It is not a snobbish thing of we being better folk. Trust me, I have witnessed enough pettiness and character flaw in myself and others of this small town to challenge anything that happens on daytime television. After all, it is only a less-than-perfect world, and we Corners folk are simply human.

But deer hunting? Those ancient rites of autumn are never violated. The sense of grace and compassion, the spirited pursuit, is brought home to us at early age. Every youngster—boy or girl—begins his/her whitetail experience with a mentor, a teacher to initiate thought. We wouldn't dream of allowing a rowdy group of young teens to tramp about the woods with high-powered rifles and little concept of nature's grace.

Of course, we have our statistical share of broken homes, but if one is without father or has a non-hunting mother, there is, it is hoped, local grandparents to nurture the necessary spirit. And if not? There are many of us to fill the gatekeeper's shoes. We are a strange bunch in the respect that we almost always hunt alone—a condition necessary to fully appreciating the treasure of autumn's gift. We talk the hunt loud and often at friendly dinner gatherings, on the street or at the cafe and Harvey's, but we generally prefer to walk the October woods alone. The exception to this mostly unspoken rule, a situation more demanding than our private times of the hunt, is the need to shepherd a boy or girl without mentor. There are many here, people like long-passed Arthur Glade, willing to take a youngster without mentor on his first journey into grace. I mention Art because he carried me along, a boy without teacher, pointing out the simple concept of thanksgiving.

A Necessary Compassion

Art had twenty acres of apple trees down a long driveway off Highway 12 about three miles north of town. He and his wife were friends of my mother, and I came to know him through her. Finding it difficult to make it on only twenty acres of orchard, he had a dental office in his living room, though I don't think he was a licensed dentist. He did make dental plates, though, out of this new thing called plastic, and made impressions of clients' gums to facilitate his craft. Although we had a part-time licensed dentist in town, you had to travel sixty miles for false-teeth work or visit Mr. Glade's apple farm down the long driveway.

First and foremost, Arthur Glade was a deer hunter. I can only hope an equally enjoyable pursuit now tickles his spiritual fancy in whatever eternal landscape he occupies. I first met Art in the early 1960s. Being just a teenager, I sorely lacked the depth of experience to truly appreciate his striking humanity. Of course, because of his reputation, I hounded him for hunting tips, picking his sixty-four-year-old brain for tidbits of deer wisdom. Never one to spare a word or phrase, Art would recount a particular hunt in the form of incredibly long-winded tales, managing to touch on every aspect of weather encountered, locale visited, company enjoyed, and thought transpired. To a restless fifteen-year-old boy, these tales could be excruciatingly tedious. Yet, from each story I seemed always to glean a snippet of sound advice, tactic, or some secret little knowledge of whitetail habits.

It was always worth the mental struggle, for in those early years, word-of-mouth was about the only source of whitetail information. The few outdoor magazines of the period covered all forms of sporting life from Cape buffalo and African lion hunting to marlin and barracuda fishing. The pursuit of America's greatest outdoor resource, the whitetail, commanded little printed space in magazines showcasing global adventure. A young hunter learned by asking questions of older hunters, then filtering the tangled mess of facts, superstitions, opinions, and outright malarkey into a working, functional knowledge.

Arthur Glade was a veritable encyclopedia of the above listings. In consequence, it was with great pride and honor that I accepted his kind invitation to join him on a hunting trip up north for the '62 opening weekend. I spent an agonizingly long month awaiting the October 15 date. Having managed to take one doe in my first two years of hunting alone, I was certain that under his tutelage, benefiting from his wealth of knowledge, I would take a buck, or at least finally see one during the season.

There was little room for doubt. Much to the chagrin of my less-fortunate and uninvited pals, a creeping confidence bordering on arrogance began to pump through my veins. And well it should have. Art Glade's living room was a theater of whitetail-hunting prowess. Four incredible trophies adorned the walls of the living room/dental clinic. Above the fireplace mantel stood an assortment of framed photographs of deer hunts from the first half of this century. In each photo, a smiling, mustached Art Glade stood with friends alongside meat poles straining under the huge weight of bucks. A museum of other American wildlife stood in that living-room office—mounted pheasants and blue-winged teal on the tables, a black bear rug on the floor, and a fully stretched cougar hide covered the wall above his wife's rocking chair. To a boy captivated by the outdoors, a visit to Art's house was a nearly sacred experience, and it was the only place my mother visited that I pestered her incessantly to come along.

And a boy's dream did come true that year. Well situated in a ground blind Art had built the week before, and following

94

strict orders to remain silent and motionless, I trembled with excitement as a six-point buck fell to the roar of my 12-gauge, the gift of Ed Timmons. But it is not that first buck, nor Arthur's museum-like home, nor his thousand long-winded tales that remain most alive in my memory. What lives forever in me is a small event that occurred some moments after the shot.

With adrenaline pumping wildly, I leaped from my blind and shouted for Art. As he walked up the small trail, I ran toward the fallen buck. Still buzzing with elation, already dreaming of the heroic tales I would tell at school, I approached the deer, wondering if it was dead. With naive and youthful excitement, I gave the buck a hard kick in the brisket to see if it would move. At that very moment, Arthur walked up and put a hand on my shoulder. With one glance at his eyes, I knew the old man was troubled.

As the buck lay lifeless in front of us, Art asked that we kneel in thanksgiving. I knew he wasn't religious; he attended none of the churches in town. I was mystified. I had shot the buck fair and square; I had spotted it myself and waited patiently. To whom were we giving this thanks?

"It is not a respectful act, kicking this fallen deer," he said softly. "You must show it honor and compassion, son. Every life taken has special meaning, for its consumption grants the gift of continuing life to the taker." Art sat us both down on the half-frosted ground, took his cap off, and spoke quietly. "Be it bacteria, bobcat, or man, we all must consume other life forms to survive. Except for our God-given ability to demonstrate compassion and grace, there is very little that separates man from the other predators. It is a necessary compassion, son."

I often think back on that October day, not solely for the memory of my first buck but simply to picture his kind face and droopy gray mustache. I can't help but smile in appreciation of the small gift Arthur Glade gave me that day, and I aspire to pass it on to the youngsters of today. The complete hunter understands the deeper meaning of his hunting fortunes. To a man of strong religion, hunting success is a blessing from God. To an evolutionist, a blessing of earth.

Whatever our beliefs, we honor the harvest by showing a silent appreciation, a thanksgiving.

We must. That quiet moment brings the hunter full circle in his experience of the earth's food chain. Certainly, it is less complicated to pay coin at the market for our meats. We are then relieved of the obligations of understanding, relieved of the silent moment of grace, relieved of the knowledge of life and death in the food chain.

Yes, Arthur, I've come to fully understand your feelings. That small grace is what separates us from the other beasts.

And it is a necessary compassion.

Chapter 10

Except for the blowing nostrils of the deer, the ridge was silent. There was no movement in the valley below. The huge buck turned to glance up again, focusing its eyes on the ridge to the south. If there was a danger about, the deer could not detect it. But as the sun offered a faint pink glow to the canyon, the buck instinctively knew it had violated the inflexible law of survival. It was not the simple matter of increasing visibility in the dawning light that twitched its alarm, but rather the ancient triggering mechanism of scent awareness.

Though lacking the ability to reason and speculate, the buck possessed an instinctive awareness of air patterns and scent. And it was dawn, time for the warming air of the valley to rhythmically climb the hills, forcing the deer to travel to a bedding area with the rising thermal at its back. The huge buck had not survived six winters in the haunt of predator by such miscalculated ventures. That rising air of dawn would broadcast its rut-drenched scent far up the canyon to any waiting nostril. This was clearly a time to be in the sanctuary of silent bed. The buck screwed its nose to the crisp air, drawing the strong drafts of birch and pine. No alarm.

A half-mile up the small canyon, Robert Altman squirmed; the frosted air penetrated his wool trousers and thermal underwear. Feeling his body twitch with little spasms of chill, he tried to wiggle without motion, letting the warming blood of activity pulse through his numb limbs. It was only 8 A.M.; he would give it at least another hour, fighting the desire to give up his stand and still-hunt back to the truck and hot coffee. He tried to block the image of warm truck by focusing his attention on the morning antics of two squirrels.

Robert closed his eyes and pictured the long main beam of the antler shed his uncle had found in this canyon last spring. It was nearly as thick as a baseball bat, with six long tines— one was thirteen inches long. He was certain the buck was still alive; the soft earth betrayed the presence of a massive deer. Huge tracks as large as his fist were crushed through the fallen leaves of birch and maple. Rubs on eight-inch-thick cedars covered the north slope of the small canyon.

Altman opened his eyes and shivered, staring through the growing light of green and gold hue. He'd already blown five days of vacation time working this canyon, five days of frozen hands and feet, seeking one deer. At least he had tried. He had done it all correctly, scheduling a week off during the heart of October and arriving in the canyon six miles north of Harland in the cold dark of every morning. Yesterday he'd passed on a twenty-yard shot at a ten-point that would better any whitetail he'd taken in his many years of hunting. But remarkably, he hadn't even hesitated in passing on the buck. The choice was clear and simple. He would bring home the largest whitetail taken in the state this year, or not fill his tag at all.

The sun cleared the eastern mountains, quickly spreading warmth on the canyon wall. The spicy incense of birch filled the deer's nostrils, and it stopped its climb up the steep slope, biting off a waxy-brown mushroom growing through the forest duff. The buck felt little strength moving through its limbs; it had eaten no more than a few mouthfuls of browse in the last few days, its appetite nearly nonexistent. The big deer was living off fat reserves—strength powered by the hormone-drenched lust of a false rut. Though it was only late October, several of the yearling does cycled early, as they sporadically do in some anomalous twitch of nature. Whenever the buck stopped to replenish its waning strength, the pheromones emanating from heated does clouded its sense of hunger. And the canyon was rich with the scent of does in the deep of heat.

With some small luck, Robert Altman had chosen a perfect time to hunt. For reasons unknown to science, more than an isolated doe had come into early heat this year; the small canyon was home to three yearling does displaying this anomaly. It was Altman's third hunting trip north to Harland, the first in many years and one he hoped always to remember. As a young boy, he'd spent several summers working for favorite uncle Sid Altman, a dairyman plying the ancient husbandry four miles north of town. Robert had driven from distant Illinois to chase a buck Uncle Sid had written about.

I remember Robert and his summer stays of years back for the simple reason that I was then driving a milk truck that gathered the local dairy output. Though I had little occasion to talk with him, I easily remember his friendly wave at the farm on my morning arrivals. Twice in the recent past, he'd saved enough money to buy nonresident tags, taking a few days off to pleasantly hunt a land of boyhood memory. This time was different. After the letters and pictures of the shed Uncle Sid had sent, he'd decided to commit—to dedicate a week and much effort in searching out the Holy Grail of North America. He had hoped to hunt November's rut, but the demands of family and Thanksgiving begged a less selfish approach. It mattered not. The muse of hunting luck rewarded his small sacrifice to family love by offering a heated false rut.

The deer swallowed a mouthful of the fungus and moved higher up the ridge, letting most of the mushroom tumble from its lips. With its hindquarters trembling from a growing exhaustion, it bounded, still gracefully, over a large jam of deadfall and stood a moment of keen watch. The buck had spent a heated night in the company of a yearling doe; her breeding clock ticking loudly through the October moonlight. It looked now for rest.

The huge buck slid into a thicket of leafless alder, turned to put the rising scents of morning to its back, and settled to rest, still focusing its eyes on the ridge line visible through the undergrowth. A strong instinctive pulse kept the buck from traveling farther up the canyon to familiar bedding grounds. It was not the light of day that made the deer hesitate but rather the stirring of remote warnings so similar to memory—the alarm of scent. It did not associate this rich and oily scent with man, but rather with that of a carnivore. A thousand years of inherited warning triggered a halt. The buck was incapable of reasoning the origin, but knew in that quiet alarm that its bedding grounds had just been invaded by the scent of a meat-eater.

The man's determination faltered, and he rose from the tangle of logs and branches comprising his blind. He stood slowly, rocking his body to feel the pin-prick tingle of circulation. Beaten again. He'd arrived at these icy confines at 5:30 A.M. after a half-mile hike in the frosted dark, only to cave at the bite of cold and silence after three hours. He smiled to himself, wondering how Uncle Sid could spend an entire day on a cold stand.

Immediately, the sinking feeling of desperation blanketed his enthusiasm. The canyon appeared to have no shortage of breeding females, yet he'd failed to glimpse the big buck in five days of hard hunting. Fear nagged that this special buck, like most trophy-class deer, was completely nocturnal, rarely showing tawny hair to the dangerous light of day or eyes of man. It was a half-mile back to the truck, and if he traveled in perfect still-hunt, it would take two hours to reach the hot coffee. He would work the north ridge on his route back out today, the crunch of even careful steps on the frozen mat of leaves broadcasting his progress. It would be a large challenge, but at least the rising air from valley thermals would be in his favor. Still, he needed luck.

The buck smelled the hormonal odor of the doe long before it turned its huge head to seek her image. She crept slowly along, dripping the calling card of pheromone-rich urine along a worn trail. The long rutting dance of last night had already faded from the buck's short-term memory; its exhausted flesh surged with fresh desire, and autumn's lust pushed the buck toward the yearling doe. At first startled by the buck's movement, the doe then slowly waved its half-raised tail from side to side, turned its rump toward the buck, and deftly stepped down the trail. A small breeze drifted across the canyon, sending a shower of dying leaf to the still frozen ground. The buck glanced at the raised tail of the doe, but instead of moving down the sidehill, it turned to stare at the ridge line above, the keen eyes capturing every movement of tumbling leaf.

It is nearly impossible for a human to fully grasp the intensity of the deer's close watch—impossible because we bother all events with much reason. Even when we believe we acted on impulse or swear we reacted spontaneously, somewhere in an unconscious microsecond we surely debated the move and reasoned at least one possible consequence of the act. It cannot be avoided. Computer-enhanced photography of brain-wave activity, done via electrode-implanted scans, proves this undeniable trait. Only the herbivorous mammals and those humans with the most severe brain damage fail to trigger a lightning-quick reasoning impulse to the frontal lobe. Because we simply can't know that feeling of animal instinct, because reasoning and memory are always triggered at near light speed before we react, it is difficult to comprehend the deer's hard watch.

This is not news. If the deer had ever demonstrated any ability to contemplate its fate, or reason out a possible outcome of its keen watchfulness, it would have developed its reasoning powers enough to improve its lot over the millennia. But, we fail to see where deer have moved up an inch on the food chain or found any control over or alternative to nature's basic challenges of hunger and thirst, let alone ever established

rudimentary use of logic or experimentation—both being first indicators of reasoning powers. Deer simply react without forethought, guided by instinct and following the never-questioned path of least resistance. The whitetail reacts much like the simple mousetrap, which goes off when triggered, yet this animal is so honed in the survival instincts of scent, sound, and sight—its triggering mechanisms—that we hunters of great reasoning skills count ourselves lucky ever to outmaneuver one.

Something was triggering the buck's amazing awareness in the vibrations of the small canyon. Alarm was twitching the swollen muscles of its neck. Again it screwed its nose to the air, winding only the odors of moss and pine and the glandular scent of the young doe. It slowly turned to glide through the tangle of deadfall and, in two soft bounds, dropped to the sloping trail of the doe.

Hesitating a moment to wonder at the sparkle of gold and red-mottled leaf floating to the ground, Robert Altman felt the cool breeze on his face. The wind had picked up, providing just enough noise of falling leaf to mask crunching steps on the forest floor. The rocky outcrop of the ridge line forced him to drop down the canyon wall, and he stopped to glass a tangle of deadfall below, searching carefully until his eyes fell on odd dark spots on the frozen, leaf-covered ground. The spots, then several more, were below a jam of deadfall. His heartbeat quickened; he was certain they were fresh tracks. He moved forward in practiced stealth, taking twenty minutes to cover a scant one hundred yards. The fresh track of a big deer seemed to leap up to greet him. Squatting to break up his silhouette, he stared down the ridge, working his eyes to pierce the stunted cedar and fir, adrenaline surging through his suddenly warm body.

"Today is the day," he whispered silently. "I've got him." In that moment of tense excitement, Altman failed to notice an instant of changed wind direction, the tiniest of reverse movement, a momentary downward swirl. Within seconds the wind righted its flow and continued its favor to him.

The buck traveled behind the doe for another two hundred yards. With a silent caution, it shadowed her trail. When she carelessly stepped through clearings in the thick woods, the buck sidestepped into deeper cover, maintaining only the contact of scent and fractured movement. Each time the buck began to approach her, testing her receptivity, little ripples of instinctive warning ran across its neck. It had already bred a few does in the small valley, and the driving urge of days past seemed tempered with caution.

Still, the rich odor of the doe controlled the buck's will, and it tensed its haunches to spring over a long-dead cedar. Then something struck the deer. Just one small jolt, rushing with freight-train force; the small pocket of human scent slammed into the buck's face, then just as quickly disappeared. The big deer froze, screwing its face and upper lip to the passing odor. Instinctively, it whistled an alarm snort. The hot doe, unaware and seemingly unconcerned, continued her courting stroll down the narrow trail.

In the piercing rush of its snort, the buck bounded over the doe's trail, through the underbrush on the small bench, across the tiny creek, and up the south ridge. It had no inclination to stop. The same oily aroma of predator pounded its olfactory senses—the same scent it had found rubbed on the brush of the hillside earlier in the morning. The heavy rack slapped against small popple, causing little veils of gold to flutter down behind the powerful animal as it climbed the slope toward the ridge top. Still, the buck did not slow down; it was now squarely alongside Robert's earlier ground blind, and the dangerous scent was even stronger. With a burst of speed fully absent of either plan or reason, it bounded over the frost-covered rock of the ridge top and slid out of control, crashing over the edge of small cliffs and into the adjacent canyon.

The human mind may think this event unfortunate. And most of humankind would find it sad indeed. They would see a great loss in the huge deer piled up against the base of a large fir, neck instantly broken against sharp rock in the thirty-foot fall. A tragic waste.

Not so with Mother Nature. This great deer is a magnificent gift, a large blessing to all so fortunate as to come across it. It will begin feeding a den of hungry fox kits tonight, a small pack of coyotes two nights later, and a passing bobcat some days after that. By the late November snowfall, it will save several jays that use what's left of meat and hide to build needed winter stores of strength. And on it will go, serving bounty to all creatures. There will be weasels and voles burrowing about the frozen remains all winter; even squirrels, often thought to be wholly vegetarian, will strip strength from the tiny crevices of hidebound fat.

Come the melt of spring, a black bear will wander close, attracted by the fetid odor of decay. With a dearth of insect life and green clover in a late-arriving spring, the bear will be well rewarded with the very last of putrid yet nutritious salvage, cracking the larger bones in search of rancid marrow. And onward, porcupines and mice will gnaw bones for calcium and other needed mineral; then bugs and worms and flies and the songbirds that feed on them, until finally the soak of its nutrient-rich waste feeds microbes and plant life, giving boost to the struggling blackberry vines seeking foothold in the barren cliffs.

But at this moment in our story, there is only the quickly dead, still warm body of the deer slumped against the fir.

Robert Altman reached his truck at noon, much disappointed at losing the buck's track in the frozen bottoms. The hot thermos and sandwiches soothed his frustration. A smile crossed his face as he reflected out loud: "I've at least got him pegged. That was the big guy's track this morning, and I'm sure the glimpse of tawny hair racing through the brush was him."

Later that afternoon he sat quietly in his ground blind a half-mile up the same canyon. As the swirl of dusk encompassed his stand, he listened to the spray of tumbling leaf stirred by the evening breeze. Through a gap in the dark canopy of trees, the early rising moon illuminated the falling leaves. "I've got two days left," he mused. "He won't leave this canyon—not with all the hot doe sign around. He's right in here somewhere. I'm damn positive of that."

And so it goes, another simple twist of fate—Providence alive in the Moon of the Falling Leaves.

I have only minor recall of Robert Altman's once-fourteen-year-old face, witnessed a few times on dairy-pickup mornings of long ago. But I do know Uncle Sid well, often enjoying a summer evening's beer with him on the faded deck of Harvey's creekside bar. Some years back, he told me of nephew Bob's disappointing hunt and how he was so close to a monster buck, the fresh track and definite sound of the big deer crashing through the brush, one flashing glimpse of hide.

A year later I drove out to the dairy on a warm but drizzly May evening and sipped coffee, telling Sid of the news I'd just garnered at the cafe. Tip Meyer had been wandering the canyon adjacent to nephew Bob's week-long hunt area, searching for the tasty morels that pop up each May. He had found the skeletal remains of the great deer, a match for the shed once found by Sid. It was lodged against a fir, jagged rocks and blackberry vines covering the area. Judging from the steep cliff above and the severely cracked antlers (he found a sheared-off tine up the cliff), Tip imagined the big deer's fall. There was little doubt in his mind. Now shrunken and faint, the white, crusty scat of fox and bobcat still littered the area a year and a half later. The large bones of the deer were cracked open and long ago hollowed.

With the rack held fast to full skull, the head was enormous. If it had been legal to glue several pieces of broken antler together, it would have scored 190 perfectly typical Boone & Crockett points. Many of us have hunted that trio of canyons in the last few years, hoping to discover an offspring of such impressive genealogy. But it has not occurred; not even a decent-size "typical" shed has been found, and I wonder now if the big deer was sterile. I have read of studies showing a decent percentile of surveyed trophy bucks to be infertile. I have yet to read a follow-up offering theories of a reason.

Chapter II

First Snows and Other Reflections

A week drifted by at Archie Weil's camp, and I enjoyed each day to its fullest measure. A warm front of southern origin moved in, bringing fine warmth and blue sky to October days and just enough chill of night to lightly frost the ground and make welcome the crackle of woodstove.

I have chased two different bucks, cat and mouse, with still-hunt stalks and well-placed stands. From the lightning-fast glimpses offered, both deer are worthy of pursuit and the use of my modern-rifle tag. If I fill the tag, I won't be able to hunt again until November 7 and the thirty-day window of the primitive arms/shotgun season. During that period, I can use only bow, shotgun, or black-powder rifle. It is a strange law to many newcomers in this end of the state, designed long ago on the premise that most deer hunters went afield during the more profitable rut period and the holidays, and their large numbers made the long-range modern rifle too dangerous. It hardly relates to us in Harland, different sort that we are, but we've had the law for so long, it's blindly accepted and a quite natural way to approach the season. The hunter is allowed to take two deer, but the time and nature of weaponry are integral to the taking. These two deer are very worthy, and I hope to find some luck soon.

Archie planted and tended so many quarter-acre food plots on these benches that they hold a large resident population and what appears to be a healthy balance in the buck-doe ratio. I am seeing upwards of six or seven deer a day, about one-quarter of them bucks, and those being of stout proportion and healthy look.

My wife came up for an overnight stay and a morning hunt this week, the demands of household and a few animals to feed at our place having previously kept her homebound. Without fanfare or much effort, as usual, she took a nice nontypical buck, nearly her best ever and a deer I had not encountered in my six days at camp. She took it in the first hour of shooting light, no less, and not more than two hundred yards from the cabin. She is always this way, and I rarely take her along because of this irritating habit of stumbling across a good buck. Of course, she attributes this lucky phenomenon to her natural hunting prowess, an ancient thing of gifted heritage, something she insists I mostly lack. I'll argue till hell freezes over that it is plain luck and, to my constant irritation, nothing but plain luck.

In hunting matters, she is the consummate fluke, no different from the lucky person who seems always to win the big drawing, the one whose name is invariably drawn out of the hat. That irritating person. The one who has never, in forty years, bought a bad used car, never paid good money for some advertised gadget that never works when brought home, never fails to have everything fall into perfect place. If the fluke ever suffers the misfortune of the slightest fender-bender, it will certainly follow that the errant driver of the other car is a Rockefeller or Perot clone offering a quick quarter-million to ease the suffering of a broken fingernail.

All towns have their own personal fluke, and though that person might be lovable or even a best friend, we always whisper "fluke" under our breath when smiling and nodding our heads at the story of his/her most recent good fortune. In the world of whitetails, it is my better half who is the consummate fluke, and though I love her dearly, after yesterday morning, I am almost glad she has left for home. It has once again become an old camp where a hunter works hard and silently for the small chance of a decent sighting.

The air turned cool this day; by evening the sky was solid gray with light drizzle, reminding me of many other late-October hunts. The battery radio, full of static up here on this mountain, was hard-pressed to grant an intelligible evening weather report, but it appears a northern front has replaced the pleasant southern flow with a chance of snow. I rarely like the snows of late October. They are infrequent, but their freak arrivals weigh heavy on trees still in full leaf, doing damage and shortening the span of autumnal landscape. This dislike wasn't always so. I remember times of boyhood, the late '50s and early '60s, when smaller deer herds dictated a shorter season, running only the last two weeks of October. With our love of the spirit, we still had large numbers of deer in our county, but we were the exception and forced to live by state law. The rest of the state still suffered the small numbers brought on by heavy Depression-era poaching, exacerbated by several consecutive winters of deep cold and heavy snow in the '50s That time of boyhood hunting, of having school days eat away an already short season, stirred dreams of a chance to hunt the snow. And this coming snow brings to mind another long-passed whitetail man.

Charlie Krause owned and operated the only feed store and mill in town, serving Harland and the surrounding rural county. I once worked for him, filling sacks of chicken feed and oats, sweeping the old building and grain mill, and loading customers' trucks during the summer of my fifteenth year. Although he was cantankerous and liable to spit a wad of brown tobacco juice near your feet to make a point, a decent friendship grew. Even though I found a better summer job the next year, thanks to the transportation of a half-broken-down '54 Chevy pickup I'd bought, I enjoyed stopping in once a week to talk farming and deer hunting with Charlie Krause.

Old Ed Timmons (of Proper Deer Gun memory) got me the feed-store work, my first real summer job. Being of the same age and cut from the same bolt of cloth, Ed and Charlie were good friends and, little wonder, much alike. Charlie Krause frightened a few with his direct and crusty manner, enjoying good argument or criticizing the style of every Harland hunter, and always bending his story somehow to show his way as the proper way, even if it required invention or embellishment. But under that show of mock disdain was a kind and gentle man, softhearted and decent. In his defense, I must admit his hunting theories made perfect sense, and whether actual or imagined, his stories always sparked a thought process to race my brain. At seventy-four and still running the feed mill mostly alone, showing great strength and stamina with one-hundred-pound feed sacks, he'd all but given up his great love of deer hunting. Still, in his opinion, he remained the vouchsafe expert on all things whitetail.

That first summer, I came to discover that Charlie had a "different" kind of religion. I also discovered Ed Timmons shared a somewhat similar belief, and I imagine it furthered the bond of their long friendship and explained their rare appearance—Christmas only—at the local churches. Charlie Krause believed in reincarnation, and as he sat one lunch hour explaining it to me, I nodded my head in a gratuitous understanding, having never heard the word in my fifteen years and too embarrassed to say so. A trip to the encyclopedia at home that night enlightened me on the concept.

Over a lifetime, Old Man Krause developed a belief that animals have little capacity for evil and are, therefore, closest to God. Although he believed it's God's plan for us to consume these animals for our survival, they remain to His Grace. This belief was just fine for the first fifty or so years of his life, but two years ago, when deep in a fevered dream brought on by a bout of winter flu, Charlie Krause envisioned himself coming back as a great white-tailed buck. Crazy or not, he was certain of this soon-to-be next lifetime, and for the next two years he walked about the autumn woods in pensive study, trying to better understand a deer's life. Oddly, he did not feel sorry for the animal—this kindred spirit—nor did he harbor any inclination to protect it from man.

Although he quit deer hunting, Charlie remained a solid supporter of the hunt, finding it a natural thing of earth and still eating any package of offered venison. But his own pleasures were now taken in close study of the land; the once minor details of woodsy tastes and smells were examined and the subtleties savored and relished, as if he was already preparing for his coming life. He understood his fevered dream clearly, even foreseeing his eventual quick death brought on by a hunter's bullet in this life of a buck. He was quite happy with his fate, and would quickly point out that the hunter's bullet was a very good thing because it saved him the painful winter starvation of old age.

I was bound by a pact of honor—much like my pact with Harry the Horn Man—to keep this dream and Charlie's odd religion a secret until after his passing. But I failed the test of secrecy by immediately asking Ed Timmons about it. Thankfully, Ed never told him of my breech of honor; Ed already knew of Charlie Krause's strange belief, did not personally believe in that form of reincarnation, and reminded me of Krause's absolute right to a personal and private faith.

The thought of October snow brings Charlie Krause's memory so clear and close—a reminder of a long-ago snow and an after-school visit at the feed store. I have told many stories of another man's long-ago hunt—this one is mine:

A First Snow

It couldn't have happened better in a movie script. On the day before opening morning, a cold front had pushed down from the North Country. By noon the cold drizzle of late October had slowly turned to snow. The golden 'scapes of autumn were now softly, silently being blanketed by two inches of first snow. With excitement and adrenaline pumping through his sixteen-year-old body, the boy drove home from school. Unable to keep the thrill of a first-hunt snow to himself, he decided to stop at the feed store and share his opening-morning strategy with Old Man Krause.

The old man shuffled over to a stack of chicken feed, tossed a sack on the hand truck, and muttered something about it being just another damn early snow. The boy was stunned. It was just another snowstorm like Bart Starr was just another quarterback. For the last three years he had dreamed of a snow like this— prayed and made promises for it. A tracking snow.

The old man shook his head in mock disgust. "They move into the wind and always mind their backtrack, son. Ain't hardly a man alive that can track down a white-tailed buck," Old Man Krause told him. "You might as well put on a tin beak and pick scratch with the chickens. And fresh snow don't make a pinch of difference, either."

At home the boy could still hear the sharp words of the old man ringing in his ears. Still, he stared out the window at the veil of white and dreamed the coming morning. It was his third year of deer hunting and, at long last, his first tracking snow. Though snowstorms were not uncommon in the Octobers of Harland Corners, the short deer seasons of the early 1960s made their timely arrival an event of kismetic proportion. Twice last year he had lost the tracks of a decent buck in the frozen bottom of a long ravine. If only he'd had a tracking snow.

That night, while checking over his hunting outfit and stuffing a sandwich and candy bars in the small knapsack, he walked several times to the window, seeking the reassuring continued presence of a miracle snow. Had it stopped? Had it turned back to rain? Each time, he held his breath while rubbing a clear viewing spot on the fogged windowpane. Each time, the muse of hunting luck smiled down on the boy. The storm was passing; a small sliver of moonlight was breaking through a crack in the dark sky. The boy had to smile to himself. There was no finer hunting than during the tail end of a passing storm front, and he pictured the wooded ravine, the noisy crunch of frosted leaf silenced by the flakes of white, the tawny-grayish hair of a huge buck standing out against the field of white. He felt his

112

pulse quicken; tiny shivers of excitement raced along his back, prickling the hairs of neck. He decided to add wax-paper bags to his small outfit to hold the epicurean jewels of heart and liver. With a long sigh of relief, the boy felt joyfully confident.

Nearly begging for his mother's permission, he would skip school tomorrow, miss a history exam, and miss playing in the heated rivalry of the season-ending football game tomorrow night. School and football were of little import now. Now there was a tracking snow.

Later that night, lost in the grasp of anticipation and insomnia, he pulled the tattered hunting magazine off the night stand and opened it to a story about whitetails. It mattered little that he'd read and re-read the piece each night over the last two weeks, or that he knew each story by heart: The Phantom Buck of Curly Creek, Old Mossy Horns of the Cedar Swamp. At times, an odd feeling crawled his flesh, as if he knew the great Jack O'Connor personally, had traveled with him on hunt after hunt, shared breakfast and camp and stalk. On barren sheep slopes of Alaska or in the wet and wooded darkness of Alabama deer hills, the boy had drawn the strong drafts of the scented lands. Tonight he simply stared at the pictures of a Pennsylvania deer camp, its cabin and meat pole shrouded in the veil of fresh falling snow.

He was a half-mile from home by morning's first light, near the long, wooded ravine running by Culver's abandoned farm and apple orchard. It was a perfect snow—the precise amount of moisture to soften steps without the alarming squeak and crunch of footfall on a wet or frozen snow. This was not a morning he could stay on a stand. Try as he might, within an hour the boy's patience failed him miserably. He could not sit in a ground blind while the first tracking snow of his deer hunting life lay wasting about in beckoning splendor. Slowly, with an imagined invisibility, he moved into the light breeze and down the steep ravine. The chatter of squirrels, telegraphing his presence, sounded through the birch and pine.

It was not long before he cut the tracks and still-warm droppings. The tracks were huge; the crush of dew claws pushed deep into the snow, reaching down to stir the bright layer of fallen leaf and betray the heavy weight of the deer. His pulse quickened. What did Old Man Krause at the feed store know, anyhow? The old man was often so cantankerous that his words were taken with a measure of quiet disregard. A good woodsman, a true hunter, could surely stalk a white-tailed buck. Again, a knowing smile crossed his young face.

In the early morning sunlight, tiny prisms of sparkle danced from the sharp edges of the tracks. With a feeling of certain success, the boy set out slowly, quietly, through a first snow, a tracking snow of long ago. . . .

Chapter 12

It did not snow that night at camp, but the cold drizzle that kept up all night did much to quiet the noisy woods. I felt it coming on that morning, a small apperception of impending encounter, the sense of a certain connection coming, a finality. It began with my first steps from the cabin in the 5 A.M. darkness. It was like a chill, a feeling, nothing special or strong, but a hunch of success. I have had this feeling before and failed miserably, and have a hard time granting any veracity to its warning—or anything psychic, for that matter. This lack of faith in all things supernatural is not the result of failing to conceptualize the possibilities—I am forever open to the proposition. Simply, I am a skeptic of the first order.

I have some heroes in life, mostly boyhood ones—old men who took the time to show me things and shape my thinking process by filling my head with reasoning and concepts of grace. I have mentioned a few of them already, and I've barely scratched the crust of what made them wholly good human beings. But it is a man who lived long before my time, Samuel Clemens, a.k.a. Mark Twain, who remains my largest heroic influence. After all, he was proclaimed as America's Greatest Skeptic.

It is not the good and popular tales of Huck Finn and Tom Sawyer that measure this man but rather The Innocents Abroad and a hundred or more published essays filled with sarcastic wit and the hilarious irony of his skepticism. No one escaped his keen eye for fraud and pomposity in the making. No snake charmer, fortune teller, magician, or priest evaded his harsh examination. Although raised a Christian and maintaining the belief in a Judeo-Christian God, he left no Protestant minister, Baptist, Jew, or Hindu holy man unscathed, finding wagonloads of hypocrisy and outright foolishness in all of them. He was despised by Catholics, Christian Scientists, and Seventh Day Adventists for his wildly humorous, unflattering essays about their creeds. The Mormons? Ditto. Moslems? Ditto again. And politicians? Whether it was the White House and Capitol Hill or some Hayseed Junction's dollar-a-month mayor, Twain's piercing eye always found the truth of the matter. And that truth was usually a large example of greed, corruptibility, or power mongering.

Even though Twain was raised a Christian, he mustered the audacity to challenge much of the Bible—a blasphemy even to close friends. While he truly believed it to be God's word and loved much of the book, knowing well the traits of humanity, he was certain that much therein had been altered by revisionists of a thousand years past and storytellers before them. He even visited the Holy Land in the 1880s, doing what he did so well: snooping, asking questions of the holy ones, and thinking hard, extrapolating from their sum a very plausible answer to his burning questions. Yes, he was a believer, but only of words and lessons he considered worthy of God's great wisdom. He believed the rest of the Bible and all religious doctrine were the ramblings of zealots and of the self-serving religious "playwrights" who insisted their words were "inspired" and demanding a cherished sanction.

With this man as my mentor, it is hard for me to believe in my hunches or feelings. The instant one appears, I am too quick in wondering about its true origin, doubting its veracity, and examining its authenticity to give it much chance for fruition. I wonder what is worse: utterly blind faith or no faith at all?

But I had the feeling that morning; I truly felt something was going to happen and headed the quarter-mile to a steep trail leading up the tangled, brushy face of Stone Ridge. After a week of hunting these lands, I had come to realize that without blind luck I wasn't going to catch a decent buck wandering the benches in daylight. Perhaps later, during the rut, a buck would make such a foolish error, but not now. Although I had the previous two sightings of good bucks, they occurred along the base of the steep face in near darkness, leaving me little choice but to hunt the beds.

This approach sets off sirens of alarm in many hunters. Even in the Corners, we are long trained in the rule of never trampling the bedding grounds. But I certainly didn't plan on trampling anything, and had learned long ago from Harry the Horn Man that bucks aren't easily driven away from habitual bedding areas. A hunter might startle them good, and they might keep a half-mile away for the rest of the day, but if it's their core area, they'll return under the cover of darkness. They might be willing to travel far in panic or in search of hot does, but their very survival is incumbent upon the vibrations—the scents, sights, and motions of a very small area.

There is large debate in wildlife circles about a deer's memory process and capacity, most believing the animal is capable of some long-term memory, others convinced it possesses short-term only—often a matter of minutes. Long-term memory of events, actions, or weather requires some analytical reasoning, and that process, in its true form, has never been verified to exist in whitetails. Some predators and upper primates demonstrate the ability, not much, but enough to show up in frontal-lobe brain scans.

White-tailed deer do have acute scenting abilities and an active recall process with these scents. While most folks believe a deer "sees" a feeding area, recognizes it as alfalfa or an oak tree, and heads to the place, it is almost always a matter of scent. Even the return visits are not necessarily a matter of visual memory but rather scent-recall of the area or of its own tracks. Most deer hunters know that the digital glands of a whitetail's hoof secretes a strong scent with each step. In fact, all trails to food plots, water, and bedding places are hardly more than paths of digital secretion plus other scent rubbed on brush and left on twig chewings. Essentially lacking an information-memory process, a whitetail's primary navigation tool is its superior scent recall, not visual-sighting memory. If one deadens the olfactory nerves with Novocaine or similar blocking agent, a deer and other ungulates are put in desperate peril. Cattle will starve to death, even when provided access routes to food, if they are unable to smell the source. A buck spooked from its bed will return to the area. Scent familiarity is a deer's primary survival skill.

The previous day, I had found a walkable trail across the face of Stone Ridge and think I can loop around to gain some elevation without my scent carrying up the slope. This bedding ground is a large area, perhaps eighty acres or more, though it is hard to estimate its size, due to the deception of steep slope. I have one chance and hope: to silently gain enough elevation in the black of morning, with penlight for guide, to find myself above the bedding deer and, by angling in from the north, keep my scent above them and the soon-to-be-rising thermals from the valley below. I know the deer are up here; the question remains, how far up?

There was a pink glow coming from the east, and I could begin to see shapes, a small hint to find a stand and quit moving. I could only guess how far up I was, but I wanted to climb at least several hundred feet and have twenty acres of brush and rocky outcrop below me. I had hoped, come daylight, to crawl around silently in search of a half-decent view of below, or at least gain one good sight line through the tall brush and stunted trees. If this was improbable, I planned to let the area settle well, then try either a grunt tube or antler rattling. If that failed, I would sit as long as patience allowed, then stoop to tossing a few small rocks down the hill. Lack of sight lines would make it impossible to still-hunt, and if one decent shooting lane could be commandeered, even the schoolboy stunt of tossing rocks was preferable to moving about.

There was little feed up the slope to prompt a bedded deer to head uphill. Though I was ignorant of brush genotypes, I'd always noticed that the particular type of scraggly bush germane to this hillside never showed signs of browsing, even in the desperate times of deep snow and cold. But I was certain that cud replacement would prompt these bedded deer to move about, if only in small areas, by noon.

With first light I stopped to rest and survey my situation. As feared, I could only see about twenty feet in any direction but skyward, and spent a good half-hour of prime-hunting, first-light crawling over shale and through brush in search of a sight line. Finally, with the rare occurrence of a bit of needed luck, I crawled into an open alley that seemed to run halfway down the slope, and was surprised I hadn't noticed it from down below. It was at least three hundred feet long, perhaps thirty feet wide, and had only some grass and a few foot-high saplings for cover; it was either an avalanche chute or a rock slide of recent origin. More importantly, it was an unexpected blessing of no small measure, and I could not help but think back on the "hunch" of good luck felt earlier at the cabin.

Making the hunch even more promising was the unique food sources sprouting here—unique, that is, to this slope of little-favored browse. How the seed or rootstock arrived in this chute—perhaps by the act of avalanche or the seed-rich droppings of birds—remains a mystery, but scanning the long sight lane with binoculars revealed tiny patches of already browsed box elder, some clumps of wild rye, and a few struggling saplings of popple. It was perfect—not only a shooting lane four times longer than hoped for, but one that offered the deer a midmorning, cud-renovating snack. And I, though uphill, was perfectly downwind of it all.

I immediately dismissed my earlier desperate plan of tossing rocks to spook a bedded deer into moving. This was a place to take a long stand, and I immediately regretted not bringing a lunch. Last night, while resting in the bunk closest to the woodstove and formulating a plan of attack, I honestly thought I'd find no decent opening on the slope and would be forced to sneak about in some vain attempt to spook a buck from its bed and still manage to squeeze off a clean shot through three-foot-wide openings—the kind of preposterous concept that only halfwits of foolish optimism manage to dream up. In other words, my standard kind of plan. In light of last night's preconceived notion of how the hunt would materialize, I didn't bother bringing lunch or pack, figuring an early return to the cabin would be in order. Fortunately, I did bring a small, two-cup thermos that fit snugly in the deep pockets of my hunting coat, and one candy bar.

When I was a young boy, a nickel candy bar—or especially one of the larger ten-cent varieties—seemed huge, took a while to finish, and properly satiated my desire. Now, not only do they cost sixty-nine cents but they seem so small and disappear so quickly that I'm scarcely cognizant of the taste and act of eating. I don't know why I bother with them while hunting. They hardly stave off hunger and seem to give me all the extra energy of a breath mint. But neither unsatisfactory chocolate nor lack of lunch mattered. Within ten minutes, and before I could pull the thermos from my coat pocket, I glimpsed the antlers.

It was only the slightest flash. For a moment, I thought that my imagination was at fault, that it must have been a bird bouncing from limb to limb in the tangled mess of tall brush running along both edges of the narrow chute. I've grown so used to my imagination getting the better of me that I foolishly dismissed the urge to lift the binoculars and instead reached again for the thermos, while staring at the spot seventy yards down the slope.

Just as I had the thermos half out, I saw the movement again. This time I was certain of antler and froze perfectly still, taking several minutes to slide the thermos back in my coat and move my hands all of the twelve inches to the binoculars. With a bedded deer there is no such thing as too much caution. One can use any modifier—from extreme to creeping to mind-boggling—in front of that word without exaggerating the situational need. And in my case, without the binoculars I could not see body or head yet and did not know whether the buck was staring directly at me through some tiny porthole of leaf and twig or if it faced downhill. The odds of the latter were slim. Most mature bucks grow to that decent age by making few errors and nearly always keep their back to the wind, gaining the needed advantage of sighting what they can't scent. I was immediately thankful that I, too, had sat in a clump of thick brush that broke my silhouette and offered good cover.

As I slowly, inch by inch, lifted the binoculars to my eyes, I knew this would be a waiting game. There would be no reason to blow a grunt tube in some attempt to move the deer out of heavy cover. Neither would rattling be a practical alternative. If either endeavor managed to tickle the buck's curiosity, prompting investigative movement, that movement would inevitably be in a circuitous loop through thick brush as it attempted to circle the "curiosity" and come in downwind of it. Rare indeed is the mature buck that will charge uphill in the full view of an open alley with no advantage of wind.

When I finally brought binoculars on the thicket, I was completely resigned to waiting it out all day if necessary and if the buck was truly worthy. The latter part of the equation was answered in first focus. It was huge—at least in antler. Even with the optics I could not see its body—only the tip of one ear and one long, sweeping branch of antler. It was difficult to clearly focus and count the number and assess the length of tines through the crisscrossing pattern of branch, but I guessed it to have four points on the one visible side, five counting an unseen brow tine. Certainly the larger of the two bucks glimpsed a few days earlier, I judged it worth the torment of sitting frozen in place with a long thirst for the coffee wasting in my coat pocket alongside the foil pouch of tobacco.

I sat there for an hour, heart still pounding quicker than normal, the cold drizzle of last night returning to test patience, and still not certain of the direction the buck stared. Just when I was sure it faced uphill, when convinced I was seeing the whiter hair in the hollow of ear and the forward curvature of antler beam through the brush, the reverse would appear equally plausible and I would squeeze my eyes shut for the needed rest and refocus.

To me, there is hardly a more excruciating eyestrain than remaining focused for long periods behind the eyepiece of binoculars. Having chased a few Rocky Mountain elk, I can report that spotting scopes are no different. Perhaps it is my eyes only, but after a minute or two, it becomes a wearisome thing for both eye and brain. I mention this eyestrain for more than the simple excuse of not figuring out which way the buck faced. I firmly believe that if the hunter spent longer time staring through good optics, the game spotted would increase in direct proportion. Many folks think powerful optics are the great aid of the Plains, Rockies, and high-desert hunters, but see little need for them in the wooded tight quarters and thickets of whitetail haunts. As the long-experienced whitetail enthusiast knows, nothing could be further from the truth. Even poor-quality, inexpensive binoculars (like my faithful pair) work wonders in penetrating thick growth, giving the viewer a fairly clear picture of the area on the other side of the thicket. Nevertheless, for all my advocacy, they failed me that morning, as I couldn't decide if the buck was facing me or not, and sat nearly motionless for an hour, thirsting for hot coffee in the cold drizzle.

The hunting muses, those minor gods of the woods that tweek serendipity, were busy elsewhere that morning—never allowing the good buck to make a foolish move in my presence. Off somewhere in the East or West must have sat another hunter who needed only an instant of luck to bring a dream to fruition. Sorry, fellow Nimrod, the muses were looking over your shoulder that morning, apparently forgetting my existence for the moment. The buck suddenly rose from his bed as if startled and stood frozen a good two minutes. I was afraid to use the binoculars, wanting both hands free to raise the rifle with the least amount of sharp movement. Through the 4X scope I could see the buck was looking down across the chute of tempting browse, and I felt sudden relief. There was still hope.

But I could not shoot under current conditions; there was no clear shooting lane to vital organs, and I'd lectured too many youngsters on the futility of desperate shots to consider such irresponsibility. One very large hope was that the buck, although seemingly startled, had actually risen for a midmorning browse (Old Man Krause, the reincarnationist, called it cud-building) and would move the thirty feet to the clear alley. Sitting back down or moving in any other direction would result in a failure to connect.

One point of gain was the better view of antler. He was truly a good buck, long in tine, a balanced-looking ten-point that I guessed to be in the 160-class range and the nicest buck I'd ever had an opportunity to take. Or so it all appeared. I was looking through a scope blurred by the close branches and leaves of my hidden spot, then distorted further by the seventy yards of brush between the deer and my position.

I have had many non-hunters, deer and elk hunters of the West, and even a handful of whitetail hunters question the need for a scope in this country of thick woods and shots generally under one hundred yards. If someone is out there who still doesn't know the answer, it is only three words: light-gathering ability. Using magnification to pull a faraway animal into visual sighting or shooting range is clearly not the purpose of a scope in the deep woods. If one is intent upon taking a trophy deer, then all legal low-light conditions must he optimized. With my old scopeless .35 Remington, my first rifle after Ed Timmons' gifted 12-gauge, I was forced to pass on too many good bucks that appeared at first or last light—not merely legal light but enough light to fall within the parameters of safety as well. Without the light-gathering properties of a scope, I was doomed, never able to clearly focus with open sights. I could see some of those deer well, even the perfect spot of vital organs. But I could not see my sights. I tried painting the front bead with a red glow-in-the-dark dot, but it made little difference. It all seemed to blur in the fuzz of low-light conditions.

At the moment, the scope offered little help, and I felt my arms beginning to ache from holding the rifle still for several minutes. And then the buck suddenly bounded clear of the large clump of brush. I thought I'd lost him for good. But again, thanks to the absent muses, it changed direction and moved toward the alley clearing.

There is hardly a better feeling for a deer hunter than to work hard at the craft, imagine a possible scenario or outcome of his design, and have it all work out as dreamed or planned. Presto! It happens so infrequently; but the day was mine. The morning hunch—with apologies to Mark Twain—was a real and relevant thing, and the buck, after two swift and silent bounds, was standing broadside in the chute. I did not wait to see if it came to browse or would scamper farther on in some other pursuit. This was not, after all, a scientific information-gathering survey, and thanks to Archie Weil and the Lord above, I had less than one second to squeeze off the single round from the .308.

As it lay before me, instantly dead from a single shot in the heart, I again felt the sad and necessary compassion of Arthur Glade, the grace of thanksgiving, and the understanding of the full circle of life. Still, I trembled from wild excitement. It was a magnificent deer, surely the best I'd ever taken, and after a minute or two of contemplating it all, I sat down on a large boulder in the steady drizzle to try to roll a much needed cigarette.

Chapter 13

That last night in Archie's cabin was glorious. No single event or thought made it so grand but rather the sum of them all, including the dinner of fresh deer liver and onions, cucumber salad, and a woodstove-baked potato. After a long drag down the slope and across one bench with the buck that morning, I was able to snake the truck up an old sapling-choked skid trail to end the small struggle. The half-mile-long skid trail was a remnant of 1940s logging, and I'm sure Archie must have worked a bit in keeping it open. Someone had; there is no way it could have existed for fifty years with only saplings bothering it. I was on my way back to the cabin for Archie's wheelbarrow when I decided the old trail was passable in my truck.

I've seen several nice deer-transporting devices in magazines and at hunting shows, but we changeless ones generally prefer an old wheelbarrow. With a little tie-down rope, a contractor-size wheelbarrow is perfect to snake around in tight woods full of deadfall and stumps with little room between trees. Sore back or not, the 'barrow seems to work best in our woods, a tangled mess of out-of-control second growth. All of this is a direct result of indiscriminate heavy logging from World War II through the early '50s It opened up the area, creating spectacularly helpful feed zones for rabbits, grouse, and deer. But because of little foresight and even less management, both public and private parcels have less fir and pine and are overrun with birch or popple. With no selective thinning, as if the concept of future timber use was abandoned, the few stands of fir and pine are so thick they are difficult to walk through, with forty-year-old trees only six inches in diameter.

I drooled over 4x4 ATVs when they first were becoming popular, and though I still wouldn't mind owning one, after borrowing a friend's machine one spring on a morel-mushroom hunt, I soon discovered I would need to hire a full-time man on a chain saw to gain the access I desired.

I learned long ago that a serious whitetail hunter should never consider the ease or accessibility of deer retrieval when planning a hunt. To do so immediately takes him out of the necessary activity of searching the hidden plots. I have also learned that the exact opposite is true in elk hunting: Nothing spoils the thrill of taking a big bull elk faster than realizing you're two miles from the nearest road, without horses, and the most elk carcass any man can carry or drag is one boned quarter. That's five trips—ten miles of heavy carrying if you want to bring out the skull and antlers as well. I've never known an elk hunter willing to leave a nice 6x6 elk rack in the mountains.

I skinned and caped the buck that afternoon at the cabin before the hide dried down tight on the carcass, and that evening I felt a little worried about the deer hanging outside. I didn't think the coyotes would come up to the cabin and shred it, but I had noticed the track of bobcat and fox close-by. With my wife having taken a deer and I planning to hunt November's shotgun season, we wouldn't be buying any red meat this year. When we are fortunate enough to take three deer, we save all the tender cuts for steaks and roasts; grind up the rest of the better meat in coarse size for future tacos, chili, and spaghetti sauces; ground another amount finely for hamburger; and put all the rest in jerky, smoked sausages, and dry salami. With this combination, all done at home, there is scarcely a package left come the following October. The only red meat we will buy is a once-a-year beef prime rib. No matter our usual preference for venison, in our humble opinion, nothing beats a beef prime rib roasted in the restaurant fashion of rock salt encasement and (it should go without saying) served with the traditional horseradish or horseradish-and-sour-cream mix. I salivate at the very thought.

Before heading home the next day, I planned to sleep in a bit, have a long, relaxed breakfast, and then walk about raising hell on the huge grouse population near camp. Wherever I had walked these last eight days, it was impossible to move without encountering grouse. I'd seen at least ten a day, and unless the irony of hunter's luck should occur—that is, seeing only grouse when packing a deer rifle—I expected to bring home the daily limit of four.

It was such a nice buck that I walked to the window several times to stare out at the large, hanging carcass and the rolled cape with still unskinned skull stuck high in the porch rafters. I'd left the head unskinned to facilitate my gawking and the necessary trip to Harvey's when I came off the mountain. I had already green-scored it at 163, my best ever, and would certainly take advantage of Harvey Mott's policy of a free drink and dinner for the taker of any buck over 140 points. Since I first saw this buck on my second day at the cabin, I would be entitled to large embellishment of a great stalking tale describing my relentless seven-day chase. I planned to make myself out as being at least as determined as the obsessed policeman in *Les Miserables*. They didn't need to know I had actually slept in on two mornings, spent one entire afternoon watching beaver work on a leaking damn, and another day picking half-frozen blueberries and shaggymane mushrooms while wandering carefree several miles into the hills on a pleasured hike.

That last night I again heard a pack of coyotes running close-by and wondered about their quarry. This sound brings me so close to the heart of nature I can nearly understand Old Man Krause's strange belief and desire. Although I'm certainly not a believer in his reincarnation, I try to be at least open to the possibility, however remote, and have often wondered if Charlie

Krause is out there tearing the bark of cedar trees with his large antlers, building neck muscles for coming combat. Unfortunately, every time I begin to drift in that romantic thought, it dawns on me that, if true, perhaps I've shot and eaten him already. That little dose of reality always seems to dash my romantic notion of Old Man Krause being some huge buck wandering October's moonlight.

Having used my modern-rifle tag, it will be nearly two weeks before I can go deer hunting again. The primitive arms/shotgun season does not open until November 7, and this is all fine by me. With the camp scouting this year, I have neglected to scout my own area at home, and with two deer taken, we have several days of meat cutting, sausage stuffing, and salami and jerky making ahead. Furthermore, with the camp scouting of September and early October, plus rabbit, grouse, and duck seasons running concurrently through it all, I've hardly spent a day in idle gossip—my second favorite pastime—at the cafe or Harvey's over the last two months. I hope to catch up on everyone's success or failure in the woods, as well as catch up on my missing quota of several cold brews a day. I'll sip an occasional coffee with brandy, but I rarely touch the old demon suds during hunting season. I brought a six-pack to camp, but didn't have one in the eight days of hunt. It isn't a fear of mixing alcohol and firearms, but simply that even one beer makes me lazy. I often hunt hard and long and prefer the pick-me-up of juice, soda, and coffee, relegating alcohol to an after-dinner, feet-propped-up-by-the-woodstove nightcap to enjoy in quiet reflection of the day's discoveries.

Another great benefit of now having close to 250 pounds of boned meat is the freedom of November's hunt. I will not be tempted to take the "nice buck" and instead will wait with rigid patience for the special one, the B&C buck. If I fail, as the odds deem most probable, we do have enough meat put away that I won't feel shamed by missing nature's true reason for the hunt—a year's supply of meat. I'm sure there are many folks out there scratching their heads over my desire to seek a special buck, as if a possible 163-point typical is not the deer of a lifetime. Rest assured I am not so jaded in selfish desire as to lack genuine appreciation of my grand accomplishment at camp. But rest on those fleeting laurels? Not on your life.

There are two reasons for the constant craving of a better buck. No. 1, as Archie Weil so perfectly illustrated, length and breadth of antler are never the true measure of a trophy. Though I immensely enjoyed the camp hunt, my first deer, a doe taken with Ed Timmons' gifted 12-gauge, is a far sweeter memory. So are several hunts my wife and I enjoyed many years ago, taking smaller deer but wildly enjoying the circumstance of challenge and camping out with a small tent and Coleman stove far back in the remote hill country northeast of here. Though only thirty miles from the blinking red light of downtown Harland, because of our youth and zeal, those hunts had all the allure and atmosphere of Rocky Mountain wilderness elk hunts.

And No. 2: It wasn't a B & C buck! It might be different if this wasn't my thirty-sixth year of deer hunting or if all of us in the Corners hadn't seen at least several 170-class (the minimum for entry in the Boone & Crockett Club record book) bucks wandering the summer fields. The wife and I often drive the back roads on August nights with a high-powered spotlight (no, it isn't illegal, as long as we carry no weapon), looking for night-feeding bucks. We have seen a dozen B & C bucks over the years, feeding casually in the safety of dark. We have also witnessed a handful or two in early morning or late evening on our own land, and in various orchards and alfalfa fields and roadsides throughout the county. Perhaps I am, along with a few others, slightly obsessed with taking a record-book buck. But it is not a matter of seeing my puny name in "The Book" but rather the combination of challenge and the opportunity here. It would be a different matter if a B & C buck were a rarity in this county, but when one sees a book buck in the early morning mist of August just a half-mile from downtown, it tends to feed the fires. In August, they seem to appear with some regularity in evening fields, fattening in the full of antler velvet. We are not so ill-learned as to fail to understand velvet's exaggerated look. A 130-class deer in full velvet can look like a book buck.

Discounting this illusion, we still see several a summer but always fail to do so during hunting season. It drives us to a bit of obsession, I'll admit, but it is a pleasant one.

Although I won't be able to deer hunt for fourteen days, I won't be far removed from the daily spirit of the hunt. Old friend Pokey Corbel called last month from Arizona and asked if he could stay with us for a week, beginning November 1. Though he partakes in Arizona's mule deer chase and has taken a few of the rarer Coues subspecies of whitetail, there is no satisfaction like a hunt in the Corners. He complains incessantly about having to pay out-of-state fees, when he was born and raised here, living his first fifty years in the Corners. But complain as he might and certainly will, he still returns every three or four years for a week of the season.

In the past, he always stayed with his brother and family south of town. But Fred Corbel, the Farm Insurance man, is a recovering alcoholic and reformed smoker now. To complicate matters further, Fred and family have also recently joined a zealous religious group and poor old Pokey feels plain uncomfortable with them. He plans on spending some evenings and dinners with them, of course, but given his habits of smoking, drinking, and an interest in chasing women at the never-too-old age of sixty-seven, Pokey asked to bunk in our spare bedroom. He is more than welcome. We share his pitiful vices and his love of deer hunting, and though my wife and I are nearly twenty years his junior, the three of us often stay up late in laughing, sarcastic attack on all things wrong or sacred in this world. Pokey often speaks in the vernacular of an ill-educated cowboy, but he is actually very well-read, sharp-thinking, and a man of fine wit. I would like to take him up to camp, but I've promised Archie's grandson and friends I would let the place settle in absolute silence for the two weeks prior to their arrival, guaranteeing them some relatively careless, unsuspecting deer.

I'll never be able to think of Pokey without revisiting the typed and very long, manuscript-style letter he sent us years ago when he learned I was writing deer stories for a few magazines. Pokey was astounded, claiming it made absolutely no sense at all, seeing that I was "the most perfectly incompetent whitetail hunter" he'd ever known. After learning I was often published, he claimed he would never again believe the advice of any outdoor writer and wondered if his outdoor-writer hero Jack O'Connor was an equal fraud. He offered every overworked cliché from "the blind leading the blind" to "those that can't do, teach" to his own invention, "It's always the true fool that ain't afraid to demonstrate the foolishness." He even titled the piece, and in his honor, I'm bound by friendship to include this manuscript-letter unedited, except for a few spelling corrections. Since it is a better piece than I've ever written; not only can the old coot out-hunt me, he can out-write me as well.

CONFESSIONS of the ARIZONA DEER WIZARD
or
THE THREE GREAT LIES
by Harold "Pokey" Corbel

Friend, if I would have spent half as much time studying law books as I invested in the relentless pursuit of deer droppings, I would now be stepping down from the Supreme Court, the gold watches and presidential handshakes of retirement dinners bothering me nightly, large pensions and book advances in the wings. But instead of passing on the memoirs of great decisions—like the single-handed saving of the Constitution by my keen rulings—my memoirs only contain the knowhow of rebuilding Ford transmissions and the following debunking of the three largest deer hunting myths.

The three great lies? Sure, those are pretty strong words, but after spending a half-century chasing whitetails, a man becomes a realist. I never intended to share these revelations with the general run-of-the-woods population—the common Nimrod—but like many of the special few, we hunters who dedicate our lives to seeking the truth, impending starvation kept getting in my way. I needed to sell this secreted information.

I thought these revelations would bring in a tidy sum, but there's not much market out there for revelations. I tried to peddle them to guide services, but every son-of-a-buck out there in guide land figures he invented deer droppings. I was desperate, and turned to magazine publishers, which is pretty damn gutsy of me, since this is the same little clan that fostered these myths in the first place. Of no large surprise, they not only declined but destroyed the manuscripts as well. I am certainly glad that I kept one copy for my records.

One final caveat: Keep this material from the eyes of any hunter under the age of thirty. I still derive a certain amount of demented pleasure in witnessing young fellas foundering in the muck of deer myth.

MYTH No. 1: *The Horizontal Line*

Now, how many times have you read this tip: "Remember, don't look for the whole deer. The woods are vertical—look for a horizontal line, a deer's back."

Ha. This myth had me in its grip for some thirty years. Finally, while sitting in my stand last fall, snapping off frozen nose hairs to placate the boredom, it came to me that every damn thing I saw in front of me was horizontal! Just where do these vertical woods exist? They surely sound like a pleasurable place to hunt. I must confess I've never hunted east of Pennsylvania, and maybe, just maybe, you folks back East are blessed with vertical woods. I did have a friend once, a fellow from Maine, but he never mentioned anything about vertical woods in his country.

Now, out West, in the high mountain forests of Arizona, our woods are strictly horizontal. I would easily spot a deer if he stood up on his hind legs in some ridiculous attempt to blend in with the "vertical woods." He would be a shish kebab on my grill before the sun set in the pines. No, out here a strange thing takes place. Each one of our vertical trees has about four hundred horizontal branches. And just to add a little spice to the brew, its many forefathers found it convenient to cast themselves at death in a horizontal tangle on the forest floor. Out here, we call it deadfall. I'm sure that you have some fancy or scientific name for it back East. Now, to throw a little ether on the fire, out here we have this stuff called "brush." The inside poop on this stuff is that, besides having about 150 horizontal lines, it grows up to just about the same height as a deer's back! Call it kismet if you must—it certainly gets my goat.

One day in my stand, after running out of frozen hairs to snap, I counted all the lines in my view. The sad truth was there were twenty-four vertical lines and 19,706 horizontal lines out there. So much for that great tip of looking for a horizontal line, wouldn't you say, fella? You can thank hunting magazines for that little clunker.

MYTH No. 2: The Twitching Ear

Here's another sucker proposition. I'm more than a little ashamed to admit I spent forty years looking for an ear twitch. It was a sincere search carried out in yeoman's fashion, for it was my first practiced magazine tip. The ghostly words still ring loud in my memory: "When glassing the deer covert, look for a slight movement, the twitching of an ear." If I read that tip once, I read it a thousand times and always faithfully practiced the ear-twitch-search method. Quite frankly, this tip is bull pucky.

The failure of my first four years of ear-twitch searching was naturally blamed on my use of the naked eye. You can imagine the joy on that Christmas morning of my seventeenth year—there she was, my very own pair of army surplus, 7x35 binoculars with a slightly fuzzy right lens. I practiced all that spring and summer, pretending many a squirrel tail flickering on a pine tree was a twitching deer ear. I'm here to report that nearly forty years of ear-twitch searching have been a complete waste of time.

Through the years I've come to think that maybe our deer out here are just not into a lot of this ear-twitching nonsense. Maybe our deer haven't caught on to this big twitching fad apparently sweeping the rest of North America's herd. We are a little behind the times out here, I'll grant you that, but I still wonder about the validity of the tip.

During the hunt of 1985 I was determined to score via the ear-twitch method. Every day I spotted fine bucks, even a trophy or two. Unfortunately, all these deer were spotted in that mundane, outdated mode of seeing the whole deer wandering the hillside. I had to pass. Finally, on the last day of the season, while daydreaming in my stand, a fine 6x6 mule deer wandered into my view. By now I had given up hope of spotting an ear twitch and was somewhat consoled by the fact this was a Boone & Crockett buck. Just as I began to bring pressure on the trigger, a sharp movement caught my eye from off to the left. Hold everything! A twitch! Not just one, but several in rapid succession. I don't mind telling you straight out—I was shook. Slowly I brought the old '.06 around to bear aim on the ear twitch. The twitch fever I felt was overwhelming; it was impossible to steady my aim. Who cared about a stinking B&C buck? There it was, a fine yearling doe standing hip deep in the manzanita brush, both ears dancing a minuet. Something struck me a bit odd about the image, so I hesitated, lifting my binocs for a closer look. Hell, it wasn't ears twitching, after all. A big mountain blue jay was flapping its wings right behind that doe's head. The excitement rushed out of me like water down my toilet. By now, the nice record-book buck had wandered off and another unfilled tag went into my cigar box. That was the last year I ever searched for a twitching ear.

MYTH No. 3 : Thermal Clothing

"Keeps you warm at forty below." Sound familiar? Hunting clothes and boots are surrounded by as many myths as the buck himself. Every piece of underwear, shirt, glove, coat, and boot in my hunting outfit is assured by its maker to keep me toasty warm at forty below. That might be true for someone jogging or splitting firewood in these togs, but, quite frankly, in my stand they fail me miserably at thirty degrees above zero. When is someone going to invent an outfit that keeps you warm at, say, thirty degrees above zero? I know I'd pay most any price for such an advantage.

I've often wondered just who needs an outfit that keeps you warm at forty below? Someone loony enough to be out hunting in that kind of weather could probably do it buck naked, running alongside a pack of screaming coyotes. I feel foolish enough hunting when it's ten degrees outside. One has to eventually realize there are gifted days meant for sitting by a woodstove, reading books and sipping a hot toddy. Who, in heaven's name, hunts when it's forty below?

And wearing wool? Here's another clothing myth that fooled me for years. Sure, wool breathes and helps wick moisture from your body. Gee, that's swell. But what about keeping you warm? The only time my woolen outfit keeps me truly warm is when I'm dragging a two-hundred-pound buck up a hill in the midday sun. That very morning, that very same wool was wicking and breathing itself limp in a failed attempt to ward off the predawn frost in my blind, leaving a shivering wool-clad fool wondering why he endures such pain. Let's get this one filed correctly—absolutely nothing keeps you warm in a deer stand anywhere north of Miami, Florida.

Once the hunter forgets the horizontal-line theory, ignores the ear-twitching method, and rejects all variations of the proper clothing myth, he or she will be free to understand and concentrate on the true secret of successful deer hunting in northern climates—pain tolerance.

Chapter 14

I am oddly in a sullen mood this last night of October, usually a time of much contentment, thick with memories of childhood Halloweens. I am neither angry nor upset, but simply wallowing on the melancholy side of it all. Pokey has arrived, but, as planned, he will spend the first night at his brother's. My mood has nothing at all to do with Pokey, but finds its root in a mix of events. Perhaps the weather is partially responsible; the wind blew hard for the last twenty-four hours and, combined with a driving rain, managed to strip much of the autumnal beauty from the hills and fields. The end of spectacular wooded plumage is always sure to come, but given some small blessing, it often creeps long into November, nearly bumping up against Thanksgiving and making for a long, color-bright autumn. Not so this year. Last night's hard rain and wind did much damage, and I was nearly shocked this morning when looking out across the pasture and up at the small hills around our place. It had the premature look of cold winter, with only scattered pockets of gold and scarlet.

Then again, it is not solely the weather change that prompts my pensive mood. I have been bothered all evening by the industrialized world's terrific waste of time. Make that Time with an uppercase T. It began subtly this afternoon as I shopped at A-1 Grocery for some fresh vegetables I know Pokey enjoys. For the first time, I really began noticing the "already-prepared" nature of many fresh vegetables in our store. It is sad enough that freezer and shelf space in big-city markets is ever growing in size to meet the demand for already-prepared dinners, breakfasts, snacks, and desserts. But salads pre-chopped in little plastic bags? Already diced and mixed vegetables with spices? Pre-peeled carrots? These types of food have been slow to arrive in the Corners and, thankfully, take up little space and receive little patronage.

I could have easily let my small disgust die a quick death, but when arriving home, I turned on the evening news just in time to hear a report on American parents' lack of quality time with their offspring. According to the report, neither mother nor father, due to job demands, has a sane moment to spare. Some perfectly pop psychiatrist was smiling the ever-present smile of glazed eye and suggesting that, for good mental health, the family should have at least one sit-down-together meal per week. I nearly fell out of my overstuffed chair, a trick of no small effort. Still, I could have let even that pass if the report wasn't followed by an advertisement for a popular "quality takeout" store. For five dollars a meal, mom or pop could take a number and line up at the counter to buy a twenty-five-dollar sack full of plastic-wrapped, still warm, complete dinners for a family of four. It was the proverbial backbreaking straw for this camel.

I realize single moms and dads have an incredibly tough task of balancing work with family, but I now wonder about traditional families where both work full-time, claiming that low-paying jobs require it so. God knows the world is full of too many low-paying jobs—I've held too many of them. But I still wonder if the "extra check" isn't totally absorbed by the costs of day care, daily transportation, clothes for work, and the constant purchase of extra-cost, already-prepared meals at grocery stores, "quality takeouts," and fast-food restaurants. The advertised takeout dinner for four (and it was no gourmet feast) cost twenty-five dollars and could have been prepared at home from scratch for five measly dollars. Where is the gain in this type of foolishness? Who are they kidding? That extra cost absorbed over half the day's earnings from a minimum-wage job.

Again, we are a slow-to-change lot in the Corners and blessed with the sweet concept of time's value. Few in this town would give up the "good time" of planting a garden and staring at the blue sky, harvesting when needed and chopping our own salad, just to work an extra job so we could afford to buy it grown and prepared. We value that time; to some, it rivals autumn's great gift. Old Mrs. Richards, 87 and still living in her house on the block behind the Kut & Kurl, claims it is the spirit of her garden that keeps her living. Even with severe arthritis and a tripod cane, she works and enjoys her ground. Because she is unable to bend over fully, the neighbors built her long raised beds to hold her lettuce and tomatoes and squash.

The whole concept of modern life often seems an oxymoron or a catch-22. We scurry around buying everything from homes, clothes, and furniture to already-prepared meals, paying dearly for heat sources, laundry, yard and mechanic work—even our very entertainment—simply to save the "time" of doing so ourselves. Yet the very act of paying someone else means less time for the simple joys, as we must now leave home and family even longer to earn the extra money at a job most people dislike, praying for the glorious day of retirement. This great wound in the soul of contemporary man seems almost self-inflicted, and, if so, it is a pitiful thing.

These thoughts and the sudden loss of my cherished autumnal beauty held me melancholy that last night of October. And it took one ghost, a pirate, and E.T. knocking at our door in trick-or-treat to bring me sanely home and contented again. They are the neighbor kids, "neighbor" meaning a mile down the gravel road toward the pavement. We knew they would come around and made double-chocolate fudge and caramel apples for their treats. When one lives twelve miles from town, with only three neighbors within a two-mile range, the quality of Halloween treat is afforded some luxury.

The sky has opened clear on Halloween; a three-quarter moon and a good chill mark the night. On the low, rolling hills in the distance, the moonlight shows the evening's dusting of snow on the treetops. Standing on the porch, small shivers dancing about from lack of a jacket, I feel the creeping pulse of a hunter's blood and wish I was now planning a morning deer hunt. But I have eight more days to wait, and with Thanksgiving coming quickly, I can at least justify seeking our traditional goose. There is a large slough—or, more precisely, a tule swamp—covering at least forty acres, five miles east of town. It is private land owned by Tom Finch and family, a part of their block of cut-over timberland, family owned for over a century. Since it serves no timber or agricultural purpose, being a natural duck, goose and muskrat swamp, they have always kindly considered it "public" land for the rest of us. We lack grain fields around here, so it is a good spot for goose blinds. The geese are still moving south. I drove out there yesterday and spotted about one hundred late arrivals resting at least overnight and, I hope, longer, as I'm going out in the morning.

Time? I am glad for my store of it—especially autumnal time. Some may argue that a writing occupation affords me unfair opportunities and it is somehow easy for me to advise spending so much time in fall pleasures. Not so. For the first twenty-five years of my adult life, I punched a time clock just like the majority of Americans. But in Harland—as it's possible to do in many areas of the country—we structure our lives to afford that freedom of time. I held that long-ago milk pickup job because it was three days a week—6 A.M. to 6 P.M.—thirty-six hours and nearly a "real" job, but it gave me four days off to hunt without rush. In the spring and summer I could always pick up a little extra cash for fall pleasures by doing an odd job or two.

Another example? The Finch family, owners of the goose slough, have a box mill that makes wooden crates for the apple industry throughout several states. It is a small operation employing Tom, two sons and a daughter, and five full-time employees. Nearly full time, that is, and it is one of the choicest jobs in the Corners for a hunter. Since most orders for next apple season come in during the spring, Tom Finch runs the place full-time from December 1 to Labor Day weekend. For the next three months he shuts it down and ships out what few orders trickle in, generally one or two a week, by himself. By budgeting wisely during the year, his three children and the five employees have an absolutely free autumn to enjoy at their leisure. Archie Weil's grandson lucked into one of those precious jobs after graduating high school. To illustrate how it takes all kinds to make this world wobble around, he gave it up and moved nearly two hundred miles away to live in a fifth-floor city apartment and sell automobiles.

Time? Quality time on earth, whether your tilt is autumn hunts or spring gardens, is always available to one who perseveres and plans wisely. It never hurts to follow the old homesteader's axiom of "Never buy what you can grow or make." Those words are inscribed over the door on the brick outbuilding serving as Harland High's agriculture, wood, metal, and car shops and home economics classroom. They impressed me at age seventeen—they still do thirty-three years later.

I do feel for those young couples starting out in big urban areas of tremendously high cost. One of our full monthly incomes in the Corners would barely pay their rent or mortgage. But if a person, or especially a couple, young or old, has a true rural leaning or a desire to escape the fast pace, then escape the damn thing! Though making foolish, ill-planned moves is never advisable, living in fear of challenge, failing to muster even the temerity to satisfy a great yearning, is a greater crime. For many of us, the goal should not be making evermore money in this life but rather having less need for it in the first place. Never buy what you can grow or make? Simple idea, but it bounces off deaf ears in a hedonistic age that relegates austerity to dirty-word status; an age that can't even self-entertain, spending as much per week in inflation-adjusted dollars for entertainment-sourcing than its grandparents spent for groceries over an equal period of time.

There are thousands of Harland Corners out there, and nearly all offer the same prize of old-fashioned rural life and low cost of living, and the same drawbacks of fewer jobs and very mediocre wages. But it all works out even in the end. Be it a big city with high wages and equally high costs or little Harland Corners, at the end of the month there's about the same amount of leftover money jingling in the pockets. In my case—none. The large reward is measured in "time." Though I generally struggle to survive and make ends meet, I just enjoyed thirty-one days of rich, earthy life and sweet peace. What money can replace that spirit?

I am wondering where Pokey will hunt in the morning. Having talked to him on the phone tonight, I know he is heading out from his brother's in the dark of morning and claims he'll show up here in time for supper and a warm bath. He advised me that he likes two well-fluffed pillows on his bed, a decent liquor cabinet, fresh vegetables with supper, and homemade desserts. He never laughs or smiles when handing out his demands of friendship, and most folks are at first taken aback by his seriousness. But he is a master of the perfect deadpan and dry wit, harmless and kind. I look forward to hearing about experiences of high-mountain mule deer as seen through Pokey's sardonic eyes. Three years back, when he last came up to hunt, we had him over for a supper that ran with laughter till 1 A.M., ruining our separate hunts of the next morning.

But we had the "time"—free time, some foolishly call it, as if all of time isn't free—a delicious, irreplaceable thing, and I feel for an America that is too easily satisfied with achieving "at least one sit-down-together meal" per week.

In the Corners, October is a month that demands the expenditure of all one's free time; save none for a rainy day. Under the glow of October's last offering, a bright Halloween moon, we sleep well in rest. Not rest simply to prepare for another day, but for a new beginning. November's own charming offering never arrives in the form of just another day.

November

"Don Quixote had his windmills. Sir Arthur, his Holy Grail. Me? Hell, I just wanna take one more good buck 'fore it's over."

Pokey Corbel

Chapter 15

And so November arrives, a time of soon-to-be holidays, colder mornings, and a coming rut. There are a thousand ways to describe the coming changes in the hunt, but there is hardly a finer example of the November zaniness now building, creeping around both buck and human, than that of Tim Buford and The Buck Naked Incident.

Tim was our deputy sheriff for nearly twenty years, of course an avid whitetail man, and we all miss him and his quirky nature. He moved to southern Texas a few years back, after his wife inherited a small ranch down there and a little cash. But for twenty years he and his deputy, Ed Torrance, were our high entertainment. Neither man was truly dense or naturally inclined to obtuse behavior on his own, but put them together and—voilà!—a mishap was certain to occur. Thankfully, they rarely ever worked together, and I suppose that saved us all.

It might serve matters if I explained one detail. We are a long, narrow county; the county seat and main sheriff's office are nearly fifty miles south, and our town is too small to require a police force. Harland Corners, as with three other isolated towns in this county, is served by its own sheriff's substation.

In our case, it consists of a part-time dispatcher, a Monday-through-Friday sheriff's deputy on the day shift, his deputy working four-to-midnight, and no one working graveyard. A part-time reserve deputy works Saturdays and Sundays. We need nothing more and, if truth be told, hardly that. There's an occasional car accident, but the deputy's job is mostly drinking coffee, serving papers in a constable's role, and settling barking-dog disputes. If the need arises in off-hours, we can call any of the three men at home or dial toll-free to the faraway main office.

Tim Buford, being the soft-spoken elder, and Ed Torrance, more youthful and exuberant, could easily remind someone of Andy Taylor and Barney Fife. Except that when they work together, for some reason they both became Barney Fife—often to the extreme.

No one has ever come up with the true story behind "The Buck Naked Incident," as Tim and Ed refused ever to discuss it or offer a candid answer to any query. But three Novembers ago, something happened out on County Road 23 that was the object of much snickering innuendo. The only eyewitnesses were a couple of teenage schoolgirls, and they were mostly blinded by the near-blizzard conditions.

Again, more detail may be needed to better understand the incident and subsequent "confession." Tim and Ed were notoriously bad deer hunters, quite an anomaly considering their Corners heritage. After a quarter-century of trying to score on a decent buck, neither had equaled the yearly and regular feats of most high-school boys and girls. But much to our continual annoyance, they both talked deer as if they had invented the very droppings. In consequence, they were always the butt of our good-natured jokes or comments on their hunting prowess.

About two weeks after the first rumors, started by a few students from Miss Chaney's Private School, made the rounds of cafe and taverns, the following "report" conveniently showed up at Tip Meyer's, the cafe, Harvey's, and most every business on Main Street. In a rare showing of good taste (or fear of lawsuit), the *Harland Herald* didn't print it. Its true author is still unknown, but many of us always suspected Harvey Mott as the culprit—it mirrors his sense of humor. Regardless, whoever wrote it took the time to type it, make it look official, print at least twenty copies, and scrawl on the top of each one: "Found in the Governor's wastebasket at the Capitol building—Nov. 25, 1991."

The Buck Naked Incident

TO THE GOVERNOR'S OFFICE: This here is my sworn testimony and account of the unfortunate incident of Nov. 15, 1991.

Tim Buford

It was late in the afternoon, sir, a heavy snow falling, when the call came into the station house. Sandy the dispatcher hollered over to my desk. "Sheriff Buford, y'all got a doe tangled up in some hog wire out on County Road 23, right past the Hansen place."

Of course I was a bit miffed. It was nearly quitting time, and if you boys down at the Capital hadn't cut the funding, we'd still have a game warden to handle wildlife calls. Well, anyhow, Ed the deputy was coming on shift and looked bored, so I asked him to come along on the call. That, Governor, was my first mistake. The second was momentarily forgetting the rut was in full swing and the deputy is the worse kind of trophy fanatic.

We arrived on the scene within minutes, and since the deputy is a much younger man than I, we mutually agreed he'd try to untangle the doe from the large roll of rusty hog wire. The deputy was doing just fine in trying to release the little doe, except for a few superficial cuts and the torn pants.

And then I saw the buck.

Now, Governor, Your Honor, I've taken many deer in my years, but this son-of-a-buck was truly sent from heaven. There he stood, across the road and not more than twenty yards back in the woods, eyeballs fixed on that little trapped doe. And that buck wasn't about to blink or back off. It dawned on me the little doe must've been in heat, and instead of being spooked, this old monster buck looked a bit angry, with kind of a challenging look on his face. Now, sir, what follows in this deposition might sound a bit queer to some folks, but knowing you boys at the Capital are all devoted whitetail hunters, I'm certain you'll understand what happened to me and the deputy in a few moments of temporary insanity. Most folks would probably just call it buck fever.

You see, the deputy had just about worked that doe free, her being caught by only a hind foot now. She seemed to relax a bit, kind of resigned to her fate and mostly looking back at that huge buck across the road and wiggling her tail. Now, when Ed spied that buck, he turned white as a sheet and leaped over to the squad car in two bounds.

"Holy cow pie, sheriff," he whispered, pulling out his .38 special from the holster. "That's a Boone & Crockett buck— probably the state record, too. I'm taking him! Got my license and tag right in my wallet."

Well, Governor, you know I've practically dedicated my life, praying and looking for a buck that big. I had no choice but to stop the deputy.

"Sorry, Ed," I hissed. "You're on duty, and it's against the law to hunt on duty." I started writing him the appropriate ticket, good officer that I am.

"Ha!" Ed hissed back, glancing at his watch. "My shift don't start for five minutes. You're the one on duty." With that, he began to slink away toward the front fender, pointing that .38 at the buck.

I was frantic. Somehow my arm jumped out—sorta automatically snatching him back by the collar. I truly didn't mean to tear his shirt completely off. Honest.

"You can't shoot him with that little .38 pistol," I again hissed. "Ain't enough foot-pounds of energy. It's against the law. Sorry, Ed, I'll have to write you another ticket."

"Ha!" Ed hissed back again. "Wrong, Sheriff Buford, it's got a hundred foot-pounds over the minimum. You ain't stopping me!" With that, he tore the ticket in two, spitting on the pieces as they hit the ground next to my shoes.

148

My mind was spinning desperately, trying to find a legal reason to stop him. Then it came to me like a bolt of lightning. "Sorry, Ed, you can't shoot across a road," I hissed for the fourth time, scribbling him a brand-new ticket.

"I ain't!" he whispered back. "I'm sneaking across the road right now, you blind jerk. Sorry, sheriff."

At this point, Governor, I might have stepped over the line of good sense. In a fit of panic I tackled the deputy, and, while we struggled in the middle of the road, I inadvertently tore off his previously shredded trousers. During the ensuing melee and fisticuffs, a foolproof idea struck me at the precise moment the deputy's nightstick did the same.

"Ed, old buddy, the law requires you to wear 200 square inches of Hunter Orange," I hissed for the last time—tired from all the quiet hissing. "Sorry, son," and I rolled on my back in the road to scribble the fourth ticket.

The deputy was stunned. I had him cold, and a large tear began to form in the corner of his eye.

"Fine and dandy, Sheriff Buford," he snapped. "Then neither one of us will get the buck. You ain't wearing no orange. I hope you're happy, you damn jackass."

As you're probably wondering, Governor, that's when I dropped my pants and cast them in the roadside ditch. You see, sir, I was wearing my pumpkin-orange boxer shorts, a gift the wife gave me last Halloween. A large smile spread across my face as I snickered, drawing my own .38 and tiptoeing across the road. The monster buck was still frozen in place, staring at the little doe.

"Oh, no, you don't," the deputy suddenly snapped, running out in the road to grab my collar. I noticed the huge goosebumps covering his trembling and mostly naked body. "That there buck is on Mary Hansen's property," the deputy went on. "She don't allow no hunting anymore—big animal-rights gal, she's turned into. Sorry, Sheriff Buford," he shivered. "You gotta lure that buck across the road to shoot it."

It was then that the formerly brilliant and now possibly suspect idea came to me. In a moment of quick thinking, I offered the deputy my nice tan survival blanket from the trunk of the squad car. In a heartbeat, the idea crystallized. It took a few minutes of begging, along with a $100 bill, but I got the deputy wrapped in that tan blanket, and he held still long enough for me to duct tape the two road flares to his head, just like antlers.

"You crawl over by that little doe and mess of hog wire; just sniff around and act like an interested buck," I whispered. "That ought to lure the big guy across the road."

As God is my witness, Governor, I never imagined the next chain of events. I never expected that school bus from Miss Chaney's Girls Academy to come around the bend. Nor that the old crate would backfire just as Miss Chaney foolishly slammed on the brakes to avoid hitting me. How could I have known that little doe would startle and tear loose, running over poor Ed? Or that the deputy would panic, snag that blanket and his shorts on the hog wire, and run off through the field buck-naked, with nothing but them two road flares, and, well, you know what else waving in the wind?

As for me, sir, what could I do? When that doe sprinted out in the field alongside of the naked deputy, both of them in a blind panic, that old monster buck took off after them like a rocket. He'd about had it with the rutting deputy business, I suppose, and was aiming to tear Ed's rear-end off. I had no choice but to follow them.

I now realize that a fully growed man that's naked except for orange boxer shorts, and running after another naked, antlered man and two deer, waving a .38 pistol and making mock-grunt sounds to slow the buck, probably don't look real tasty to a bus load of schoolgirls. But that idea suggested in the recall petition the town folk and Miss Chaney signed against us is pure poppycock. Me and the deputy is both Christian family men and hardly never break no laws, especially that stuff about moral turpitude they mentioned. And aside from all of this, Governor, sir, I never even got a shot off at that buck.

Yours truly,
Deputy Sheriff Tim Buford

Chapter 16

The hunting muse smiled down on me at the slough. In the first hour of shooting light I took two mallard drakes with two shots, a rare event considering my wingshooting skills. Not seeing or hearing any geese across the forty-acre swamp, I put down my honker call and poured a cup of steaming coffee. No sooner did I screw the top back on the jug when, out of the corner of my eye, I spotted a silent fivesome flying thirty yards to my right and only twenty-five feet above the water. This type of pure luck seldom visits, and the cup of hot coffee went over on my lap; the thermos ending up out of the blind and floating in the muck. Within a span of two seconds, I upended everything in the blind, carelessly lurched for the propped-up, loaded shotgun, and swung hard to the right, taking a wild snapshot at the trailer. When things are going right, even careless acts that merit punishment rather than reward bring bounty. The trailing goose piled up in the swamp within easy fetching distance—that span always measured by exactly how far I can move in hip waders without getting stuck or soaked.

As terribly unromantic as it might sound, I am not a dog man, preferring to do the fetching myself. It's not that I don't harbor a secret affinity for the furry buggers but rather that they require a stay-at-home daily attention and much training, and I enjoy neither kenneling them nor allowing them to roam free chasing wildlife. Still, it warms my heart to see a hunter with a finely trained golden retriever or Lab—one that sits in tight silence until shots ring out over the slough, or walks so well-mannered and gracefully quiet, promptly leaping into the back of the truck when the "kennel-in" order is given. But good dogs have had literary volumes written about their loyalty, love, and loss. It is not my place to speak of them, having owned only one dog in my adulthood, and he a mutt of ill-breeding—a damn good barker, though, with an extraordinarily keen habit of crapping in the petunias.

It is a huge goose, twelve pounds or more, and will make a fine centerpiece for Thanksgiving. A wild Thanksgiving. My wife and I have borrowed a custom of the Tip Meyer family: presenting a near totally wild Thanksgiving feast. Of course, there are store-bought items; we could hardly grow a pepper tree, sugarcane, or coffee tree here, or find a decent salt mine to keep the taint of A-1 groceries from the table, but the rest is painstakingly hunted, gathered, or grown. If this Thanksgiving is at all like previous years, we will have the goose stuffed with wild pine nut, morel mushroom, and wild onion dressing. Even the bread for the stuffing is wild and homemade, its flour hand-ground from wild grass and oat seed the wife gathers in September. She bakes the goose with a wild honey and huckleberry glaze, and instead of potatoes, we have a "wild" acorn squash. The modifier "wild" is a bit of a reach. The seed stock of this squash is quite domestic, but they are heirloom seeds passed along for generations in my wife's family. The squash, not being a hybrid, are very small and hardy, self-subsisting on summer rain. We planted over a hundred of them along the tree line ten years ago, letting them go native. Thanks to squirrels that pirate them and spread the seed, they now pop up all over the twenty acres and feed a variety of wildlife.

We will again have smoked grouse for appetizers, along with spicy pickled trout caught last summer. The other vegetable will be the fiddle-neck fern shoots, tasting much like asparagus and growing wild in all the wet areas. We pick and freeze them every June. All other hors d'oeuvres and salad makings are wild or garden-grown, including sweet and dill pickles, pickled garlic, deer salami, and extra-sharp cheese. The cheese is another reach. Although it is homemade and aged in our root cellar, the milk and butterfat come from Altman's dairy. I once advised the wife that if she insisted on parading the cheese around as wild, it would better serve the matter of integrity if she would lasso a lactating June whitetail and draw the milk. But as usual, when I am saying something quite insightful, she is conveniently banging pans around or safely out of earshot in the bathroom. It is an uncanny talent, and one I have yet to fully master.

Harvey Mott took a grand buck yesterday morning at approximately the same time I was dropping the Thanksgiving goose. In a small example of Harvey's integrity, he told all that the taking was purely a fluke and no reflection of his skill. For six days he had been hunting Ed Timmons' old spot on Popknee Ridge, about ten miles west of town, chasing or at least often glimpsing a nice 140-class typical buck. He would have likely passed on this deer if it was still October, but now, on November 2, with only five days of modern-rifle season left, the lofty standards of opening day seem to shrink.

With a busier-than-usual night at the bar and grill, Harvey missed his early-to-bed call, failing to answer the alarm clock's 4:30 A.M. ring. Waking up surprised and disappointed at 6 A.M., first light scratching at the window, Harvey nearly gave up the hunt for needed sleep. As he rested on the pillow, contemplating his choices, the reality of November whitetail hunting quickly returned to sober his thoughts. Like many of us, Harvey has taken the majority of his bucks between 7:30 and 10 A.M. Arriving in the dark of predawn is not necessarily an absolute of successful hunting.

He pulled his pickup into the overgrown skid trail on Popknee Ridge at a late 7:30 A.M., grabbed the daypack, binoculars, and rifle, and turned to head up the trail to a tree stand. Much like the happenstance of my lucky goose, Harvey caught the slightest movement out of the corner of his eye and slowly turned his head. Stepping out of a stand of stunted second-growth fir alongside the logging road he'd just driven was a beautiful but strange nontypical buck with five-inch-wide palmated main beams. When fortune is generous, she is often blindly so. The buck stood eighty yards away, head cocked in a gaze in the opposite direction, seemingly oblivious to the red Ford pickup that had passed its spot less than a minute earlier. With the buck's attention momentarily distracted, Harvey was able to set down the pack and chamber a round in the .270, two time-consuming and noisy acts that are mostly impossible to pull off when encountering a surprise deer. With one shot, the buck immediately slumped dead alongside the logging road, leaving no long drag or carry through thick undergrowth and timber.

He was back in town by 8:30 A.M., embarrassed by the ease of the taking, nearly feeling it ill-deserved but still willing to haul the buck to Walt's, Tip's, the *Herald,* and the cafe for the flattering accolades. Because the twenty-three tines rising from the palmated beams were all short, the longest seven inches, it green-scored only 186 nontypical points, short of book entry for nontypicals. But it was an amazing rack nonetheless, with drop tines and double brow tines—a pretty enough thing in its symmetry and "look" to be at least as valuable as a true record-book buck.

I can't begrudge Harvey's fluke of double luck—stumbling across an unknown deer on a road and having it stand frozen in place for a full thirty seconds. Harvey is not like my very own and precious 'fluke' at home. She does those lucky things year in and year out. Harvey, on the other hand, works harder at his hunting than anyone in the Corners, spends more scouting time in the summer woods than anyone since Harry the Horn Man, and rarely, if ever, enjoys the blessing of hunting luck. In fact, Harvey is so dedicated to the hunt that he almost never takes more than one deer per year. With all the free creekside barbecues he hosts every summer, he could easily use more than one buck. But Harvey patiently works and waits out a good October or early November deer, takes it, then spends the shotgun/primitive arms season in search of a B&C monster only.

And he conducts that search with the patience of Job, never wavering to take a smaller but still excellent buck.

Ten years ago, he asked if I'd help him work a dense ten-acre patch of stunted cedar bog south of town, convinced a huge buck lived in there and could not be taken without a small drive. Harvey posted at the end of the bog where it narrowed in a funnel that slowly rose up to a small bench. We both had unfilled shotgun tags, and Harvey insisted I feel free to shoot the big deer, one he had personally scouted, if I had the chance, adding that my job was not simply the helpful driver but a hunter as well. Sure enough, halfway through the tangled mess, I jumped one of the largest deer I'd ever seen in legal light and didn't need Harvey's appreciated approval to shoot—adrenaline immediately took over and ruled reason. But it hardly mattered. Although I got a good look at antlers of certain 170s-class, a clean killing shot was never offered. Somewhat consoling was the fact that the magnificent animal was heading directly at Harvey, posted less than 150 yards away. I held my breath, listening for and anticipating the roar of Harvey's 12-gauge pump. Nothing. After a three- or four-minute wait with no shot, I carefully stalked those 150 yards, hoping the buck had pulled up to hide or double back.

It took twenty minutes to reach Harvey's post, and by that time the buck had grown in my mind's eye from a certain 170-class deer to a possible 180 or more. He was very tall in tine, twelve or more inches, I'd guessed from the fleeting glimpse, had maybe five or six points per side, and the rack was very wide. And there was Harvey, sitting calmly and smoking a cigarette, a small smile on his face.

"Jesus," I whispered. "Didn't you see that monster? He was heading right for you, Harv."

"Saw him coming all the way," Harvey whispered back. "Nearly ran over the top of me."

"Why the hell didn't you shoot? Couldn't get a clear shot off?" I stammered. "Geez, he was so big, I was tempted to take a bad shot, wound the bugger, and track it down. God, that was a book buck!"

Harvey smiled again and shook his head. "Naw, I had a good, long look at him. Maybe 155 or 160 tops, pal. If you'd have nailed him, I'm afraid you would have experienced a whopping ground shrink. He had two long tines that gave the overall look a deceptive largeness. Nice buck, though. A good kid's buck," Harvey winked in small exaggeration.

I was flabbergasted. Before taking my 160s deer at camp the previous month, I had never squeezed off a round at that large a buck, never had the opportunity. But so it goes with Harvey Mott. He'd already taken a nice three-hundred-pound ten-point in October and would not waver in November's rut for anything less than a certifiable Boone & Crockett 170-point minimum for typicals.

I have finally learned that level of self-discipline. It was a long time in the coming, but our quirky setup of two different but continuous seasons lends itself to showing some patience. If I lived in an area where only a single buck was allowed, I'm not certain I could maintain the stoicism. Back in the 1960s, when we were allowed only one deer, I held out for a trophy-class deer I'd been chasing all month. I was proud of my new-found patience and bragged about it regularly until the final darkness of closing day. At that instant, I felt overwhelmed with regret and foolishness and, sure enough, spent the next spring and summer with no smoked sausages or venison steaks on the barbecue. I had seen at least one hundred does and fifteen decent bucks during our old one-month season and felt the fool when staring at the high-priced packages of beef at A-1 Grocery throughout the year.

After all these years, Pokey Corbel still won't tell me any of his spots, and while he was out hunting one of them today, my wife and I drove northeast to an area we'd hunted years ago. It is only twenty miles away, but the rough road makes it over an hour's drive. It is a small plateau on a ridge of jagged hills rising nearly a thousand feet higher than our valley. We often camped there twenty years ago to enjoy its scenery, small creek, and wilderness feel, but never really saw any trophy bucks on our otherwise successful hunts. This year we drove up there simply because it was shrouded in fresh snow, whereas the valley and rolling hills were still bare. We hoped to use the fresh snow to scout for a decent set of tracks. The shotgun season opened in a few days, and we wanted another option in case our homelands and a few local spots failed to produce a big deer.

To our surprise, there was a tent set up by the creek and a pickup with Louisiana license plates parked alongside it. We rarely see an out-of-state hunter in the county, and, when we do, it is usually someone we once knew or a relative of someone we know. With no one in camp, I was reluctant to get out and trample about the area and was just turning the truck around when the wife spotted a man coming through a grove of half-naked maple. He was a young fellow, mid-twenties and, remarkably, hunting alone, having driven nearly two thousand miles to do just that. I was immediately impressed with his fortitude, endeared by his style, and we spent an hour sharing his coffee and our cold fried chicken and listening to his story. He had never heard of Harland Corners before and had picked it out on the road map because the name struck him "right." He had purchased out-of-state tags by mail and had come to our area for one simple reason: a lifelong desire to hunt the snows of the North Country. He'd found "our" road and place by stopping at Meyer's Sporting Goods and asking about any remote areas he might hunt.

I was so impressed by this young man's confidence and determination that I drew a map to our place and invited him to stop by on his way out for a meal and cleanup shower before the long drive home. I committed his story to memory, and I'm happy to know there are others besides the folks of Harland who hold the spirit of autumn so dear.

To Hunt the Snow

The young man stood at the door of the tent, his gaze fixed on the thin beam of flashlight searching the darkness. Little specks of snow crowded the air around the light. A smile crossed his face. For years he had dreamed of this hunt, imagining the look and feel of it, the smell and taste. To hunt the snow was a large and lasting dream.

He closed the tent flap and huddled by the gas lantern, watching half-frozen beads of condensation sparkle across the ceiling of the canvas tent. He was fifteen hundred miles across the middle of America from Louisiana, far from the cypress and Spanish moss of home, the sour-sweet odor of methane gas rising from the swampy bogs of chigger and snake.

Closing his eyes, he again pictured the twelve-point moving slowly below his tree stand, its swollen neck bent toward the ground in search of pheromone scent from the recently wandering doe. How had he missed? Nearly two thousand miles he'd come to bow hunt the huge bucks of the North Country, and he had cleanly missed a twenty-yard shot, with not a bothering leaf or branch to share the blame.

At least he would have tomorrow, and two more after that, before having to pack it in and head home. In the end, in the final overview, it mattered little whether or not he took a good buck. He had already spent four magnificent days in the land of his boyhood dreams. Four days bathing in the crimson hue of maple and rich golden popple, four frosted nights around the campfire, the pungent aroma of maple smoke clouding the northern night air with incense. And now, at long last, the snow.

The man was glad to be alone. It was his private dream, spawned by the hunting stories he'd read as a boy. In those magazines of the '70s and '80s, the great hunts and spectacular whitetails, the precious moments, were always moments shared in the ancient deer camps or deep woods of the North Country. He had promised himself that one day, while the blood still pulsed young and strong in his veins, he too would sit on a stand surrounded by the autumnal explosion of North woods, or start out a morning silently tracking a buck, its heavy hoof print crushed into the fresh snow.

"Why the hell would ya wanna drive thousands of miles to hunt whitetails?" his friends had chided. "Got plenty enough deer sneaking right behind Old Man Colter's store down the road."

There was no way to properly explain the dream, no way to explain the intangibles of alluring sights and scents. To a southern lad who had never touched snow and was weaned on the deer stories of the North woods, there was only one burning desire: to hunt the snow.

"Now, if you was a-heading to Alaska to hunt grizzly or up to Colorado for elk, hell, boy, we could understand," the friends had commented. "But going that dang far for a whitetail—hooey, boy, that's twisted," they continued in good-natured harassment.

Again the young man opened the tent flap, this time reaching down to scoop a small pile of the sparkling white into his hands. The snow was letting up; a small sliver of moonlight escaped from between dark, boiling clouds to cast a soft glow on the darkened woods. It was a good sign. Those very same magazines always claimed that deer moved willingly on the tail end of a snowstorm. Tomorrow might just be the day of dreamed success.

The man squinted into the night, shaking his head in childlike wonder. Just five hours earlier, these very woods were alive in spectacular foliage that defied description, brilliant shades of autumn intensity he'd known only from pictures. Now an alien landscape returned his stare—strange and white, but quietly inviting.

He thought morning would never come. The anticipation of what waited outside, the long-dreamed snow of the deer woods, robbed him of deep sleep. Although groggy and still tired upon rising, he felt the adrenaline rush of anxiety fueling his morning ritual. With practiced patience he forced himself to slow down and eat a small breakfast, supply his daypack, and give the bow a thorough once-over.

Outside in the predawn darkness, he moved toward the tree stand he'd placed in a grove of hardwoods on a small rise. As his feet bit into four inches of November snow, he was thrilled with his decision to invest in the luxury of felt-pacs. They were expensive and would serve little good back in southern Louisiana, but had been worth their weight in gold these last few frozen mornings. Today, they were simply priceless.

The storm was not quite over; little flakes fell to spot his camo, and he smiled childlike, tipping his head to catch one on his tongue. He was not long in the stand, watching the antics of a frolicking squirrel, when he spotted the doe picking her way through the grove. Though he'd spotted several deer over the last few days, he was still astounded by the size of northern deer. This lone doe was easily larger than any buck he'd taken back home. He studied her nervous twitch, her head turning to watch her backtrack, the white flag of tail bent to the side in a hormone-spurred invitation. He all but knew what was coming next and, within minutes, spotted movement down the trail. The hunting muses were smiling down on the young man; it was the same nice twelve-point of yesterday. With a pounding heart and the pinpricks of tingle crawling his neck, he drew the bow and sighted on the thirty-yard pin. A tumbling spray of silent white flakes blinked past his straining eyes, framing the buck in a manner of grace usually reserved for the painting masters.

No, the boys back home would never understand this moment, never feel the drenching waves of thrilling vibration. They would never know this rarest of sweet gift, a lifelong dream realized. Or understand that all humans need a dream, something coveted to live for and plan for. To a whitetail hunter from Louisiana, it was a simple thing, long held and precious. A chance to hunt the snow.

Chapter 17

Much Ado About Tarsal Glands

I learned a great trick from Pokey last night. Some would say it was an obvious thing, but, to my feeble mind, it made good sense and is now part of my arsenal. We had enjoyed a good supper of garlic-rich, roasted grouse, marinated all day in equal parts sherry wine, soy sauce, and salsa. It was served with hand-harvested wild rice I picked from a spot planted long ago in Tom Finch's swampland, and a side dish of steamed Swiss chard and beet greens that had still been growing, despite much frost, in our garden. To Pokey's delight, dessert was Coffee Royal with brandy, homemade coffee liqueur, and piles of chocolate-sprinkled, fresh whipped cream. This type of supper is not out of the usual for us or dished up simply for Pokey's sake; nor did it cost over two dollars. At the risk of beating a dead pony, never buy what you can grow or make. Again, as mentioned earlier, one always has a choice between settling for second-best and the pedestrian, or spending the time needed to create a grand life. Yes, it took some time to put this meal together, but the choice is clear: Either spend that time creating it at your leisure and peace, or set the alarm clock, work for someone else, and pay another to provide you with a lesser meal at higher cost.

But it is not the meal that measured the night. Pokey had rambled on for an hour about chasing Arizona mule deer and the strange differences between the deer species. And although mule deer have little bearing on his incredible knowledge of whitetails, it was an enlightening conversation.

"They wander miles for water out West, hoss," he began. "Not like your deer back here that got a spring or wet bog in every canyon. That's how we hunt out there—wait near the water source. Hell, sometimes they're two or three miles apart."

With little pause, the old coot went on: "And their feed is so damn dry; hell, when them old deer chew up some sage or green bunchgrass, it doesn't have the moisture content of your driest January browse back here. They need water, hoss, that's the secret of hunting the West."

And on he went, describing how easy it is to see many does and small bucks wandering open hillsides on the edge of aspen groves, the obvious location of most water sources.

"If I was desperate to eat, hoss, I'd take the mountains of the West. Ain't no sneaking and hiding in the dark, wet woods out there. A man can just hike the mountains and find a deer for food." Pokey had finished his first Coffee Royal and asked for another, this one minus the "mess" of whipped cream and chocolate. "But don't expect to find a buck that way. Good buck, whether it be muley or whitetail, is a special damn thing. Big muley bucks don't wander no hillsides in the daylight like a fool hen. And the scent? Hell, you're dealing with mountain canyons and swirling winds that make hunting downwind a dream."

But I've drifted from Pokey's remarkable scenting game, the small advantage that helped his tremendous rattling success in days of old. When we Corners folk first read magazine accounts of the near certain results of proper antler rattling, we all jumped into the fray. That was some twenty years ago, and when I reference "we," I do mean we. As a hunter in the Corners, it is impossible to read some new whitetail theory in an obscure publication and keep it to oneself. If silent in matters of politics, we are loud in our cries about new deer wisdom. Outdoor

164

knowledge is the Rosetta Stone of Harland Corners, opening the door to friendship and conversation. Everyone in the Corners respects good woodsmanship, whether the topic is a newly discovered morel or huckleberry patch, or the latest whitetail science from the University of Minnesota; regardless of gender or age, all offer an attentive ear. If it is a gratuitous listen, then so be it; I am at least happily unaware of the deception. Prozac need not come from the physician's prescription pad, after all.

I mention the tranquilizer *du jour* because I often feel some guilt in our mode of lifestyle, wondering if we Corners folk are any better than New York's Sixth Avenue Prozac zombie. When visiting there on business a few years ago, I was shocked to see how many middle-level executives, male and female, moved about in the tranquilizing fog of the prescription drug Prozac. As I rested in my hotel room that night and wondered in my best Mark Twain fashion about the nature and fate of humanity, thinking so much less of my New York brethren for their need to numb the savagery of the senses, I wondered if we in Harland, so proud of our drug-free style, aren't metaphorically doing the same thing. Because we sip a brandy and coffee at night or must have a chicken-fried steak at the Four Corners Cafe and talk whitetails to feel sane and whole, is this really any different from the New York executive popping Prozac in the morning to survive the day? Can't almost everything be a diversionary "drug" of some sort? Yes, we are basically drug-free in the normally accepted sense and receive possibly undeserved accolades for our old style, but is the way we handle life really any different? What we do—our love for the outdoors and expression of the hunting spirit—is simply a tranquilizing agent of a different composition and delivery. While I mock the Prozac zombies of Manhattan, I can't help but wonder if we are not guilty of wandering around in a fog of our own design, seeking the pleasure of its euphoria.

Despite much laughter during his story of mule deer and my drifting thoughts of Prozac zombies, I still managed to extract a jewel of whitetail hunting from Pokey Corbel. I'm not certain this jewel is relative to all whitetail hunters; it requires a year's forethought and the desire to do things quite free and proper. It involves the deer hunter taking the first step on the lightly trod path of never buying what you can grow or make.

"I told you long ago I hardly bothered with cover scents." Pokey spoke softly, nodding in appreciation of the new Coffee Royal, this one absent the chocolate and whipped cream. "That's not perfectly true. What I meant is I don't search for something to buy. Nature is a hunter's best friend, hoss."

I knew a decent piece of information was soon coming down the pike. Pokey is the most tight-lipped, secretive, and sarcastic booger I've ever met. It is all a great and sweet game to him. He loves the little push-push of "I know something you don't know" and therefore, "You're a miserably stupid S.O.B., ain't you, hoss?" This is Pokey Corbel; take him or leave him. And many do prefer to keep some distance. But I like the old coot; I did when he was a younger coot and hope it remains forever.

"I think the best trick a common man can pull," Pokey whispered, "is to use a buck's poison right back against him. Ever notice how strong a buck's tarsal gland is during the rut?" Pokey set down his coffee cup and scratched at the three-day growth of white whiskers. "That's because he pees on it intentionally every time he stretches out to do it. Elk do the same thing. Hell, even domestic goats do the same thing." Pokey fumbled around in his pocket, searching for a cigarette and probably wondering if he should share one of his tricks.

"I cut them glands off any rutting buck I take. Just skin around the inside of the hock and cut off a two-inch square. You don't have to take the bladder for later use, like I do; just the two glands will work wonders." Pokey found his half-crumpled pack of Lucky Strikes, lit one, and continued his rare offering of advice.

"Take them patches of hair and gland and stick 'em in one of those zip-locking freezer bags and freeze them away. Listen, hoss, next year when you're out rattling, hang one of them by a string on a nearby tree. Take the other one and safety-pin it to the top of your hat." Pokey leaned back on the couch, flicked an ash toward the open face of the fireplace, and again nodded his appreciation at the coffee he swallowed.

"Where does the heat leave your body, hoss? Most of it outta the top of your head, right? If you use a tarsal gland or any scent, dab it right on top of your cap. Making 98.6-degree tarsal scent waves in the twenty-five-degree cold sends out an incredible flow of cover scent, running out a hundred yards or more. And rattling? Hell, when an old buck hears the action and smells the rich odor of tarsal gland, he won't be tiptoeing when he comes in. That tarsal scent is so strong and real, it damn near covers any scent sneaking out of your privates."

It was a grand and simple idea. I had often bought doe-in-heat urine for the outrageous price of five dollars an ounce, and I'm certain that capturing an in-heat doe and collecting her pee is the best path to financial freedom. But even though the market is crowded with buck scents, I'd never given them much consideration.

Pokey always left the bladder in the field-dressed carcass until he returned home. For the uninitiated, the bladder is a nearly clear, plastic-like bag no larger than a tangerine. If one does not sever it with a knife when field-dressing, it will hold its six or seven ounces of liquid for days. When soaked with tarsal glands and frozen for next year, this represents at least forty dollars worth of "rutting buck scent." Again, homesteaders' axiom aside, it is not simply a matter of the dollars saved, but rather that one has finally discovered a vital piece of the woodsmanship of the Hunter's Moon.

Just as many others do, my mother called the October full moon the Harvest Moon. Where she deviated a trifle from the norm was in November. The sainted lady called that full moon of November the Hunter's Moon—as did her mother, and before her, another mother, and again another before her, until we drift back to a time of early fires and rough clubs.

One does not have to collect tarsal glands or bladders to demonstrate a kindred spirit with the Hunter's Moon. It only takes a clear and cold night, the crunch of footfall on frozen ground or snow, and much imagination. The Hunter's Moon of

November is a time of sneaking deer. The cautious buck behavior of the previous two months slowly erodes with the irresistible pheromones of each new doe coming into heat. The bucks sneak about in darkness, heads bent to the ground, to draw the sweet odor of hot does. To catch one so foolishly occupied in the light of day is every hunter's dream.

Although I've offered Pokey's method of creating your own potent scent for pre-rut hunting, it is not tarsal glands or grouse dinners that freeze that night in my memory. It is a story Pokey told of mule deer and his grandfather's early life in the West. I was unaware of Pokey's grandfather, Peter Corbel, and his life in the wilds of the nineteenth-century American frontier.

While talking laughingly about chasing mule deer through high-mountain aspen groves, an experience I'd also enjoyed on a mule deer and elk hunt in Colorado, Pokey turned suddenly serious when talking about his grandfather. Considering Pokey's quite perfect sense of deadpan, it would have gone unnoticed by the casual listener. But my wife and I could easily sense the man's mood.

Peter Corbel had left Missouri in 1849 at the ripe old age of sixteen, seeking the adventure and fortune of a Rocky Mountain trapper, a mountain man. Unfortunately, he was two decades late. Silk hats had long ago replaced beaver pelt in the fashion circles of Europe. The era of the mountain man was long dead. Beaver had fallen from six dollars a pelt, equivalent to two weeks' wages in the St. Louis of 1830, to four bits a hide, and that only if the trapper was willing to brave hostiles and a thousand miles of roadless plains to deliver his goods back in St. Louis. The fur-happy days of Seeds-Kee-Dee rendezvous, with buyers traveling to the Wind River Mountains of Wyoming, were long past.

Peter Corbel wandered the Rocky Mountains for thirty-five years, serving as guide for Mormon settlers and California and Nevada gold seekers, and hunting elk and buffalo for the ubiquitous army forts dotting the Indian frontier. Peter Corbel hadn't seen a whitetail since childhood, did not miss them, and persevered to provide for his new wife home-based in Taos, New Mexico, and the impending birth of Pokey's father.

I can't fully recall how the story even came up, but in retrospect, I think I was enlightening Pokey on my experience of exquisite torment on a deer stand in a recent bitter cold November, arctic air so penetrating that twenty minutes on stand was a damn long time.

Pokey began to slowly talk about November cold in the Rocky Mountains, and a story his father had told him as a child in the 1930s. Peter Corbel, having conceived Pokey's father at the ripe old age of fifty-five, was long gone by Pokey's birth, and Pokey knew of him only in story. This particular story was about his grandfather's days as a railroad crew hunter in the Wyoming mountains of 1877 and how he lost the tip of his nose to frostbite on a deer hunt. I don't know if it was the day's fresh dusting of snow on our fields, the high-pitched wail of a Northern blowing outside the house that night, or Pokey's innate ability to fully transfer a thought or mood, but the tale is forever real and locked in my heart. Much like Archie Weil's story of a last night at his cherished camp, another man's story, especially one told originally in the third person, is difficult to re-create. Still, by closing my eyes and again hearing the howl of cold wind, I can picture the railroad camp in Wyoming mountains and the small herd of mule deer, feel the bitter cold, and for the moment know Pokey's grandfather, Peter Corbel, a man missing the tip of his nose.

A Nose for Deer

That November was a constant struggle, but they did not play to it anymore. It was bitter in those mountains, freakish— no haughty shades of gold and scarlet, just all-day ice and sage, and darkness came so very early. About the camp, a stink of wasted kerosene from ten unnecessary lamps floated in the thick warmth of ten necessary warming fires.

There were many deer hanging from poles—blue-frozen carcasses, little chunks whittled from this flank and that shoulder and pockets of fat scooped out to grease the griddles. The stiff flesh swayed in the wind, carrying odors of meat and kerosene up the steep canyon. The frozen air gnawed at lips and fingers and would not stop.

They came to camp each morning from earthen dugouts by the aspen grove, or down across prisms of ice on the watercress bog. Some came from the rock cliff where blanketed lean-tos and stone shelters jutted. One of the ways was very long down the steep slope of shale. From up the hill, eyes closed, they felt the waves of heat rising from tents and fires long before entering the compound. It was wildly pleasant there; the coffee and biscuits smelled of warmth and blood. They came each morning hungry.

Peter Corbel watched them swarm around the fire, snatching bits of half-raw meat from the grill. They suffered much in this cold, each one of them gaunt and poor of oxygen. Peter sat on a frosted log and studied the curious faces in the small light of fire and predawn. Fifty of them, all Chinese railroad workers, all horribly miscast in the pointy cold of a Wyoming mountain. None spoke English; all spoke pain and weariness.

The wolves and hostiles and iced winds of mountaintop nights mattered little; they were not allowed to sleep in camp— not with their queer faces and annoying, squeaky voices. To be Chinese, the most disposable labor of the mountain West, meant a life of little and easily replaced value. They were the means to labor's end and nothing more. To be regarded as only muscle, a creature nearly devoid of form, was no easy thing.

Peter Corbel had their lives in a marrowless grip. He was the hunter, paid sixty dollars a month to feed fifty Chinese laborers, six white crewmen, and a foreman of ass-breaking pomposity with the flinty experience of his hired eyes and carbine. In the times of summer and early fall, it was an easy thing, a sea of buffalo wandering close to the mountains and great herds of elk moving a hundred miles to wintering range. But that was before the frozen air of this poor morning.

But filling his nostrils now was not the scented blood of fresh buffalo or the odor of half-rancid meat hanging in the once-warm air of September, but rather the glandular stink, the hormonal odor of piss and fear. The three hanging deer offered little comfort. They would feed fifty-eight men for two days on half-ration. For the previous two weeks the full ration had been cut in half, no longer matching the contractual guarantee—five pounds of meat and a half-pound of biscuit per day. There was not much game in these high peaks. To someone unacquainted with the rigors of labor and the science of metabolism, even the half-ration might seem satisfactory. But that is far from the reality. Given the caloric demand of hard labor (3,000 calories per day) and without loaves of bread, vegetables, oils, and butter, or the boost of sugar and milk, the body requires nearly eight pounds of meat daily—the standard ration of Hudson Bay trappers in the nineteenth century.

Peter scratched at the graying stubble of beard and squinted at the crew. He felt the coming trouble crawl slowly up his spine. The constant dynamiting of the rock face had spooked the few remaining deer from the adjoining canyons. Those that remained were the ancient bucks, poor of flesh and lacking the life-giving energy of rich fat deposits. Fat is the precious fuel of an all-meat diet. Poor in fat or not, these remaining bucks were wise, willing to suffer the high mountains to avoid falling prey to the wolves of the Plains. Providing food for this large group under these conditions was no easy matter.

He watched them squawk and holler in Chinese at the uncaring foreman, pleading their case of weakness and chill, cackling in wasted effort. Peter Corbel's thoughts drifted from today's hunt to a time of Missouri childhood, when he'd dug through a huge red anthill behind the barn. In the little tombs inside the mound were a hundred cackling grasshoppers, stunned and wiggling, their shells being drained of life as a wet yellow juice soaked the dirt and ants. Outside and scattered about the mound were a thousand dried and empty shells once carried to the tombs alive, their inhabitants cackling like the Chinese of this morning.

Peter rode far that morning, bringing only one packhorse and little hope. The first light of dawn broke over the jagged eastern peaks, dancing a pinkish glow on the snow. Peter shook his head in small disgust. Every bone in his body warned him of the coming storm. Unlike the others in camp, he had spent thirty years in these mountains and knew the little harbingers well; it was how one survived, and mistakes were seldom forgiven. While earlier sitting on his frosted log at camp, the signs had been clear: low pressure forcing the smoke from fires to cling to the ground; sharp cold and biting wind. A storm was coming.

In that same eastern direction was a stand of aspen, their naked, leafless remains woven with manzanita brush and covering an acre of steep draw. It provided cover enough; there would be deer. Of this he was certain.

It took an hour to move quietly downwind of the draw, using the ridge line of the adjacent canyon to mask the stalk. Twice he had stopped to feel the cold wind building and pick the crusted ice from his mustache. There was no choice but to ignore the clear warning. Fifty-seven sets of pleading eyes had pierced his back two hours earlier, gaunt faces pinching up to stare at the hunter riding out with little hope. That pressure forced him to ignore the building winds from the north.

Although it is wet storms from the far-off Pacific that bring deep snows to these mountains, the north wind was the thing to fear. After growing sharp-pointed in the scratching cold of its Arctic birth, a Northern sweeps down across the frozen plains of Alberta and Montana, building, unfettered by bluff or tree, spilling its hardness in gale-force fashion on the Wyoming mountains, freezing unsuspecting birds in place, crushing much life in its path. But Peter Corbel would not stop. He felt it coming, saw it, tasted it, and had noticed it when first rising at 4 A.M. but he had a contract to fill and, more importantly, lives to save— fifty-seven of them dancing about his head, pushing him forward.

And then he saw the deer. From a small rock bluff paralleling the aspen grove, three mule deer quickly rose. Hardly frightened, they ambled up the shale slope, stopping to look back at the silent intruder. All three were bucks and still light in weight from the recent rut—all poor blue meat, with little of the precious fat reserves. Within seconds, all three were down, the sharp reports of the carbine drowned by the strong gusts of wind. He noticed the muzzles of both horses were covered in long stringers of ice as he led them across the slope in the darkening 10 A.M. light. Above him, the pointy crags of rock were shrouded in gray; the first spit of ice-pellet flurries slapped his face.

"Damn," he muttered out loud. "This hoss thinks it's too cold to be snowing. It's gotta be ten below, or worse."

As he gutted the deer, the stark realization that one packhorse could not carry all the meat ran about his head. He'd have to pack his own mount and lead them both, head-to-tail, back to camp. Six miles, he mused silently—it must be six miles back. After lashing the last deer down and stuffing both panniers full with hearts and livers, Peter stopped to peer out across the mountain canyon. Nothing. The nearby aspen grove was gone, already lost in the whiteout. Slanting horizontal in 60-mph gusts, the ice-pellet snow raced up the canyon, stinging faces of horse and man, screaming notes of warning, of coming pain. Peter pushed on, sensing the southwest direction of return; little was visible to offer signposts of reckoning.

After ten minutes, it all became a hopeless thing, beyond safe and far from sane. His face was numb, the graying mustache crowded with frozen condensation, little feeling in feet and hands. A stiffness crawling. Scrambling up the shale, he found a small rock ledge, its small, slotted opening facing away from the wind. Struggling to unload the already frozen carcasses of deer, stacking them like bricks against the mouth of the ledge crevice, and jerking the two saddle blankets off the mounts, he lay back in the sheltered, frozen dirt. There was little else to do. Fire was a certain impossibility, warmth mostly improbable, and life tenuous at best. Wait it out. Fight the cold.

The two horses stumbled down the shale and stood, ass to wind, against a clump of sage, their muzzles hanging long with ice. With the sour-sweet smell of sweated horse blankets creeping up his nostrils, Peter squinted out at the suddenly forty-below scream of ice wind. He could last five hours, maybe less, and quickly rubbed a gloved but frozen hand against his face to coax some needed circulation. The tip of his nose, once burning wildly, was void of all feeling.

After squeezing his body into a tight ball of protection, he jumped, startled by the sound of a too-quickly-freezing aspen branch exploding in the frozen air. Peter closed his eyes and listened to the high wind, silently praying for a letup and wishing he had a smoke. Be a shame to die without a last smoke, he mused. "This hoss could use a small piece of pleasure," leaked from his lips.

He slowly opened his eyes to again peer out at the still-growing darkness, and the frozen eyeball of a deer stared back, offering no sympathy and even less hope.

Chapter 18

Pokey in the Pit

Pokey and I have planned a hunt together, our first ever, and it is quite simply a hunt of small desperation. The day after tomorrow is his last day in the Corners; he will pack up the truck and camper and head back for Arizona on Friday. Tomorrow is the shotgun/primitive arms opener for me, and we have formulated a "flawless" plan to execute on the unsuspecting whitetails of a long canyon near my place.

Pokey has hunted five of his six days here, always alone and in his favorite haunts of years past. Each day he has passed on smaller bucks, seeing only one worthy of an expensive, out-of-state tag. But now, on the eve of his final day, the strict standards of a quite special trophy hunter have dropped several notches.

"If I ain't gonna look the fool, hoss," he laughed that night, "driving two thousand miles home without a stitch of venison. A man might hunt the horns for the great challenge, but only a fool drives off without a winter store of farm-fed whitetail. Hell, I already gave Tip Meyer twenty bucks for the dry ice."

I decided to offer Pokey a chance at a decent buck, one that I knew frequently traveled a long ravine next to our place. The wide canyon runs a good half-mile into the thickly wooded hills, ending finally with a small climb up to a bench of spring bogs and birch thicket. At its lower end, the canyon opens out into our small pasture, the one with two ancient apple trees. Its mouth is the very tree line where we watch summer does and velvet-clad, yearling bucks dance nervously about, building the courage for a bright-light stroll out to check for fallen apples. Through the years, day or moonlit night, we've never witnessed a mature buck join in the dangerous folly, as if one never wandered or lived in that canyon. But come September, the rub lines and wide tracks of at least two decent bucks appear. By late October the first scrapes appear along the half-mile trail leading to our pasture.

I have jumped the very same buck in this canyon at least four times over the last two seasons, but have never seen him there at any other time of the year. I believe his home ground is probably a mile away, and he works this canyon only during the rut and pre-rut, solely for its good resident population of apple-spoiled does. If he has grown this last year, he may save Pokey more than the embarrassment of going home empty-handed. I figured the buck to be in the 140s or 150-class last year, and with good growth from last year's mild winter and warm spring, it might be pushing the book minimum this November.

Pokey at first wasn't interested in hunting the buck or muscling in on one of "my spots," but when I mumbled something about the canyon being impossible to hunt, his old eyes brightened. It was the intended and perfect challenge, and not far from pure truth. Because of some combination involving the dynamics of wind shear, thermals, and atmospheres, all beyond the reach of my weakening brain, there is never a constant wind direction in that canyon. Try as I might, I could never successfully attack it, because the wind shifted in 90- or 180-degree patterns every five minutes. I did take two small bucks there many years ago, but both bordered on pure luck or fluke. Still, I've always thought it a great place to rattle or take an all-day stand.

We hiked in there today at noon, after his morning hunt across the valley, so Pokey could get a feel for the place, build a stand, and not stumble in there blind in tomorrow's early dark. I cannot carry a slug gun until tomorrow, so I carried Pokey's shovel and camp hatchet while he carried a just-in-case .270. He immediately loved the place—and why not? The canyon is perhaps two hundred feet wide, choked thick with stunted cedar and fir, and has gradually climbing walls that rise about seventy feet in elevation. A veritable network of heavily trodden doe trails leads down to my pasture. Rub lines on six-inch trees run along each sidehill, and there are at least ten large scrapes on the bottoms.

Though the place is state-owned and therefore public, the only decent access is through our property. I've never seen another hunter in there in all our years here and rarely hunt it myself, having long ago grown disgusted with its betraying winds. Nearly every time I tried rattling in there, I would hear the distant approach of a cautious buck. But in that wicked place, a buck need not circle to the downwind side, possibly exposing itself for a shot. It would simply halt its approach a hundred yards off in thick cover and wait two minutes for the inevitable wind shift, and a loud, whistling snort of alarm would serve as my only reward for the effort. It was no different still-hunting— always a distant crack of deadfall or far-off snort, and when I arrived at the sound source ten minutes later, it was always the same: ground chewed up and sprayed about to mark the sign of a quickly fleeing, panicked deer. Over time, I've caught a few careless does unaware, but that is no large accomplishment, and I'm certain that surprising mature bucks there is next to impossible.

Not so Pokey Corbel. After an hour of scout, he chose a spot about twenty feet up the sidehill offering a remarkably good view in nearly all directions and began digging a hole in the soft dirt. It took nearly an hour, but Pokey managed to dig a pit about three feet deep and just large enough to hold one sitting human. He spread the rich-smelling earth around and covered it with the wet and molding leaves of birch and maple. As I sat against a decent-size tree and enjoyed a smoke, I had to marvel at his mostly silent engineering. Next, he gathered dried boughs of fir and pine and built a small fire in the bottom of the pit, adding chunks of rotted birch log until he had a fire going underground. With a smile, he finally broke a long silence to justify his act.

"I learned this from a book about Native American deer hunters of the eighteenth century. The pit, that is; the fire is my idea."

Pokey bent over his smoldering fire and held his hands to the warmth. "The Indians up in what is now Pennsylvania used to dig a ground pit and cover the top with pine boughs. Then they'd hop in there with a bow or spear, with just their head poking out and covered in more boughs, waiting days, if necessary, for a deer to come by." Pokey stopped to borrow my tobacco and fill his pipe. "Now, the idea behind a pit ain't just camouflage, hoss. If you just want to hide yourself, this here idea is one hell of a lot of work. Be easier to pile up some brush or deadfall. No, a pit is for scent control. I once told you a man's gotta own the wind. If you can't, a pit is the next best thing. It's how I took that nice buck in '69, the one hanging at Fred's insurance office in town. It was in a canyon east of town with this same shifting wind problem and always home to good bucks."

Pokey let the fire smolder for a half-hour while he explained his pit theory.

"When you sit in a pit, the wind doesn't work your body over, snatching bits of scent to broadcast. A lot of the warmer scent coming from your body will be absorbed in the loose dirt of the pit walls, and the fresh earth is also a great cover. Now, here's the real trick: When your body heat naturally rises in the pit, it has to pass through the fresh boughs of pine or fir covering the pit and your head. If a hunter crushes those fresh fir needles between his fingers when sitting quietly, each one releases a large dose of scented oil and turpentine. Here, smell these." Pokey had been crushing an inch-long sprig of fir needles as he spoke, and now thrust his fingers toward my face. The scent of pine and turpentine was very strong.

"See the oil on my fingers, the shiny stuff? It's potent, hoss, damn potent. And because of its oil-based nature, it's long-lasting and will just about dominate the warmer air rising from your body in the pit. I not only continually crush these little sprigs when I'm in the pit, I rub this oil behind my ears, alongside my nose, and around my mustache to help cover my glandular scent."

I stood up and walked over to his smoking pit, reaching out to enjoy the small warmth, while Pokey took the hatchet to the bottom branches of a stunted fir, stacking a little pile of fresh boughs alongside his pit for morning's use. Slowly he began sprinkling moist dirt back on his fire until, now smothered, it drew its last breath of oxygen.

"So, what about the fire, Pokey? What purpose does it serve, besides stinking up the whole damn canyon?"

Pokey smiled a long smile and mooched another pipeload of tobacco. I am always amazed at this man's eccentricities. Here we hike nearly a mile into the woods from my house and he has the forethought to carry his pipe but not his own tobacco, obviously planning on pinching mine the whole time. He is not a cheapskate by any means and, in fact, is a very generous man with his money. He is simply eccentric to a fault, and I feed those fires by letting him know he is my whitetail mentor. Because this is no secret, Pokey quietly plays the role to the max, having his protégé serve his whims. If I had asked him just what the hell he'd be doing if I didn't have my pouch of tobacco, I'm certain he would have calmly replied: "Guess I wouldn't be smoking, hoss." If I had then shaken my head in disbelief, he would have added: "'Course, I'd expect the protégé to always be thinking of an old man's needs. Where's the pleasure in being a mentor if the protégé ain't tending to business?"

He lit his pipe and sprinkled a last handful of sand over the covered ashes in the pit. "The smoke odor will act as additional cover tomorrow. What's the most common smell in this valley all fall? Woodsmoke, hoss, woodsmoke. Can't think of a single family without a stove or fireplace in the whole damn county—plus, all the logging slash piles and orchard prunings they light off in the first October rains. There ain't a field or canyon a man can hike around here in October and November without picking up that faint odor. Just remember, it's the same for the deer. If there's one scent the whitetails of this county are damn comfortable with, it's the aroma of woodsmoke. There ain't a better masking agent for this area, hoss."

We walked the mile back to the house, Pokey hurrying his steps, wanting to get back in time to drive out to an old favorite spot for an evening hunt. As we tied some fluorescent flagging strips along a trail he would use in tomorrow's darkness, Pokey explained that later tonight he wanted me to fire up my homemade smoker, a converted refrigerator. He would put his fur-lined cap, coat, and trousers in there overnight, letting their fibers soak up the pungent apple woodsmoke. I was overwhelmed by his strategies and fully understood his theories. Since the wind was consistently shifty and always betraying, Pokey would use the ground pit to reduce his scent broadcast. The heated air rising from his body in the icy morning would be rich with the oils of freshly crushed pine needles, after it passed through the woodsmoke of his hat and clothes. The cold ashes in the bottom of the pit would serve as both scent-absorber and woodsmoke scent-maker.

I've long considered myself a dedicated whitetail man, more than willing to take the extra step or push the envelope. But this man, at age sixty-eight, so enthused and rich with enough style to dig a pit, build a fire, and later put his clothes in a sausage smoker? It is now easy to understand why he is often argued as our "best man in the woods," and I can further understand why he always took the best buck year in and year out.

A little after 6 P.M., Pokey returned from his evening hunt and immediately chided the protégé—right after accepting the offered scotch and water—about tomorrow's hunt.

"Best be a good buck in that canyon of yours, hoss. Just on your account, I passed on a nice eight-point at last light. Nothing special, but a husky damn thing, probably touching three hundred pounds."

Right after dinner we formulated our strategy—or rather, Pokey did. It won't take a brain surgeon to see I had the stooge's role in this plan. His plan of "hunting together" was simple: I was to lead the old coot close to the pit in the dark, then get out of there and leave him alone. As consolation to being thrown out of my canyon, I was assigned the duty of wandering up an adjacent canyon and hopefully spooking any deer over to Pokey in the pit. He planned on rattling and working a grunt tube in the first-light hour, and if that failed to produce results, he would let the canyon settle in midmorning silence, hoping to catch a wandering free-roamer, as he called them. As an afterthought, he had the protégé for backup. His plan for me amounted to my walking a half-circle around the canyon, always at least a quarter-mile away and possibly moving a buck over the ridge line.

It was an all-day operation, and we both were going to pack food and coffee. Pokey was bringing a veritable banquet of dill pickles, salami and cheese, cold grouse breasts, a thermos of hot soup, and an empty plastic jug for the spent coffee. As the stooge and constant hiker, I packed much lighter. I actually liked my role. Much like Br'er Rabbit pleading not to get tossed in that briar patch, being asked to hike and still-hunt is my kind of stooge work. I am the type who easily abandons a stand for the thrill of still-hunting and its instant reward of warming frozen limbs. Besides, my scent would be caught in the swirling winds of that place, defeating all of Pokey's work and planning.

It was a good evening, this last one, and we sat long by the fire. This has been an extraordinarily cold autumn, always visited by the icy chill more familiar to late December. Tonight is no different. It is only November 7; the night temperatures should normally be in the mid-thirties. The days should be often sunny and warming to fifty degrees. But it is cold out there tonight, in the mid-teens; the week was marked by gray, ominous skies, and I catch myself now wondering about the coming winter. It is a good night to sit near the fire, the crackling orange glow giving more than physical comfort. And it is a good night to hear tales of Indian and pioneer hunting techniques.

Pokey is a scholar of sorts in one particular field, deer hunting, and to that end he's read all the information available—not simply modern how-to information in magazines or studies on whitetail behavior from various universities, but the history of deer hunting on this continent. This little search led Pokey through a lifetime study of Native American and pioneer history. He visited many accounts and stories that night and offered his opinion of the greatest hunters among the hundreds of tribes or nations.

It is purely foolish the way we modern folk—both white and Indian—group the incredible diversity of Native Americans into one catchall, the generic American Indian, as if the Seneca of New York had a thing in common, other than a distant shared gene with the desert Paiutes of Nevada, the Tillamook of Oregon's oceanfront, or the buffalo-hunting Crow of Wyoming. It is much the same as naively grouping all Europeans as "white" and therefore of the same bent. It doesn't require a doctorate in history to realize the Spaniards of sixteenth-century Barcelona were wildly different in lifestyle, religion, and food-sourcing from the Vikings of Norway and, in fact, bore no resemblance or kinship to them. It is no different with the early Native Americans.

"I figure the Indians of the northern and eastern woods were the best deer hunters," Pokey opined. "The southwestern tribes had good year-round weather and practiced sound agriculture. Up in the Northwest and around all the coastlines, they had tremendous fisheries to provide year-round food. The Plains and Rocky Mountain bands had the incredible store of buffalo to counter starvation. But in the north woods, folks had tough winters, little agriculture, and no blessing of buffalo or great salmon fisheries."

He explained that the hunting Indians were well aware of scent and did everything to counter it. Hunting with a bow or spear required bringing a deer into kissing range, and to that end, the north-woods tribes excelled. Not only were pits and tree stands employed, but grunt tubes and fawn bleats as well. Various pungent plant life was crushed in bowls to make cover-scent potions, and some even coated their entire naked body in heavy mud, mixing it with the urine from a recently killed deer and letting it dry to form a scent-busting encasement. Though this fact is fascinating, I can't imagine the freezing pain of rolling naked in lakeside mud on a frosty autumn morning.

Perhaps their favorite and most effective method of masking human scent was the fresh hide from a deer. Draping a hide over the body while out hunting wasn't simply a process intended to camouflage the body but was an early method of scent deception. The fresh skin of a deer, especially the hormone-rich hide of a rutting buck, not unlike human skin, is very porous, holding thousands of pockets trapping oils of scent essence. With a little herbal or mud masking of the human scent, an Indian hunter draped in the pungent blanket of a rutting buck could travel the woods with some invisibility.

These folks did gather some wild grains and nuts and put up a store of dried fish and pemmican, but because they lacked the bounty of southwestern agriculture, salmon fisheries, or buffalo herds, a north-woods whitetail was cherished, much needed, and utilized to its every organ and very marrow. Cold Allegheny or Vermont winter days were not survived by sucking on a gruel-ish paste of stored nuts and ground seeds. The flesh and precious fat of a whitetail, and even a gelatinous brew of boiled hooves, was the life-giver.

Much is made—again reflecting the misconception of Indian-generic—about the Native American's propensity for sound environmentalism and never wasting Mother Nature's gifts. At the risk of offending my Native American brethren, this often-taught concept is romantic, self-aggrandizing bunk. Waste was and is always in direct proportion to available bounty. While a north-woods Indian was compelled by starvation to waste not, a Plains Sioux or Columbia River Umatilla was often afforded the luxury of waste. With less than 60,000 humans occupying the strip of Great Plains running from Canada to Texas along the Rockies, and ten-million buffalo as fodder, waste was a common occurrence. One has to only visit the journals of a host of explorers and mountain men who roamed that country to see the true picture.

When the massive salmon runs of the Columbia River occurred—three separate species and runs—the Umatillas and other tribes living along that river were buried in salmon. Pokey recounted a journal story from a Willamette Valley-bound group of pioneers in 1843. They were traveling west along the mighty Columbia when they encountered an Indian salmon harvest near present-day Dalles, Oregon. The river tribes dried thousands of pounds of salmon, their entire year's store of food, during these runs, and each run was a wild and hectic ten-day event. Pokey claimed that at least 100,000 salmon, all ten to thirty pounds, churned the waters each day during a run. With spears and nets, the men hauled fish after fish from the crashing swirl, throwing them on the banks where children clubbed them. In their enthusiasm, thousands more were caught than the women and elders could daily process, and the banks for hundreds of yards were littered in rotting carcasses; thousands of oceangoing gulls and other seabirds flew the three-hundred-mile trip for the feast. Pokey described an account of one pioneer group claiming the Natives walked over a carpet of squishy, rotting salmon flesh that covered the ground from river to village. The oxen pulling the two-wheeled carts of the homesteaders balked at walking through it, forcing the caravan to circle above the village.

It was no different on the Plains; and I am always bothered by the Hollywood image of Indians always wisely utilizing the bounty of buffalo. Yes, the Sioux, Blackfeet, Crow, and Cheyenne did go on summer and fall hunts with nearly the entire village participating, building a store of hides, sinew, and dried meat for winter and utilizing Nature's gift to the best of their ingenuity. But what Hollywood never shows and modern Native Americans refuse to imagine is the simple fact that two Crow or Sioux travelers, scouting or journeying the Plains, would take a nice fatted cow for a summer evening supper and enjoy the liver and prized, fat-rich hump meat over their campfire. In the morning, they would cut off a slab of meat that might resist spoiling for a day or two, load it on the horses, and continue the journey. Behind them in the tall grass lay six hundred pounds or more of wasted flesh and hide. Of course, Nature wastes nothing, and the wolves, coyotes, and other creatures of the Plains likely rejoiced in the bounty. Still, Hollywood and Indian activists paint a different picture in which only those of European ancestry practiced waste.

Even more distorted is the portrayal of our shameful buffalo slaughter. I am well aware that some of the slaughter was politically motivated and much of the rest was a product of the imported European morality of the marketplace. We Americans have a storied history of applying that morality of the marketplace to our natural resources with devastating consequence—be it buffalo, watershed, or timber. But the Plains Indian often demonstrated much complicity in the shameful act.

While visiting a Plains History Museum in Montana many years ago, I was mildly surprised to view an old ledger belonging to a major hide buyer operating out of the Fort Shaw area in the 1870s. The largest sellers by far of buffalo hides were the Blackfoot Indians. I realize we planted that little seed of consumerism in their unknowing souls, showing them how they couldn't possibly be happy without wool blankets, metal pots and kettles, candles, and, of course, whiskey and inordinate greed. But they joined and participated in the slaughter with much gusto.

One band of Piegan, a tribe of the Blackfoot nation, sold over 15,000 hides in one four-month summer season. This band lived in and traveled the Milk River country of northern Montana and southern Canada, and their ambition and sales numbers stirred my curiosity. With help from the small museum's curator and the Great Falls library, I researched the particular band and discovered they totaled less than 1,000 in population. I was stunned. For years I, too, had believed the Hollywood precept that only "whites" possessed the evils of greed. It is wholly impossible for a 1,000-member band to consume or utilize some 15,000 buffalo over a summer season. That is roughly 10,000 pounds of boned meat for every man, woman, and child to eat in a few months, or nearly 2,000 pounds of dried meat for each child to carry around. Suffice it to say that the Milk River country was thick with rotting carcasses those summers of the early 1870s, and its "environmentalist" residents were entirely responsible for the waste.

The tone of this discourse might mark me as no large fan of Native Americans. Nothing could be farther from the truth. I am forever envious and admiring of a people and lifestyle so often perfectly sane and quaint. But as a devoted scholar of the American West, I often take exception to the Hollywood propaganda, and some Indian activists' portrayal of the Indian-generic as a sainted being, devoid of the greed, power, and ruthlessness fundamental to any human society.

But in the matter of wasting Nature's bounty, the many tribes of the north woods were nearly without sin. They had little choice and, in consequence, were the craftiest of all deer hunters. Come morning, Pokey's pit-and-smoke-scent technique will hopefully demonstrate their long-ago prowess.

He spent most of that evening describing deer hunting techniques of the original Cherokee bands of the Southeast, Seminoles of the Florida swamp, and a tribe from northern Maine—not simply their hunting style but how they prepared and preserved the precious gift and their reverence for the antlers of great old bucks.

Perhaps the strangest hunting tale involved the poor and somewhat lowly Paiutes of Nevada far from the wooded haunts of the whitetail. All early travelers encountering this group of Indians living along the tiny, muddy Humboldt River of northern Nevada were stunned by their haphazard style of survival and lack of hunting tools. The first recorded encounters, in the 1820s, are rife with descriptions of a people so backward in matters of weaponry, it borders on the implausible. To these scattered groups, often numbering only twenty or so members per encampment, a deer wasn't merely a great thing, its taking was an act of godlike magnitude. In the 1820s these poor folks were still without bow and arrow and the technology of obsidian-tipped weapons. They hunted with clubs and wooden spears sharpened by rubbing the point over a coarse rock. With this technology, taking a deer was indeed a godlike act.

They made all their clothing and shelters out of the hemp-like bark of sagebrush and subsisted on a summer diet of seeds munched raw from the stalks of river-bottom grasses and grasshoppers. The very same locusts that caused much tribulation in the later Mormon settlements of Utah were the staple of several Paiute bands in the Nevada country of the early 1800s.

In the cold winters, lacking both grass seeds and insects, they wandered into the hills to collect piñon pine nuts and conduct large jack rabbit drives. With the same hemp-like sage bark, they wove three-foot-high nets hundreds of feet long and strung them across narrow draws. Then several women and children would run through the surrounding sagebrush, scaring out all the rabbits in a quarter-mile area and chasing them down the netted draw to waiting clubbers. When the rabbits piled into the nets at high speed, often entangling themselves, the club-wielding men bashed their heads. Yes, to a people of such limited weaponry, taking a deer was an act recounted in the high praise of honoring tale.

Pokey spoke of mountain men who encountered these Paiutes on an 1820s journey, just minutes after shooting a nice mule deer doe on what turned out to be the edge of the Paiute village. Although the Indians were in natural awe of the black powder report of a long gun and the first look at odd, bearded white men, the entire village surrounded the fallen doe, squealing and pointing at its lifeless carcass. In the spirit of travelers crossing another man's land, the mountain men made the appropriate signs of a gift, and the Paiutes quickly dragged the doe to camp. The preparation and cooking was done in pre-Neanderthal style, with several men holding the deer, without field-dressing or evisceration, over the flames for twenty minutes, singeing off most of the hair. Now hairless, the carcass was dropped whole into the coals, and the same wooden hunting spears were used to push mounds of ash and coal over its body. Lacking earthenware, stone, or wooden pots, the concept of stewing was lost on them. But the deer body served as a perfect vessel, and after spending an hour or two buried in coals and hot ash, the stomach and organs were boiled into a hot, sloppy brew. The carcass was dragged out on the dinner table of desert sand, and the Paiutes used those same spears to punch large holes in its belly. With the deer propped up on its charred back, burned hooves pointing skyward and its opened belly serving as a large stewpot, the villagers used their hands to scoop out the steaming stew of stomach, blood, lungs, and liver.

These were Indians who wasted nothing but some of the hair; the deer would feed the village for three days. By day three of the feast, they burned the remaining bone and hoof to nearly charcoal black, then crushed it between flat rocks, added enough water to make a paste, and mixed it with seeds or any passing insect. Rare is the species of animal life or race of mankind that so properly consumes its harvest.

And in this illustration, one can see the folly in grouping the aboriginal Native Americans as Indian-generic, as if they were a common family of much similarity. Though some Indian nations possessed a wisdom rivaling the best of Greek philosophy, and others demonstrated a high order of social grace and personal hygiene, at the very same time, other nations and bands dotting America were not even acquainted with the Stone Age and were devoid of practiced grace, more resembling the Neanderthal spirit of brutality. But, good God, did they ever utilize their deer! To those living on the edge of perpetual starvation, much like the black bear that finds no carrion too unsavory, the crime of wasting food is not even conceived, let alone practiced.

Pokey Corbel is a fascinating man to engage in conversation. Though I'm pretty sure he couldn't pick out Romania on a world map and his grasp of Iraq and Iran, the Persian Wars, and the biblical Garden of Eden setting in that famous Tigris-Euphrates valley would boil down to the one-line comment, "They ought to go in there and shoot that goddamn Saddam," he is still a wise man. Wisdom is not necessarily a product of great knowledge stores or accumulations of history and the body-politic, but can be manifested quietly in our manner of grace, appreciation of moment and place, and in how we live with ourselves and others. Pokey has all the mannerisms and wit of a modern-day Will Rogers, speaks in a tongue flavored with slang and soft curse, yet tosses in quotes from Dickens's *Tale of Two Cities*, Chekovian short stories, and Shakespeare—in between patches of "If that don't suffer my skinny ass, hoss," leaving the listener wondering on the man's brain.

And we talked long that night, till nearly eleven, much too late for those planning an early rise. First light will dawn around 6:15 A.M., and the canyon pit is an hour's hike from the house with the cautious steps of darkness slowing the pace. Still, I had a deep, restful sleep and felt strong at the 4:30 A.M. ring of alarm clock.

Chapter 19

The heavy crunch of footfall on frozen leaf echoed across the
pasture and up the small canyon in the darkness. Any deer within a
quarter-mile of our approach to the trail leading to Pokey's pit was
well aware of the intrusion. Thankfully, deer have very short-term
memories. This is always a difficult time to hunt in the Corners.
Although a few does are already cycling, it is still pre-rut, the bulk of
does coming into heat some ten days from now. And the weather is
often uncooperative. On this day, November 8, it would be more
common to find a drizzle and gray sky, morning temperatures in the
thirties, with maybe a small chance of a snow flurry. Under those
favorable conditions, it would be a pleasure to hunt. Nothing quiets
the fields and woods like a day or two of misting drizzle, and I always
relish those days to still-hunt. I can move so perfectly quiet, with only
my scent to worry about, completely surprising feeding does and small
bucks when I stalk within fifty yards of their position. And even scent
proves a lesser worry, the drizzle saturating the rising odor of heated
body, preventing the alarm siren of human odor from reaching out in
large broadcast. I am certain this scent-repressing effect of fog or drizzle
is the reason for my inordinate hunting success on those favored
November days.

But this year is quirky and cold, the porch thermometer showing a near-record fourteen degrees as we left the house. The forecast for bright blue skies and a thirty-five-degree afternoon will hurt my chances as I wander in the loudly crunching hills flanking Pokey's pit. It is all fine by me, as I'm still not mentally prepared to take an all-day stand in this cold and would rather still-hunt than shiver in the cold silence. I wonder about Pokey's durability. He is so determined and dedicated, I have no doubt he will remain in his pit all day if necessary, but he is not thrilled about our early cold snap, his intolerance of cold being the sole reason he moved to Arizona fifteen years ago.

As we entered the wooded mouth of the canyon, the penlight caught the flash of fluorescent pink flagging we'd left in place yesterday.

"This is far enough, hoss," Pokey whispered. "I can find my way now. No reason for two of us to stink up the area."

So off I went in the black of morning, still a half-hour before dawn, heading for an adjacent draw that paralleled Pokey's. At first light, I intended to slowly work my way up this draw and climb the small hills above Pokey's canyon. This would take several hours, and if I heard no shot ring out from the main canyon or didn't stumble across a book buck myself, I would hunt the small hills and benches until afternoon in my style of thirty-minute stands combined with slow still-hunting. I planned to head back about two hours before darkness, dropping directly into the head of the main canyon in hopes of pushing something Pokey's way. At least this was the original scenario; the day's happenings would soon alter all best-laid plans.

Around 7 A.M., an hour after first light, I was nearly halfway up the draw, probably in direct line with Pokey's pit and a quarter-mile to the north. There was little chance to move silently on the frozen bottoms, and I was encouraged only by the chance of spooking something toward Pokey. I decided to sit and rest against the trunk of an old-growth pine, one that had somehow miraculously escaped the timber cruiser's eye back in the days of a booming logging industry in the county. Considering the conditions, I knew my chances of seeing a decent buck ranged from improbable to none and decided to fully enjoy the day as a hike in the November woods. To that end, I poured a half-cup of coffee from the thermos and rolled my first cigarette of the day.

As it always seems to happen, when I am least expectant of activity and enjoying a snack, smoke, or coffee, pandemonium breaks out. Certain that every deer in this draw, even the most incautious yearling doe, had vacated the area in consequence of the morning thermals pushing my scent ahead and a racket equivalent to a D-8 Cat coming from my footfalls, I was caught off guard by the small buck moving down the sidehill. Without large movement, I tried to crush my just-lit cigarette into the pile of frosted leaves by my leg. And just as had happened in the goose blind last week, the plastic thermos cup balanced on my lap dumped its load of hot coffee on my crotch. The small buck, eighty yards off and closing ground, acted as if it were fully unaware of my presence. If it continued on its present course, the little buck would pass ten yards in front of my large tree and head over the ridge to Pokey.

It was a strange buck, no more than 1½ years old (a yearling, we used to call them), but carrying a pretty basket of ten-point status. It was thin-necked and slender with a nearly feminine look, as if the small but pretty basket of antler was fastened to a yearling doe's head. Though I've never hunted in the Southeast or over in Texas country, this buck reminded me of pictures in deer hunting magazines of wildly beautiful, high-scoring racks on southern and Texas whitetails that have the body and neck size of our northern does. The accompanying stories stated that many of these mature bucks field-dress at 150 pounds, which explains the slimmer look.

In our northern climate, a mature buck often pushes three hundred pounds on the hoof, giving the hunter a 240-pound carcass to drag after field-dressing. Though perhaps not as big as the hefty Alberta-Saskatchewan deer, ours nonetheless have that same steerlike, stocky body with tremendously swollen November necks. When you gain only a fleeting glimpse of a bounding buck in the North country, the antler size is often underestimated, guessed at about 120 B&C points. But because of the large head and body, the exaggeratedly fat neck, and the long, coarse hair of a growing winter coat, it actually might be a 140-class buck offering that millisecond glimpse.

The little buck seemed to be on a mission, nearly trotting and still unaware of my presence. Though now only thirty yards away, it had yet to make eye contact with my wet-crotched but perfectly still frame. While it was still half-trotting and nearly ready to pass in front of me at ten yards, both front feet of the little buck shot forward nearly horizontal and stabbed into the frozen, leaf-covered ground. There was no doubt it had finally scented me, and I could actually see a nervous twitch ripple its shoulders. Still not bothering to eyeball me sitting against the tree at spitting range, the buck collected itself, coiled, and without snort or other fanfare bounded across the bottoms and up the sidehill toward Pokey in a few graceful leaps.

If, as I believed, I was directly across from the pit in the adjacent canyon, the little buck would soon wander into Pokey's view. But I did not expect the muffled roar of his shotgun to break this silence. Yes, he would feel much disappointment and shame in going home skunked, but knowing the man, I knew it was too early, only 7 A.M., to settle on the prize of last resort. Knowing his confidence and hunting spirit, he would thankfully take this little buck if its arrival coincided with the last light of his last day. But not now, last day or not. To the eternal optimist, it is only 7 A.M. and much opportunity could still wander the day.

I retrieved my crushed and hardly smoked cigarette from the mess of frosted leaves, lit it again, and poured another coffee, this one held tightly in hand. Closing my eyes, I tried to picture Pokey Corbel in the adjacent canyon, sitting crossed-legged in his little pit, his butt resting in the ashes of yesterday's fire. Across the top of the pit would be the cover of several limbs of fir and pine, their needles bruised and crushed to release the strong odors of forest turpentine. Only his head would stick through the mat of boughs, giving him full view of the canyon. Even his head would be camouflaged in fir, as Pokey always had a black elastic band sewn on the outside of his hunting cap to hold tiny sprigs of fir or pine. When he gave me this little tidbit of information fifteen years ago, it made perfect sense; it still does today, and I wouldn't be caught deer hunting—be it stand or still-hunting—without Pokey's trick.

Mr. Corbel's reasoning was simple: Since all experts on hypothermia claim that 70 percent of body heat escapes from the top of the head, Pokey imagined the head much like a glowing, heated mantle sending out thermal waves of scent to drift the woods in betrayal. Considering the experts' claims, I could see little reason to disagree. Whenever he enters a hunting area, Pokey will break off five or six sprigs of fir or whatever indigenous growth gives off a strong scent, crush them between his fingers to release the pungent oils, and stick the little sprigs in the elastic band around the top of his cap. The residue left on his fingers is wiped behind his ears, an area that harbors the largest scent glands of the head. His hope and theory are that the escaping body heat and incumbent human scent would rise from his head, be filtered through the stronger odors of pine or fir, and mask his own scent when broadcast. I believe this one gimmick, garnered from Pokey years ago, to be the single largest aid in my ability to see many deer while hunting.

After a ten-minute calming-down from the rush of letting the little buck pass unmolested, I repacked the thermos and tobacco, crushed another handful of cedar needles to wipe around my face and ears, and headed up the canyon. Even after seeing the little deer, I'm still certain my chances of surprising a wiser animal are dismally remote. The brighter side of the situation is the opportunity to hike a small hill and ridge about a mile ahead, one I've visited only a few times over the years. With its four-hundred-foot rise in elevation, it affords a sweet view of our country. At the base of the rock ledge on its summit, always bathed in warm noontime napping sun, is a small spring covered in watercress. Fully convinced I will see no "shootable" buck in this mostly hiking journey, I had already planned on picking some pungent watercress to add on my salami-and-cheese sandwich and take a long midday nap. It was nearly 8 A.M., and the smallest temperature rise began to fill the still-frozen woods.

Pokey Corbel slowly tilted his head down to squint through the boughs at his watch. It was 8:05 A.M., the sun finally climbing high enough to offer more than cold light to the canyon. He wondered on the chance of taking some careless minutes in a coffee and smoke break, nearly doing so about an hour earlier when he'd heard the crunch of hooves on frozen leaf. For twenty minutes he had watched the little buck come down the canyon sidehill and wander aimlessly through the bottoms, stopping occasionally to browse. After it had casually wandered up the canyon a hundred yards or more and been lost in the green thickets of stunted fir and dusty scarlet of frosted blackberry vine, Pokey decided to try calling it back. He still did not intend to take the buck, though he'd twitched with the inclination twice earlier when it passed his pit at twenty-five yards. If it had only been later—even noon or one o'clock—he would have taken the little buck and thanked both God and the animal for the blessing. But this was not the deer that had left heavy rub lines on eight-inch trees along the sidehill, or the one making huge scrapes of bed-mattress size along the narrow bottoms. Still, the urge to experiment, to draw in a buck searching for battle or doe, prompted his hands to grope about for the rattling antlers stashed alongside his crossed legs.

Without lifting hands or shoulders up through the boughs, he first clashed, then lightly tickled the sheds together. Slipping the rubber O-ring up the tapered reed of the grunt tube to imitate the higher pitch of a younger buck, he blew a few long and soft grunts while still tickling the antlers. Within minutes, the lighter footfall of now carefully placed steps reached his ears. Still not seeing the little buck, Pokey lightly clinked the antlers and blew one last soft grunt, nearly a bleat, and stilled himself in silence.

With slow and exaggerated high steps, the buck moved from a tangle of leafless box elder and stunted cedar, exposing itself at sixty yards—within the range of Pokey's old smoothbore Remington pump loaded with slugs. Pokey had shunned the new generation of shotguns of calculated barrel length and twist of rifling that stretch slug accuracy to 125 yards. It was not that he disapproved of the shotgun's evolution; if given one, he would surely use it. But having been an avid bowman in his younger days and pleasured with the thrill of luring a buck within spitting distance, truly challenging its great senses and enjoying the

breathtakingly close look, he naturally aspired to bring any deer into the seventy-yard range of an old smoothbore shotgun.

Much pleased that his scent wasn't reaching out to the little buck and satisfied with his choice and plan of the pit, Pokey relaxed for the moment to watch the buck sneak toward him in exaggerated stiff steps. After closing the gap to thirty-five yards, the little buck suddenly froze, then stabbed a forefoot in the ground, lifted its tail in readiness of flight, and stared back up the canyon. Pokey's heart sank, certain the work of pit, ash, pine oil, and his clothing smoked all night in apple wood had failed the moment. The little buck gave every indication of a full human scenting and quickly bounded up the hillside and over the ridge. If the buck had scented him, then a smoke and coffee would make little difference. Slowly, with much disappointment, he reached for the daypack.

The crashing report of snapping limbs froze his reaching hand in place. The sound came from up the canyon, perhaps a hundred yards or more and far from the route of the just-departed little buck. A thought quickly formed in his brain, forcing a deep breath to settle his nerves. What if the little buck hadn't scented him, and the earlier rattling had called in another buck, the big guy, resting farther up the canyon? In Pokey's mind it became immediately plausible that the pit was working well. Perhaps the little buck had not scented him but rather scented and saw a large, dominant animal coming.

He gave one more soft grunt on the higher-pitched tube and pulled the shotgun around, sticking its barrel through the boughs in better readiness. Within thirty seconds he saw the flash of warming morning sun bounce off the whitened tip of a long main beam.

I was nearly to the top of the draw, realizing a need to slow the pace if I was going to make an all-day event of this hunt, when the roar of a shotgun echoed across the hills. A distant single shot— 8:20 A.M.—then a long, fine silence. I knew Pokey would not fire without a certain killing shot, and a small smile crawled my face. Knowing further that he would never miss a certain lethal shot at that yardage meant the hunt was over. Heading back on the thirty-minute walk down and over the ridge line to Pokey's stand, I felt an odd disappointment, surprised and almost saddened that Pokey had taken the little buck wandering his way so early in the day. I am good at doing this very thing, holding someone up on such a high pedestal of character or prowess that I am doomed to suffer an eventual letdown. There was no sane reason for my minor disappointment; Pokey had worked hard and patiently for six glorious days of November hunt, passed on three or four bucks of the 140-class, always a difficult thing to do, and was certainly entitled to take the little buck on his final day. Still, my romantic notions, flavored with childlike hero worship, always imagined the old coot holding out to last light, forever stoic, patient, and awaiting the good buck.

Pokey climbed out of the ash and dirt, let out a half-squealing war whoop, and danced a little jig of adrenalized happiness about the still-frozen ground. Piled up against a clump of stunted cedar less than forty yards away was a magnificent twelve-point of long tine and incredible width. It had come in to the rattling as Pokey earlier imagined, and it was this huge buck's presence, not Pokey's scent, that had sent the little buck scampering over the ridge. After a minute or two of jigging, crying out, and finally settling down, he filled his pipe with the tobacco of two hours' delay and walked over to the great deer to kneel in silence. As if suddenly realizing for the first time his own increasing age—that turning sixty-nine in a few months and living two thousand miles to the southwest surely hinted of a possible last hunt in the land of musky whitetail and gold leaf—Pokey reached out and softly stroked the buck's huge forehead, bending over to press his lips in a large thanksgiving on the great deer's head. Although he would tell no one, never mention these moments, small tears clouded his tiring blue eyes as he whispered a heavenward thank you for the blessing of a year's meat in the rare form of a truly grand buck.

Closing his clouded eyes to momentarily drift back in time, Pokey pictured a seventeen-year-old boy stalking similar hills and canyons in 1945, the closing year of World War II. It was only a three-day season, Friday through Sunday, and the high-school boy had slept in the woods to better his chances, not wanting to bother his mother to drive him from town to the hills at 5 A.M. He remembered wondering how his father, lost at sea in a cargo ship crossing the Atlantic in '42, would have hunted that frosty hillside on a 1945 morning. And later, near midmorning, stalking with an already rare skill, young Harold Corbel dropped his first buck, a little eight-point yearling. He was thoroughly exhausted from lack of sleep, having spent the night shivering with cold, woefully ill-prepared with cotton pajamas serving as thermal underwear and one green woolen army blanket as his sleeping bag. With much struggle and large swelling pride, seventeen-year-old Pokey had dragged that buck nearly two miles to the roadside ditch of Highway 12 and waited patiently, happily, for a passing car or truck to flag down.

He opened his eyes, blinking away the tiny tears of joy and fear to stare at the great buck, feeling a sudden warmth of heart. If by some twist of fate or time this was his last hunt in the Corners, it had all been perfect, six days of sweet silence wandering the frosted but still colorful • 'scapes, six nights of good supper and much laughter. And alongside his slightly trembling legs, still numb from two hours of pit sitting, rested a buck of enormous size—a lifetime score for any one of America's ten-million deer hunters.

When I finally rounded a small bend in the canyon bottoms, a place that opened up a bit, allowing the warming sun to take hold, I found Pokey smoking his pipe, a large and bright smile on his face as he rested next to the field-dressed deer. I stopped in stunned surprise at the picture in front of me, silently cursing my earlier dismissal of Pokey's legendary patience. In place of the little yearling buck I'd imagined when first hearing the single shot was a deer that seemed to dwarf my great and lifetime best score at camp. Weighing easily over three hundred pounds, the buck carried a rack that would have made the book at 175 points, except for an odd, inside drop-tine sticker on the left branch that carried a seven-inch deduction in its beautiful spiraled twist.

When Pokey asked if I'd give him a hand filling in the pit, I immediately balked and told him to leave it be. I would drag a few chunks of deadfall to temporarily cover the dangerous, leg-snapping pit. When he gave me a questioning stare, I offered up the truth.

"That isn't the big buck I've seen in here many times before, Pokey. That isn't the old-timer I was talking about. My buck has large, rainbow-like tines that nearly meet in half-circle arcs. I'll be damned if I'll fill this pit in. I aim to use it in the morning. This canyon must be worked by two dominant bucks—I'm surprised they haven't killed each other by now."

I was thrilled—foremost for Pokey's great score, but also because my buck was still alive and now had the run of coming-into-heat does. Duplicating Pokey's nearly scent-free setup, I could now hunt this canyon of constantly shifting wind.

This huge deer changed Pokey's travel plans. Perhaps because of his short bout of mixed joy and melancholy, or that creeping apperception of his own mortality, he decided to spend an extra day in town. He had taken a break from hunting during a couple of lunch hours this last week, sitting at the Four Corners Cafe and visiting with old friends who had seen him through the window. He'd spent one full afternoon visiting Tip at the hardware, Old Pug at the barbershop, and Viola and the ladies at the Kut & Kurl, but now, for the moment, he wanted more.

By the time we got the deer home, took some pictures, and cleaned up, with Pokey deciding a celebratory cold beer was now in order, it was midafternoon and the day all but shot. With two beers under my belt, I was compelled to skip an evening hunt, enjoying instead a restful afternoon bathed in warm sun but still-chilled air. Pokey had decided to go out with a bang, and instead of us skinning the deer promptly, he wanted it hung in the cold shade of my woodshed overnight. Rather than leaving for Arizona in the morning, Pokey decided he would park his truck and camper in front of Harvey's tomorrow, right next to the old wooden scale beams of Orville Pert's design. He'd had his first buck of 1945 weighed hanging from that wooden scaffold, after earlier in the month putting up his fifty cents for the old-deer contest. He fully intended to borrow my block and tackle and once again hang a great deer from the ancient beams for all to see, keeping his living-legend status alive and well. He would sleep in the camper next to the hanging buck tomorrow night, after enjoying a full day of free lunch and dinner and far too many free drinks bought by old friends stopping in to see him and the buck. Harvey Mott, no stranger to friendship and well acquainted with methods of drawing a large, till-ringing crowd, made it all happen. He immediately got on the phone and called both old-timers and young men, young men who were only children when Pokey first moved south, inviting them down to see a grand deer and a good man.

It was a loud and happy time all afternoon and evening at Harvey's, with many folks, the wife and I included, giving up another evening hunt to celebrate friendship, hunting tales, and life in general. Early the next morning, the sky still black with nightfall, Pokey would head off to Arizona with a full thermos of coffee and a large hangover.

I suppose it was all meant to be, and I'm forever glad we came into town to enjoy the friendship and long farewell of that night. Six months later, in early May, we received a short phone call from Fred Corbel, Pokey's brother, explaining with much pained rasp in his voice that Pokey had collapsed dead from a heart attack that morning while unloading his little aluminum boat on an Arizona bass lake. He'd always had a strong heart and never gave an indication of a problem; he had more stamina and strength than men twenty years his junior.

I don't believe an autumn will ever visit here again without his spirit being there in full accompaniment. He was a good man, an incredibly wise hunter, and I will forever miss him, hoss.

Chapter 20

It was November 21, a week into high rutting activity, when I sat in a cold ground blind in Lagormore Canyon, about seven miles from home. In the twelve days since Pokey's departure, I have hunted hard with no success. I've seen plenty of action—perhaps six does and one or two young bucks each day—but have been surprised that seeing a fairly common three-year-old, 130-class animal has become increasingly difficult this year. I suppose I'm the anomaly, as the more serious hunters of the Corners have fared well. Tip Meyer took a beautiful buck two days ago; so did Hank Miller. Even Ed Torrance, our new deputy sheriff, took his lifetime best—a 140-point buck found wandering Wilcox's apple orchard. And the whole crowd reports daily sightings of decent bucks.

I hunted Pokey's pit for several days after he left but saw only does and that same yearling with the pretty ten-point basket. I watched him stay with a doe in heat for nearly two days, and I now think the other big buck, my deer with the rainbow tines, is not about, as I couldn't imagine him allowing the little guy to have the run of local does. I haven't been back there for five days and may try again in the morning. With almost a year's supply of meat in the freezer, I'm holding out for the always-hoped-for book buck and will not pull the trigger unless positively certain.

Because I firmly believe in Harry the Horn Man's repeatedly demonstrated theory about big bucks sticking to their chosen home range, I don't think Pokey and I ran off the rainbow-tined buck that has always used that canyon near my place. Rather, I think the big deer has been led astray by heated does and is temporarily miles away. Radiotelemetry studies have demonstrated that some bucks will range up to eight miles during the rut. This little tidbit of information is often misunderstood, the reader imagining the lusting buck wandering off in determined hound-dog fashion, with little territorial limit in his intense search. Not true. They are "home boys," these bucks, and it is the secret of their long survival: living a lifetime in a square mile patch surrounding their core bedding area. If they end up far from home during the rut, it is not from dogged search or design but rather a simple matter of the buck wandering the fringe of his core area and encountering a cycling doe on the fringe of hers. He will follow her throughout the night across her adjacent square-mile until he services her two or three times. At that point, he might come across another hot doe or the pheromone-rich scent trail leading into her area. After a few days and nights of this wild but careless pleasure, the buck can find himself miles and miles from home. When the hot does of the strange areas are bred, the silent warning of instinct will overpower the lust, and Nature's gift of a direction-fixing mechanism, much like the one possessed by migratory birds, will make the buck head for the sanctuary of his core area, using old scent trails as additional guideposts. The great wandering of rutting bucks is the "domino effect" without design, and I'm hoping that's the case with the rainbow-tined buck.

The November weather in the twelve days since Pokey's departure has been strange, a difficult pattern to hunt with confidence. The day after he left, we had our first major snowstorm, a large dump of seven inches followed by two days of record-breaking cold for the second week of November:

Mornings of bitter minus-three temperatures and days warming only to twenty degrees. January weather. This was followed by a true Indian summer: eight days of balmy, sixty-degree afternoons and the worry of spoiled meat with a hanging deer. And now the land is again frozen hard with record cold.

I mention a true Indian summer because the misuse of old expressions by modern journalists and television news people has become a pet peeve. It was bad enough when our television weatherman advised us of a coming week's warm Indian summer weather in mid-September, fully ignorant of the fact it was still "plain old summer" and would be until the autumnal equinox. This year our television forecaster had the audacity—on a hot Labor Day weekend—to say, "The coming week looks to remain hot, an Indian summer." If the expression is going to be so abused, then he might as well call a hot Fourth of July weekend Indian summer.

Although there are at least five accepted versions of the expression's origin, it is accurately defined as a freakish warmup always occurring after the first snows and hard cold and usually in November or even early December. And though its origin is claimed by several eastern Indian tribes and also accepted as wholly European, an expression of early colonists, the one I find best suited to my senses is an obscure version granting mountain men the creation.

The Plains were a dangerous place for mountain men and buffalo hunters, with at least ten different Indian nations living there and claiming territorial ownership. They were selfish and protective of their areas, and rightly so, for land was the very heart and soul of their existence. In the warmer months from March through October, a wanderer was certain to encounter natives, be rightly judged a trespasser, and driven out or killed. Not so come November. Given their limited technology, it was impossible for the natives to survive a Plains winter with arctic cold blasts traveling unmolested by mountains or trees, building eighty-mile-per-hour winds, chill factors of eighty-below and twenty-foot-high snowdrifts that could bury a village in five hours. Come the first snows and high winds of late October, and the Moon of the Falling Leaves, the Sioux headed for winter shelter in the Black Hills in South Dakota, the Crows for Wyoming's Big Horn Mountains, and the Blackfoot for Montana's Bear Paw and the eastern escarpment of the Rockies. In those places and dozens more like them, the Plains Indians settled in winter camps that broke high wind, warmed chill factors by fifty degrees, and provided ample firewood.

November and December on the Plains were safe times to chase late-migrating buffalo and herds of elk coming down from higher grounds, safe times to travel and hunt unmolested and unthreatened. But every few years a freakish warmup, often lasting two weeks, would cover the Plains after the first warning snows of a coming winter. In the version I prefer, the mountain men called those warmups Indian summer, simply because the warmup brought the large bands of natives temporarily back out on the Plains, looking for straggling buffalo, grazing horses on the dried grasses, or just scratching about for a boredom-provoked skirmish. It was the dreaded "Indian summer" weather. As a longtime American West history buff, I prefer this obscure and quaint version, but regardless of the term's true genesis, Indian summer is never the common and expected warm days of September or even early October.

I longed for that heat on a recent morning in Lagormore Canyon; it was just two degrees above zero, another record breaker, and only one doe had been spotted in two hours of frozen stand. I have hunted this canyon at least once a season for the last thirty years, and as a high-school boy I drove out here daily to check my six-trap mink line. It is a long canyon, perhaps three miles or more, beginning narrowly back in the rolling hills and widening to nearly a half-mile where it opens out on the flats of the valley. I've taken several good bucks here, but only in late November, as if they rarely wander the place except during the rut. I believe there are many places like this, though I've never read a similar opinion in hunting magazines—places I call "doe grounds," where there are both convenient water and year-round easy feed access, with only one drawback—the daily exposure to open space and human eye.

The cover adjacent to orchards, alfalfa, and cornfields around the county can always be considered doe grounds, maintaining a year-round population of chance-taking females enjoying the convenience of the rich food sources. Although one might spot velvet-clad bucks temporarily sharing such an area, it is rarely their home base and they are witnessed again only in November, lured by the rich doe scents emanating from the doe grounds. But just as with most of my November trophy hunting, I am in the wrong place or embracing the wrong time. It is a rare November rutting day when I fail to spot at least a small buck skulking about this area. I have several ground blinds built on the canyon's hillside above a tule-choked pond at the fork of four main deer trails. This pond is the only water in a half-mile area, and its moist seepage is surrounded by favorite browse and acres of clover and grasses. At least eight does and their fawns, generation after generation, live in this area of less than eighty acres, spending their lives without ranging more than a half-mile from the tule pond.

The doe grounds are always this way. The mouth of the little wind-shifting canyon of Pokey's great buck empties into the pasture, spring, and apple trees of our place, and for years we have watched the year-round life of its resident does, feeding them a bit in hard winters and always keeping a salt block in our field. Even if the oldest doe dies from predator, starvation, or age, it is her progeny and eventually the progeny's offspring that live in the area. They rarely range more than a quarter-mile up the canyons and hills and can always be found bedded in the first hundred yards of cover surrounding the pasture. I cater to them not simply for altruistic reasons. I haven't shot a doe in thirty years, leaving their odds for survival and the healthy balance of a good buck-doe ratio up to predators, the unpreventable highway carnage, and the shotgun reports of teenage boys and girls rightfully thrilled in taking their first or second deer. And though I don't shoot "my" does, I use them shamefully as bait, and I suppose that in some people's mind I'm not a friend of wildlife, though I believe differently.

By keeping my resident family of does contented with their layout, it naturally follows that nearby and far-off bucks will wander into my home area throughout the rut. Yes, it is self-serving—shamefully so, some might suggest—but is it really any different from an animal-rights vegetarian feeding wildlife as a way of courting them for viewing pleasure? My wife and I truly enjoy watching our wildlife, but whether one caters to the animals for hunting and meal potential or viewing pleasure, isn't either reason self-serving and designed to bring the human a gain? I'm not sure the non-hunter wanting to "use" wildlife for visual or ethereal pleasure is less guilty or more sanctimonious than the hunter. With their loud chants and protests of hunting, the antis certainly seem to believe they are more attuned to Nature's harmony. But they are selfish-minded as well, though none ever hesitates a moment to think about it. Not only do they have a religion of export, not unlike the annoying, door-knocking zealots of some Christian faiths, they are so self-proclaimed righteous that they fail to realize that their desire to see deer wandering an evening field is solely a selfish desire for entertainment or gratification, hardly different from a hunter's love of these animals and undeserving of the media-offered pedestal of selfless guardianship. If the antis truly wanted to protect some species from a real or imagined fate, it would better serve their process if they tried to understand the unchanging laws of Nature, the life-and-death struggle in the food chain, before attempting the save. It does not serve the sighted to have a blind man pick the colors of the clothing we wear.

With that thought, I sat above the tule pond, shivering from the cold and the lack of deer sightings. But with the luck of Nature's quirk, I fortuitously witnessed that very drama of food-chain struggle played out in front of me.

The pond below me, frozen hard from the last three days of early cold, covers at least a half-acre of canyon bottom. There is little open water in that half-acre—a little glimmer here, a small pool there—but mostly it is shallows grown up with thick tule. After driving out here yesterday afternoon on a minor scout, seeking reassurance of the pond's continued presence and ample deer sign, I found several paths of bobcat track locked in the frozen shoreline mud. Oddly, alongside the cat track was the easily identifiable bounding pattern of a large buck mink. It is odd because our mink, since trapping and wearing fur have come to be deemed politically incorrect and are now held in the same light as child molesting and devil worship, have only two worrisome predators—large owls and bobcats. I tried to study the spoor and visualize a possible stalking, but the mink track disappeared across the ice, the animal perhaps going to investigate the several tule-and-mud domes of muskrat huts pushing up through the ice of the pond. While I sat in a frozen blind overlooking the fork of four doe trails and the pond, I watched a small play of life, an event every animal-rights activist should be required to witness.

It was nearly 8 A.M., freezing cold, and I was ready to give up the stand and return home, comforted by the "quitter's excuse" that only a fool would hunt in such deep cold, unless faced with starvation. No reasonable man would do so for the pleasure or spirit. And when I saw the mink, a loud popping sound, like a muffled gunshot, filled the canyon.

After the first startled twitch, I realized it was the branch of a sap-rich birch exploding with the too-rapid swell of below-zero cold, the still-wet birch bearing perfect witness to the rigors of late December. The Plains Indians called December the Moon of the Popping Trees for this very reason. The first deep cold of December always catches the deciduous family of trees unprepared. Though leafless from autumnal metamorphosis, their woody pulp is still wet with late summer's flow of sap. Those first days of deep December cold swell those still-wet cells of tree limb too rapidly, tearing fiber with quick expansion until the limb explodes and breaks off with a loud report. The Popping Tree Moon is one of my favorite descriptive names, but I was hardly thrilled to hear it happening in November. The cold of northern climates is so long in its stay, forcing spring to scratch and claw its way back in late April or early May, that only a masochist of intemperate status would welcome its early arrival.

The mink, first slinking snakelike, then comically bounding like a trained circus animal, leaped in mid-stride at the exploding sound, landing tense and worried. I watched it for a half-hour as it scratched and sniffed at two frozen-mud muskrat domes, and wondered about its large hunger. The animal's willingness to expose itself to the bright light of a frozen day reflected the desperate hunger of an early arriving Popping Tree Moon, and I wondered again if we were in for a long and tough winter. I sat there and shivered, picturing the still-alive-and-well Pokey Corbel cooking deer steaks on his barbecue in the tee-shirt-and-shorts weather of an eighty-degree, November day in Arizona.

After giving in to the hard cold and the depression of seeing only one doe in three hours, I gave up the Lagormore Canyon blind to head home, hoping this evening or tomorrow would bring back the more normal forty-degree temperatures germane to late November. It is always foolish to give up a stand during the rut; noon is often more productive than first light. But I am bitten hard by this two-degree morning and would rather view my whitetails in hunting-magazine photos by the fireplace than in this frozen landscape. It is a good time to warm up by the truck's heater, drive back through town, and have a late breakfast at the Four Corners Cafe, telling all who will listen what a good hunter I am, rather than stay here and demonstrate that reality. I am not always so weak-willed and can generally tolerate long hours of patient stand in near-zero temperatures. But those frozen hours are best driven by a large need for meat, and aided by seeing and hearing much deer movement. After three hours of bitter cold, one wayward doe spotted at first light and a careless mink are not enough to fuel the fires of psychological body warmth. In my case, mind over matter requires a bit of diversion or hope.

When I dropped off the hillside and walked along the edge of the frozen pond in the half-mile hike to the truck, I noticed a small thing unobserved from the distant blind. One of the several muskrat-hut domes was nearly ripped off, a hole of three-inch diameter torn into its side above the ice. A few small specks of blood and mud dotted the pond ice around the hut, and I now realized the mink had recently, perhaps last night, found success in its hunt.

After arriving at the truck and warming up by its blessing of good heater, I thought better of leaving, thinking a snack and a short nap might invigorate my cold-tolerance. This was once a good canyon to hunt in November, still should be, and I planned to go back and wait out the muses. At least two mature bucks, antler size unknown, had left sign of working the area daily for does, and with a warmup and a restful nap, I could resist the temptation to turn tail and head for sausage and French toast at the cafe. With Pokey's long stay, I'd already spent the extra dollars I'd salted away for autumn's restaurant lunches and hunting talk at the cafe and Harvey's.

When I turned the truck engine off and drifted in the haze of a midmorning nap, the opened muskrat mound and specks of blood remained vivid, and a running theater-like movie of last night's imagined mink attack played clearly in my mind. I don't really know if I was asleep and fully dreaming, or merely groggy and consciously imagining it all, but the night was cold and clear, a Popping Tree Moon shone, and I think, silly as it sounds, I was there in the form of a mink or muskrat.

The Popping Tree Moon

The blue glow of moonlight reflected off the ice, a silvery hue wiggling across the fur of a mink. With its nose screwed to the faint odor of life still drifting in the frozen air, the mink twitched. It was the sweet smell of rats, fat, warmblooded muskrats. Weeks had passed since its spit had mixed with the warm flesh of a rat. It was the cold moon of December, the Popping Tree Moon of the Plains Sioux, but to the animal it mattered not the posterity of this time; there were no Sioux to bother the mink, no Plains, and, except for the tick of starvation, no time to measure. There was only the frozen moon of tight cold and the mink's shrinking stomach.

The mink had spent last night digging machinelike in the frozen mud, its nose hinting of a frog burrowed deep in the bank, a shrunken stomach crying agreement and encouraging action.

After an energy-consuming hour, the mink reached the frozen nugget of a small frog. In ill-conceived autumn haste, the frog had not burrowed deep enough to ward off the stabbing ice of a Popping Tree Moon or the nose of starvation hunting the small creek. But those chunks of an icy frog, gulped frozen to melt in a shrunken stomach, only replaced the precious fuel expended in the digging. The mink had grown weaker; finding warm blood tonight was a necessary thing, and the dark-furred hunter darted its nose to the moon, squeezing nostrils and rolling lips to better scent the musky odor of urine. The rats had to be close.

Where the mink now hunted, the small creek slowed, spreading out to a half-acre cattail pond. Dropping to all fours, it bounded along the stubble of tule standing upright and frozen in the ice. The silhouette of a muskrat hut loomed ahead. In the words of man, the temperature hovered below zero, inhibiting the betraying odor of muskrat life, but the keen nose of the mink pointed toward the hut's silhouette. In two swift bounds, the mink gained the peak of the tule-and-mud dome and began studying the hut in radar-like fashion, seeking a blip of stronger scent, a radar-like blip of air current warmer and sweeter than the frigid night air. That tiny signal would reveal a potential path to the sanctuary of rats.

The human senses could never feel that few-degree temperature change of rising air, or pinpoint the stronger scent of muskrat in the frozen mound, but that change betrayed to the mink the smallest of vents, no larger than a stalk of wheat—a necessary air vent, but one that often dooms muskrats on cold winter nights. The small vent would be the starting point in the dig, the weakest link in the frozen-mud armor of the hut. The mink had no training in this skill, had not been taught by its mother after its birth two springs ago. And it did not plan the assault; it merely happened. Programmed on a microscopic sliver of DNA and passed along at the mink's conception was the faint memory-like knowledge of a million moonlight assaults on frozen rat huts occurring from the beginning of muskrat time, and the act required no thought or plan but simply spontaneous action. The mink began the dig.

Inside the dark chamber, the solitary rat was startled by the digging sound, its nose contorted to scent for danger. It found none and sat quietly, ears tuned to the scraping sounds from above. The muskrat had no inclination to slide through its underwater entrance tunnel in escape. On the contrary, it sat immobile, eyes fixed on the watery tunnel. Its dark memory-like motivation, its gift of DNA, forced it to remain still and safe in the chamber. Danger, Nature had programmed, would usually approach from the watery tunnel entrance, not from above. Danger lived outside the dark chamber in the waters or under the ice ceiling of the frozen pond or on the banks. It was not a thing that came from above a hut's dome. The survival instinct commanded the muskrat to stay in the hut and avoid the haunts of mink and cats and owls of the outside world and water. It could not challenge this order, possessing no working brain cells to consider alternatives. No planning, no future, no doubts, just blind submission to instinct. The muskrat concentrated its attention on the watery tunnel, somehow knowing it to be the passage of invasion, and ignored the digging from above. Nature cared not if it erred in this directive. The celebration of Nature involves the survival of the species, not the individual, and Nature's directive of instinct served the muskrat well—most assaults did come from the water or a careless moment spent on the banks. The rat moved to the corner of the hut and quietly chewed a tender shoot of tule. The sound of digging grew louder.

The mink flinched from the loud explosion crashing across the pond, but its mindless digging did not slow. In the last week, it had grown accustomed to the gunfire-like popping of alder and birch filling the night air. But out of the distance and darkness the mink did pick up a warning scent. The triggering mechanism of caution suddenly halted the digging action. A mink too consumed by the blood search, too intent upon celebrating its fortune in the musky odor of rats, often failed to muster at the roll call of the morning sun, becoming a meal to a great horned owl, a full stomach to a daring fox, or, as the present scent indicated, a cold moon's supper for a bobcat. The mink's fearless style and pugilistic skill often persuade the larger predators to pass on a potential meal, but not in the Moon of the Popping Trees, when shrunken stomachs erase fear. It was only a slight odor of bobcat, but the piercing eyes and crinkled nose of the mink pointed toward the canyon it had traveled earlier. Although alarmed, the mink was overcome with the urge to continue digging; hunger overruled caution, and perhaps, somewhere in that tiny brain, the memories of a million ancestral experiences suggested a bobcat possessed very poor scenting abilities and was not an immediate threat. Whatever the reason, some primordial dictate commanded it to continue the dig, and the layers of mud and tule grew thin.

The muskrat's heart began to beat faster. The sounds from the roof of its hut grew louder by the moment, and now a pale glow of moonlight began to flood its chamber. The rat forced itself farther into the corner and away from the sounds of the dig. Unaware of the consequence of its action, the rat placed itself farther away from its only route of escape, the watery tunnel. Most of humankind would call the muskrat confused at this moment, but how certain are we that the rat experiences confusion? In our rush to assign animals a full complement of human characteristics, we often gift them with the potential for confusion. Are we so sure that a deer that seems to dash in three different directions at once is confused? Surely such action must be a prime directive of instinct, each step a deliberate move coached from the primordial darkness. The state of confusion denotes a temporary lapse of analytical reasoning, and if the muskrat was so possessed, it might cease its biological function of consuming cattails to keep the wetlands open and instead build rockets. It is no different with the mink. But since neither animal can reason, the digging continued, and the rat stilled itself further, not fearful but aware of imminent danger.

In the previous month, two of its family unit had fled in fear through the watery tunnel and never returned. Minute traces of their urine-scent still remained in the lodge, stimulating a vague memory—a memory devoid of emotion, a glandular memory that would fade altogether with the final evaporation of their musk. But enough memory remained to support the instinctive feeling of danger existing through the watery tunnel. Safety existed in the hut, in the silence and stillness that offered a cloak of camouflage. And in that moment of safe huddle, the flash of moonlight glinting off ebony claws slipped through the matted roof.

The mink felt its claws break through the final layer; the flush of heavy odor and warmth raced up through the opening. It had begun this dig on a faint scent, a cold probability, and the reward of success was another week's life. If a mink could dream of a future, it would surely dream of muskrats. It would dream of its strong jaw paralyzing the rat, the first taste of the life-giving fluid oozing through the puncture holes, the acids and juices of its stomach churning and triggering the swallowing saliva, frothing its mouth with blood and spit. It would prefer, in this mink dream, to keep the rat alive for a while. Like a wingless vampire bat, the mink would enjoy suckling the warm blood, feeling it pulse strength through its emaciated body. Its needle-sharp teeth would pierce the spinal cord to paralyze but not kill the rat and a slow feeding would ensue, replacing the lost energy spent in a six-hour search for rats on a frozen night. For an extended time it would rest alongside the still-breathing rat, slowly sucking warm fluids until the rat neared death. At that point, the mink would begin the pleasing evisceration.

But mink do not dream of the future, and in the present, in this moment, danger was approaching. The mink quickly withdrew its clawed hand from the lodge and sat upright on its haunches, crinkling its nose to the night air. The scent of bobcat was much closer. In the hut, the muskrat was unaware of its temporary reprieve. So convinced was the rat that its ploy of stillness offered invisibility and safety that it expected the invading mink to pass through the lodge without incident. Not so the mink. Perhaps being a predator tuned its instinctive reactions to a less gullible level. Water was safety to the mink; on land or ice it was no match for the cat. It had earlier scouted the small pond for an opening around its shore, but the peat composition of the soil allowed the ice to penetrate deep into the bank, offering no fissure or shelf under the ice for the mink to enter.

As the mink contorted its face, gauging the distance to and direction of the bobcat, its legs trembled and tightened in readiness to bound away. Suddenly, its ancestral memories stirred. It sensed an escape, saw it happening. It might have been a few generations back or a million years ago, but escape from bobcats existed before through a watery tunnel in a muskrat lodge. Much like a human experiencing déjà vu, the mink sensed those memory-like instinctive moves of a thousand previous escapes. Ironically, like the rat, the mink's safety now existed in the watery tunnel offering escape under the shelf of ice. The mink quickly dropped to all fours and slashed at the opening. After several blows that sapped its remaining strength, the opening grew to a three-inch hole, into which the mink, glided silently like quicksilver, gaining both safety from the cat and the promise of a two-day meal.

Outside the hut, some forty yards distant on the fringe of the frozen cattail pond, the bobcat pricked its ears. The muffled squeal of a muskrat leaped through the cold night air. And though the cat could not smell it yet, the scent of the sweet and red life-giver, the warm blood of a muskrat, rose in heated waves from the hut to dance across the ice in the Moon of the Popping Trees.

Chapter 21

One Last Chance

I went out today for the season's final moments, honestly not caring if I even saw a buck, simply intent upon enjoying the last day of chance. It is December 7, Pearl Harbor Day, and unlike the cold of two weeks ago in Lagormore Canyon, it will be a pleasant morning—temperatures in the thirties and expected to rise close to fifty degrees by afternoon. Again, a strange autumn. Now that it is December and the last day of deer season, we are having October's warmth. The crabapple tree by our front door, long ago leafless and settled in winter dormancy, is trying to limber up and form tiny shoots of new bud, given five days of heat.

I have invested in a long-shot chance this last day, rising at an early 4 A.M. to drive the two hours to Archie Weil's camp. I had meant to spend the night there and avoid the small misery of a too-early awakening, but returned home so late and tired from last evening's hunt that I caved in to the luxury of sofa, electricity, and a moronic television movie. Early rising is fine in October and early November, when the benefit of first-light hunting demands an early start. But in December, first legal shooting light doesn't arrive until 7:15 A.M. and a lazy sort like myself can stay in the sack till nearly 6 A.M.

I am going to the camp because of a "tip" and feel a bit shaky about the source. Archie's grandson and friends, all warm and likable fellows, stopped by the house on their way up there two weeks ago and again on their return, four days later. The grandson had taken a nearly mature eight-point; one friend took a little forkie and the other a small doe. I'm sure the doe numbers up there can use the thinning, but I was a bit surprised that someone would drive over two hundred miles, spend much money, and be happy taking the type of small doe ubiquitous to all of whitetail country. At any rate, the grandson claimed he had twice spotted a rocking-chair-racked buck of certain trophy status, wildly nontypical, roaming the upper bench near the steep slope, but was unable to get off a shot. It is not that I doubt the lad's word, but rather that folks who don't often see large bucks in season have a tendency to grossly misjudge size. This little error is quite natural, even occurring with our youngsters in the Corners and, in fact, with yours truly. I remember the season of my nineteenth year and that very happenstance, referred to as "ground shrink"—discovering that your nice buck on the ground is much smaller than it appeared moments ago at one hundred yards.

In that season of 1966—after taking a doe in each of my first two seasons (we were allowed only one deer back then) and three bucks in the subsequent three years—like many nineteen-year-olds, I thought I owned the woods and had invented buck hunting. I remember the day well: It was the last day of the modern-rifle season, and I can still picture the huge buck coming down a hillside toward my stand. We had not heard of rattling antlers back then, and though I'd heard from Old Man Krause that Tip Meyer, Pokey Corbel, and a few other serious hunters made a grunting sound in the back of their throat to lure or stop a buck, I hadn't heard of a grunt tube and could not practice a sound I knew nothing about. It was a matter of taking a stand along scrape lines or in an area of heavy doe use and hoping for the best.

When the buck came down the trail, I immediately began trembling—my first and last case of buck fever—and raised the brand-new and only target-fired .35 Remington carbine. It was the biggest buck I'd ever seen during open season, and it was coming in at a trot, less than one hundred yards away in the thick woods. At that point it must have picked up a slight scent, not a panic-prompting disaster but enough to stop the buck in its tracks. It slowly swung around and began to move back up the same trail, now with tail almost upright. If I thought it was massive coming in, the view from the rear as it began to head away was spectacular—a wide and very tall rack of trophy proportions. Somehow I managed to still the shaking and squeeze off a perfect quartering-away shot that struck heart and instantly dropped the big deer.

I was thrilled. Climbing down from my tree-stand perch, I hooted in joy, picturing the face of Orville Pert when I brought this monster in to win the Hideaway's deer contest. This was not only a B&C buck but a probable state record as well. Even when the necessary compassion teachings of Arthur Glade began to take hold and I was whispering the most serious prayers of thanksgiving, I could not help smiling wildly, thinking myself the new heir-apparent of Harland Corners' hunting prowess.

Although it was my biggest buck and would remain so for ten years, I began to swallow hard, uneasily, as I approached within a few yards. Don't misunderstand: I was grateful then and will remain so forever for the big deer's blessing, but I was shocked by the "ground-shrink." It was as if a different deer had somehow replaced my certain record-book buck. It scored 151 in the Boone and Crockett-style measurements of Orville Pert and took fourth place in the Hideaway contest, winning me a woolen buffalo plaid shirt and a free dinner. Of course I dug deep in my pockets to have it mounted. More important than my contest prize, minor fame, and the year's good eating was the clear lesson in judging antler size at a glance. One needs to see many large-racked deer—both long looks and millisecond glimpses—to enjoy any chance at consistent accuracy. And for this reason, I wondered about the story told by Archie's grandson. I know he has little experience in judging true trophy-size animals.

I've read many tips and pointers in hunting magazines suggesting the use of visual measuring guides to help a hunter estimate antler size in the field—the seven-inch length of a whitetail's ear, the circumference and diameter of the eyeball, and the ear tip to ear tip spread. But this slow-paced and time-consuming method is often impractical in the cornfields, thickets, and woods of whitetail country. I have taken bucks passing my stand in thick woods that never offered one decent look at antler in a protracted three-minute approach. And when that moment of a good, clean shot presented itself, there was little time to compare eyeball diameter to tine circumference.

I don't dismiss the tips; they work well when you are afforded the luxury of time and clear view. But for my money, a far more practical approach is the flashcard style of instant judgment. Because the moral responsibility of every deer hunter is to take only a humane, killing shot, doing just that should be the focus of our attention when a buck is sneaking through thick cover. Visualizing the needed vital organ shot on the approaching buck and trying to keep a bead, sight pin, or cross hairs confidently placed, awaiting that millisecond of perfect opportunity, requires maximum concentration. It is not a time to be painstakingly comparing ear length to G-3 tine. After that year of 1966 and the amazing ground-shrink buck, I trained myself, with help from Tip Meyer, to flash-judge any buck.

It is a simple process, but can take years in the perfection. Paramount to its success is first picturing the buck of your dreams, both typical and nontypical, and holding that image in mind. The next step, which should become a lifelong habit, is deciding yes or no the very instant you see a buck. I do mean quickly, in that first glimpse, while the eye and brain are still in the process of announcing a deer sighting. This should be done year-round, whenever bucks have antlers, and can occur in summer woods or fields or along nighttime roadsides when a buck is spotted from your passing vehicle. The essence of the flashcard style of judgment is to always say yes or no when spotting antler. By constantly maintaining a clear image of your dream buck, be it a good 135-class deer and your area's best offering or a 190-point state record, you'll be surprised at how quickly and often you say no with unfailing accuracy.

If you live in an urban area or a rural setting where you get few field and roadside sightings, the deer-hunting magazines become a tool of perhaps unsuspected value. Years ago, Tip Meyer taught me to flip through the pages of deer magazines. Counting advertisements, there are often fifty or more photographs of bucks in a single issue. By playing the yes-or-no game when turning pages, one develops a mindset for flash judgment. Thirty years later, I sometimes still play the game when first looking through a deer magazine, and I'm happy to report near-perfect success. I will occasionally say no on first glance, but given a good twenty seconds to stare at the picture, I might squirm and hedge my way toward a "maybe." But at least the reverse seldom occurs, and, in consequence, I never suffer the dreaded ground-shrink of seeing more in that moment of excitement than truly exists.

I have decided to hunt Archie's camp on this final day for more reason than the grandson's story. It has been a strange rut and November for me in my regular spots. Besides the wind-shifting canyon next to our place, I have six prime locations I scout and hunt yearly. Year in and year out I will spot at least one good buck in each area during the rut, and often two or more. After all, besides heavy sign, yearly sightings are what make an area "prime." But this year I have seen nothing but smaller two- and three-year-old bucks of the 120-class—perfect freezer deer, or what Harvey Mott calls "a nice kid's buck." I have been recently wondering if the Lord above or His underling, the hunting muse, isn't giving me the stiff-arm in consequence of my great October camp deer. If so, I can accept the dressing-down of November's poor luck with some understanding. That was and is such a magnificent deer, I suppose I should be forever thankful and content to rest on the laurels of its taking. But the law permits taking another, and this is, after all, Harland Corners. One does not sit by the television or woodstove and let all of November's season waste away because a good October buck was taken.

I've gone back to Archie's camp for even more reason than the hope of a good sighting or the grandson's story. Still new to me, wildly charming and full of unknowns, it is a fitting place to spend the last day of autumn. Although the fall season will not officially end until the solstice on December 22, we here hardly pay heed to those parameters of regular calendar or science. The last day of deer season, be it in October or December, is always the last day of autumn in Harland Corners.

I have often noticed that the big nontypical bucks seem to come out of the woodwork near season's end or right after that, and I've finally read a few stories and opinions confirming this quirk in magazines. If there is truth in the stated size of this twice-spotted nontypical at camp, it should still be wandering the area.

The day seemed to sail by so quickly. I sat near the clearing on the upper bench, my scent again carrying up Stone Ridge to spook the bedding grounds. I wasn't too concerned; this was December 7, and deer movement now follows a much different pattern from that of October. With the lost leaves of the last forty-five days, this bench hardly seems the same place. Where I once had restricted, forty-yard views down narrow aisles between foliage-rich trees, I can now see one hundred yards in many directions. With late-cycling does or others that failed to conceive last month, there is a small rut still going on, and it should prompt some daylight movement on these benches. It would be nice to have the opportunity of hunting these clearings, after October's limited choice of hunting only the beds of the tangled brush slope.

But it was not to be, and dusk came so quickly up here. I did see three different groups of does and watched a small eight-point sneak by my position at sixty yards. This buck has a good chance to gain age and size, as it moved in textbook stealth past my stand. A light breeze was blowing, robbing the buck of any chance to scent my presence, yet it still moved as if a boogie man hid behind every tree. I had the opportunity to watch it sneak over a 150-yard stretch of bench, and it never once took a careless step, halting at every opening over ten feet in width to scent and stare before quickly moving across. This is rare behavior for so young a buck following a doe-in-heat trail. At this age, when after a hot doe, they usually plow along with nose to the ground, showing little fear and paying small attention to surroundings, shocked into sobriety only at the scent of man. This deer might grow to trophy class; already it was wise enough to outsmart the average hunter.

Walking back to the truck in the growing darkness, I couldn't help wondering if I shouldn't have come up here sooner. The grandson and friends have been gone for over two weeks, and I should have made better use of the camp. I think that taking the big deer in October at this place held me back—a small, nearly awkward feeling, as if it would have been wrong or wholly unappreciative to come back this year expecting more. I won't make the same mistake next year and will hunt the camp in October and again when the grandson and friends leave in November, catching the last week of the remaining rut.

I also hope to spend more time at camp with the "fluke," paying the neighbors to feed our chickens, her horse, and our yearly raised weaner pig, so she can get away for a few days in a row. I've talked to Harvey, and he is already thrilled and planning on spending some days and nights up here. But with my rather selfish desire or need to hunt without company, basking in the coyote howl or the silence of nights alone, I will surely spend most of the time here by myself. It is a place that seems to beg the silence of thought and reflection, and, like Archie before me, who enjoyed it best when alone, I plan to keep that spirit of mountain stillness a precious thing. I've never understood the mentality of those hunters who see deer camp as a place for raucous behavior, late nights, and much alcohol. Isn't that the very same daily atmosphere of town, tavern, and home? At the risk of sounding hopelessly outdated or romantically eccentric, I can't help but see deer camp as hallowed ground, deserving the reverence held for ancient places and early days.

It was difficult not to walk over from the truck, parked twenty yards away from the little cabin, and fumble in the darkness for the key. It would have been nice to spend the last night of the last day in the glow of its kerosene-lamp charm. And I do not necessarily mean just the last day of deer season, but any last night of any last time on earth. Still, I couldn't bring myself to walk over, preferring instead to keep the memories of October's great stay and impressions in the spirit and place they now reside. It would not be the same place, now dark and cold, without the orange glow of fire escaping the cracks of the woodstove, flickering on the little forked horns, and the smell of baked potato and fresh coffee swelling to fill the small room.

It was a long, peaceful drive, an hour of perfect contentment, down the winding, muddy road to the highway. I never drive anywhere without the radio on, always enjoying, if not needing, its melodious companionship. But without forethought or design, I mindlessly reached over and turned it off. There was something to cherish in this quiet drive, made easy by the recent warm spell. I'm sure my thoughts and mood of this last evening would have been much different, bordering on hectic or desperate prayer, if the truck was in four-wheel-drive and pushing a foot or more of fresh snow. But not in this odd year, and I was free to drive leisurely, watching the flash of headlights pierce the woods on each sharp turn. I had not driven more than a half-mile from the cabin door when a doe leaped across the narrow dirt road. Just as I reached the point of her crossing, I slammed on the brakes to witness a nice buck with the palmated main beams of nontypical fashion leap across in the exact spot. Knowing it was pursuing a doe, I had to wonder how many does were still cycling. It is normal for a few does, perhaps 10 percent or so, to still be "open" at this time of the year, prompting December's post-rut activity. But I've seen far too many this last week.

For many years I have read over and again how weather does not affect the rut or the cycling of does, that the rut is purely and simply a process of photoperiodism triggered by the lack of intensity or the angle of sunlight, perhaps aided further by the new or dark phase of the moon. But this year throws a wrench in those once-smooth-meshing gears of wildlife science. With our odd weather of both temperature and snowfall, the does seem to be coming in heat at irregular times, defying the written word of zoologists and pundits. For the first time in many years, we did not have a heavy rut period in mid-November. Instead, it seems to have been equally spread out from early October to early December. Knowing the does' standard gestation period of 195 days, I plan on watching closely this spring and summer for evidence supporting my observations. If we have many early and late fawns this year, I will be compelled to argue a bit with the reproductive experts and insist that weather could be a larger factor than presumed. Old friend Pokey Corbel insisted weather patterns are important, with this speculative premise: If light intensity is the quintessential determining factor, then the reflective properties of early snow cover or the reverse effect of week-long periods of dark skies and gray, drizzly days have to influence heat cycles. Of course, if the angle of sunlight, not simple photoperiodism, is the determining factor, Pokey's argument is specious.

As every year, there will be a dance and potluck dinner tomorrow night at the VFW hall to ring out the season, a time for the whole town to gather and swap tales of the big one only glimpsed as it bounded over some ridge or into a swamp. Or to step outside and check the nice rack someone has brought along in the car trunk. There will be drawings for prizes donated by local businesses, prizes for every youngster who filled his or her tag, one for those youngsters completely skunked, and another for lady hunters only.

We Nimrods of a more serious bent have our own prize waiting at Harvey's Bar & Grill. Just because the bureaucrats in the Capital ruled our once-advertised and famous deer contest illegal does not mean we haven't found a quiet way to circumvent their hard line. The trouble with well-intended government action is that the bureaucratic moralists save no souls and tend to make minor criminals out of honest folk. As we've done every year since the public contest ended, long before the season started, some forty-two of us each put a twenty-dollar bill in an old pickled-egg jar at Harvey's and the highest-scoring typical and nontypical quietly split the pot—this year $840. Since Pokey wasn't entered, I believe I might have the biggest typical with the camp buck, marking my first-ever win. Of course, that was at last checking four days ago, and much could have happened since then.

It is not the little jackpot (actually, a damn good jackpot) of prize money that interests me the most, but the win itself. Though I certainly hope not, perhaps it's just ego pushing me. But I truly feel it's more the matter of worry about the shoes I'll soon fill. We have lost so many of our old-timers, our mentors in this simple place, that, though just nudging fifty years of age, I'm slowly beginning to fill that role. I was asked before this season if I'd mind taking one fatherless fourteen-year-old on his first hunt this year, and another brother-sister combo whose father is working overseas. Not knowing the youngsters or their families very well, I cringed at the asking, uncomfortable with the prospect and, unfortunately, rather selfish with my desire for solitude in the autumn woods. But on the other hand, it was a first asking, something of an honor, and I ended up enjoying it immensely, managing to help each one properly experience the hunt. To top it off, all took deer—two does and one yearling buck.

What bothers me—somewhat foolishly, I suppose—is that although no one enjoys the season as much as I do, or pays as much attention to whitetail habit and habitat, I have yet to join the honored circle of "a damn good buck hunter." All the old mentors who taught my generation were not only decent and wise human beings but also made incredible yearly scores. This mentor-in-wait, the prodigal son, is a little light in that department—the tarnish on my badge of wannabe. Perhaps the camp buck will put me up alongside the others, if for only a moment.

It is a storied place of the hunt, this Harland, and men like Ed Timmons won Orville Pert's old weight contest many years in a row. If not him, then Old Man Krause, Arthur Glade, Archie Weil, Rolly Harper, or Orville himself—hell, they took turns beating each other year in and year out. Finally, in the early '50s, after the contest switched to a Boone and Crockett style of measurement, a young fellow named Pokey Corbel stunned them all by winning or placing no worse than third for ten years in a row. I think if Harry the Horn Man, who never once entered the contest and thought it childish, hadn't been such a hermit and so antisocial, he would have topped them all. I've yet to meet a man who knew more about whitetails, or who moved and even thought more like one.

But the mentor-in-wait? I've yet to make my mark. I think I have a shot at winning this year, and after the dance we'll head over to Harvey's to see. He plays the role of secret well, and if one of the forty-two entered took a huge deer in the last day or two, Harvey will conspire to keep it quiet.

Going to Harvey's after the potluck, or the Hideaway in earlier days, is an old ritual and not necessarily tied to the town's social calendar. Since the season closes each year on December 7, it is more often than not a weekday. The potluck, always the following night, naturally faces the same weekday problem. With school the next day and many folks having job-related early risings, the potluck and dance have always been an early evening event, stating at 5:30 and ending before 9 P.M. Thereafter, it's often a mad dash to Harvey's or the Hideaway by a large group of us to see the posted list of winners and sit around the fireplace with a nightcapper—one a bit stouter than the straight eggnog and fruit punches of the dance.

As I turned off the highway to travel the gravel road home, the realization sank in fully. It was over. I am never remorseful at this thought; after three months of early rising and spending full days in hunt or hike, I am generally exhausted and need the winter months to recoup and write; the spring to work around the place, repairing and tending to its constant needs; and the summer to make a few extra dollars and complete the chores others leave for autumn—a never-ending cycle, utterly boring in some folks' view, I suppose, but my own little circle of life nonetheless.

And it seems to go by so fast anymore; weeks pass like days once did, seasons like months. I will no more than blink my eyes and spring will be upon us. Then I'll scratch my head in wonder of it all, and it will be the Fourth of July picnic rich with children screaming laughter and joy, tumbling over in sack races, the evening air thick with barbecue as we await the twilight and fireworks.

And then suddenly it's August. And like Rolly Harper before me and others before him, I will see it. Maybe there will be just the right amount of dust in the air, or the smoky haze of some faraway forest fire—perhaps something only imagined or ethereal. But a faint orange glow, softened further by the suddenly noticeable declination of the sun, will fill the air.

And in that late-August moment I will first notice the light, feel that first trickle of autumnal blood pulse through me. All things will seem sweeter—the smells and tastes of whitetail land.

And I will know it is almost time.

Epilogue

The Gatekeepers

I have been asked by many anxious hunters, just exactly where Harland Corners is, as if the questioner was planning on moving there tomorrow. They are always saddened to learn the truth. The character sketches in this book were drawn from very real people, once alive with the passion and soul of whitetail hunting. And though I've taken some liberty in the embellishment, their individual hunts and the events of happenstance are equally real. But Harland Corners is a mythical place, visited only in spirit.

It is not a purely fictional or fabricated town, but rather an amalgamation of three whitetail hunting areas in which I've either lived or had the pleasure to visit long. A permutation might be a better description, since I've taken the best of their individual spirits and gifted the sum to Harland Corners. Although I owe the actual towns the blessing of anonymity, I can divulge their general regions. They are all small towns, under 2,000 in population, with histories showing nearly every resident to be a deer hunter, some passionately so. One is a small town in central Vermont, another a similar place in northern Wisconsin, and the third is a large area along the Canadian border encompassing corners of British Columbia, Alberta, northern Idaho, and western Montana.

More importantly, Harland Corners is anywhere you want it to be. When the nature of a town manifests itself in human spirit, the intrigued are capable of breathing that life into the reality of their own place. In simpler terms, it is a place for you to create—in fact, a place you must create if you are passionate in your love of autumn and whitetails. It is up to us to live the life of Harland

Corners, to teach our children of its storied past and ways, and, in exercising that very grace and compassion, to keep the spirit of autumn alive. If we are not ever-vigilant in this matter, if we fail to kindle the hunting spirit, fail to keep it alive with our manner and deeds, persevering to create a small piece of the Corners in our own life, it will soon disappear, taken from us by those in power who know nothing of its wildly beating heart or the perfect reality of Nature. It is up to you. Never count on another to perform the task for you. That too-common strategy of doing nothing offers shelter to the greatest dangers.

I cannot imagine an October without shotgun and the rocketing adrenaline rush of grouse exploding from a sapling grove rich in autumnal plumage, the purple-pink sunrise viewed from a duck blind of thick cattails, or the silent still-hunt in the colorful 'scapes of whitetail haunt. But a slow but certain end to such scenes seems to loom on the horizon as each new generation grows up without outdoor mentors and moves farther from the ways of autumn, from hunt and harvest, from the spirit and place of Nature's ways. It is not simply the move from rural house to urban life but a move away from the earth's own soul.

I have sadly noticed that many young hunters across America are now more pleasured with shooting their rifles than silently stalking or waiting quietly in stand, more thrilled by just killing a deer rather than by knowing the reason for doing so or anything about the animal or Nature itself. For them, hunting is simply a surge of excitement lacking compassion, grace, or forethought. A quick thrill, not unlike the trigger on a video game and the flash of its colored screen.

If this is the future of the hunting spirit, it will do little good to lobby Washington or write your State House—the ancient rites of autumn will disappear regardless of your political efforts. A better solution is to kindle that spirit, to live your own Harland Corners, however small, and, by fine example, to show youngsters and family your passion for this grand season of harvest and wild beauty.

This book is not fiction—men like Ed Timmons, Orville Pert, and Pokey Corbel truly existed. Perhaps you've known one or two like them in your life or town. It is up to us to keep their fire burning, to ensure that autumn is never stolen from us. If we fail, then we are surely the last of the gatekeepers.